STARTING IN OUR OWN BACKYARDS

HOW WORKING FAMILIES CAN BUILD COMMUNITY AND SURVIVE THE NEW ECONOMY

ANN BOOKMAN

ROUTLEDGE
NEW YORK AND LONDON

Published in 2004 by
Routledge
29 West 35th Street
New York, New York 10001
www.routledge-ny.com

Published in Great Britain by
Routledge
11 New Fetter Lane
London EC4P 4EE
www.routledge.co.uk

10 9 8 7 6 5 4 3 2 1

Library of Congress Cataloging-in-Publication Data

Bookman, Ann, 1948-
    Starting in our own backyards : how working families can build community and
    survive the new economy / Ann Bookman.
        p. cm.
    ISBN 0-415-93588-1 (hardcover : alk. paper)
    1. Work and family. 2. Work and family—United States. 3. Family. 4. Community
    life. 5. Working mothers. I. Title.
    HD4904.25.B66 2004
    306.3'6—dc22   2003017127

To the memory of my parents
Ruth Lowe Bookman
and
John Jacob Bookman

Their devotion to family, passion for their work,
and contributions to community
continue to inspire me
and all those whose lives they touched.

CONTENTS

PART III. INVESTING IN COMMUNITY: EVERYBODY'S BUSINESS

ACKNOWLEDGMENTS

My work on this book commenced in 1997, but it actually dates back to 1969. That summer I traveled by seaplane from central Alaska to the Yukon Delta to do my first anthropological field work in a Yup'ik Eskimo village. Like many anthropology majors, I was initially drawn to the discipline because it provided a window into cultures where family bonds were close and people worked together and cared for each other—a way of life I believed needed recalling. When I arrived in the village, however, I did not find a band of hunters and gatherers living in communal harmony; I found Yup'ik families living in extreme poverty, with children subsisting on dried fish, pilot bread, and Crisco. Adolescent children were forcibly sent away to Bureau of Indian Affairs boarding schools, and adult men spent months each year working at cannery jobs far from home.

I also found that many Yup'iks combined Catholicism and traditional religious practices to ensure a connection to their ancestors—a part of their community. Many households, now headed by women, devised new inter-family support systems to cope with the absence of fathers. It was my first and perhaps most powerful lesson in learning that "community" is not a static ideal. It is a real, often imperfect process in which people seek to re-create the forms and meaning of human connection, adapt to changing external conditions, and ensure the future of the next generation.

A few years later, when I traveled to western Kenya to do field work for my master's thesis in a Luo village, again my preconceived notions of community were wrong. I expected a tight-knit agricultural community where women maintained subsistence plots of maize and millet, men spent the day herding cattle, and extended family lineages were the backbone of community. Instead, I found families torn apart. Many men had left the village for low-wage jobs at tea plantations in the highlands or menial jobs in Nairobi.

Women spent several days a week miles from home, selling their produce in local markets. The introduction of a cash economy had disrupted traditional communal forms, and the Luo who remained in the village were creating new child-rearing practices that included school and school teachers, new roles for elders, and new supports for female-headed families.

When I began to do research in the United States on work and family issues, I took a job in an electronics factory. Through participant observation I learned that the Azorean immigrants I worked with sought economic integration into American society, but largely resisted cultural assimilation. In the Azores they had been farmers, in America they were blue-collar workers. In their urban neighborhoods, new arrivals quickly joined social clubs named for the specific islands they had come from. These clubs helped people get jobs, organized festivals, and provided a place for families to socialize. Re-creating old communal ties in new associational forms eased the transition of these families into an inhospitable land.

This book tells another story of community and changing economic conditions—this time among knowledge workers in the biotechnology industry. I have learned from the middle-class American families featured in these pages that new forms of community are emerging to mitigate the insecurity of living and working in a competitive, global economy. To these families—and *all* the families that have so generously let me into their lives and into their homes—I want to express my deep appreciation. You challenged my romantic notions of community and taught me that the bonds of authentic community are constantly being reinvented.

This book has benefited from the moral and material support of many individuals and institutions. I thank the Alfred P. Sloan Foundation for support of this project during many stages of its development, in particular my program officer, Kathleen Christensen. She encouraged me to bring a community focus to work-family research and has generously provided both intellectual and personal support. I also thank the Gender and Institutional Change Program of the Ford Foundation, and its director, June Zeitlin, for additional support at a critical juncture.

This book owes its existence in no small part to the guidance, support, and infinite patience of my colleagues at the MIT Workplace Center. Co-directors Lotte Bailyn and Thomas Kochan have been exceptional mentors throughout the process. Their scholarship has inspired me, and their encouragement has helped me develop and define my own ideas. They have also "walked the talk" about the family-friendly workplace, providing a creative, flexible work environment for all of us who have the honor of working with them.

I thank my colleague Mona Harrington for her vital role in the completion of this book. From the development of a book proposal, to conversations about content and organization, she has been a consistent supporter and an insightful critic. Her conviction that women can pursue their professional dreams *and* care for their families has helped me to persevere.

Special appreciation goes to my editor at Routledge, Ilene Kalish, who has given enormous time to the manuscript. She helped me purge it of academic jargon, clarify ideas, and crystallize key arguments. She extended understanding when family circumstances made deadlines impossible. For her editorial wisdom and personal compassion, I am most grateful.

My thanks to all members of the Radcliffe Biotechnology Project—Paula Rayman, Françoise Carré, Lotte Bailyn, Susan Eaton, and Constance Perrin—for sharing their ideas, providing helpful feedback on mine, and encouraging me to continue my research.

I have been fortunate to work with a talented group of research assistants: thanks to Sandra Resnick, Meg Lovejoy, and Dana Ansel for their contributions in the early stages of interviewing; thanks to Holy Cross students Carrie Ann Croucher and Cara Gleason for help with secondary data collection; and to MIT students, Kevin Choi and Caroline McEnnis for work on the Community Index and library research.

For their guidance into the world of trade book publishing, I thank Deanne Urmy, Liz Allison, Susan Quinn, and Jill Kneerim. Their advice was honest, their knowledge extensive, and their time greatly appreciated.

This book has benefited from conversations with many people over many years, about anthropology, feminism, working women, childcare, the family-friendly workplace, building community, the well-being of families and children, peace, social justice, writing, and the creative process. I have been inspired by the work and benefited from the wisdom of Martha Ackelsberg, Fred Adelman, Stephen Ainlay, Bertram Ashe, Dianne Bell, Ellen Bravo, Christina Bi Chen, Jacqueline Cooke, Jane Cooper, Delores Crockett, Cynthia Costello, Gary DeAngelis, Shelton Davis, Lisa Dodson, Roslyn Feldberg, Elaine Fersh, Stephen Fjellman, Robert French, Mindy Fried, Fran Froelich, Karen Furia, Ellen Galinsky, Nance Goldstein, Mary Jane Gibson, Heidi Hartmann, Barbara Helfgott Hyett, Mary Hobgood, Morton Klass, Louise Lamphere, Joan Lombardi, Margaret McKenna, Karen Nussbaum,

David O'Brien, Tillie Olsen, Achola Pala, Mamphele Ramphele, Gail Reimer, Kris Rondeau, Civia Rosenberg, Jane Sharpe, Pam Solo, Roberta Spalter-Roth, Jack Stauder, May Stevens, Kip Tiernan, Joan Vincent, Yasmina Vinci, Kristin Waters, Beatrice Whiting, and John Whiting.

I am very grateful to my readers, Lotte Bailyn, Mona Harrington, Tom Kochan, and Sandra Morgen. Their thoughtful comments and perceptive critiques immeasurably improved the final manuscript; the weaknesses that remain are mine alone.

I thank Jane Leavy, who understands what it means to me to complete this book and has been a wise and caring midwife to its delivery.

On March 22, 2001, my then eighteen-year-old son, Nick, was diagnosed with leukemia. It was as if the tectonic plates of our own tiny world had shifted; the landscape of daily life became unrecognizable—we were standing on new ground.

Although the impetus for writing this book was never impersonal, when my son became ill the central concerns of this project took on heightened meaning. Nothing mattered except being with Nick. I needed—and was very fortunate to find at MIT—the kind of workplace I was writing about, a "family-friendly" workplace that would allow me to leave work and care for my son until I could return to my job. Even the biotechnology industry was no longer a subject of academic interest; it was the source of the drugs that were critical to my son's survival. Sitting in Nick's hospital room, watching Cytarabine and Daunorubicin flow from IV bags into his bloodstream, I knew that it was women and men just like the workers I was writing about who had discovered, tested, and manufactured these life-restoring therapies.

And our community became the essential, nourishing context for Nick's recovery. The many communities of which my family is a part surrounded us, supported us, fed us, prayed with us, and buoyed us up until we could regain our bearings. As I was writing about the vital role of community in the lives of working families, I was learning that my own communities were the key to my completing this book.

My close women friends have been a continual source of sustenance and strength. They encouraged me to write from my head and my heart and believed in me in the moments I could not believe in myself. For providing, as the poem says, "an unending circle of love," my deepest appreciation to Andrea Cousins, Susan Levin, Sandi Morgen, Arlene Pressman, Polly Allen, Carol Conaway, and Mary Murphree.

My faith community at Temple Israel, clergy and congregants, has provided countless *g'milut chasadim*, deeds of loving kindness. I especially want to thank the members of my Women's Study Group: Joyce Antler, Paula Brody, Carole Diamond, Ellen Ogintz Fishman, Fran Godine, Louise Lowenstein, Pam Paternoster, Susan Porter, Fran Putnoi, Joan Rachlin, Heidi Vernon, Mary Wright, and our incomparable rabbi, Elaine Zecher.

The teachers and staff of Associated Early Care and Education have inspired me to keep going through the example of their dedication and tireless work with young children. The president and CEO, Douglas Baird, and my fellow board members have supported my efforts to complete this project; their commitment to a world that values all families and all children has deeply informed this book.

Finally, my extended family has provided ongoing support and enthusiasm for this project. I want to thank my brother and sister-in-law, Richard and Milica Bookman; my parents-in-law, Joan and Clifford Buehrens; my brothers-in-law and sister-in-law, John Buehrens, Gwen Buehrens, and Paul Buehrens; my uncle, Charles Lowe; my cousins, Sarah Lowe, Elizabeth Lowe, Stephen Lowe, Cambria Lowe, and Ellin Levy; and a particular thanks to the youngest members of my family—Erica, Mary, Karla, Aleksandra, Thomas, Daniel, Sage, Rory, and Simon.

This book could not have been written without the love, support, and encouragement of my husband, Eric Buehrens. From concrete technical assistance—especially translating the "maps" into computer graphics—to unusual patience and flexibility, the book has benefited from his help. He cheered me up when I was down, celebrated small milestones along the way, and most important, gave me the gift of time. I want to acknowledge his strong intellectual example; to delve deeply into territory that is unfamiliar, to continually reexamine basic assumptions, and to dare to have ideas that go against the grain. He has my deep respect and deepest appreciation.

Last, I want to recognize the contributions and very special support of my children, Nick Buehrens and Emily Buehrens. In their own lives, they are strong, resilient, and brave. In my life, they are a source of great joy, always there with humor and big hugs. They have taught me what is most important in the lives of families, not with words, but with loving, caring deeds. If this book can, in some small way, ease the journey for their generation, it will have surpassed my hopes.

THE ENGINE THAT COULD

The alarm goes off at 5:00 a.m. in a single-family suburban home west of Boston. Julie Taylor gets up; her husband, Peter, continues to sleep.[1] If she is not too tired—a rare state—she exercises for half an hour on her treadmill. She'd like to join a health club but doesn't have time. Every early-morning minute is precious: "It is my only time alone." At 5:30, Julie goes downstairs to the kitchen. She makes lunches for her two daughters, her husband, and herself—she has memorized who likes mayonnaise rather than mustard, whole wheat rather than white bread, American rather than Swiss cheese. Then she gets the girls' backpacks ready. Her older daughter, Sara, now in second grade, has a planner for homework assignments and several note-books, an assortment of pencils, pens, and markers, and a large collection of hair elastics. Julie signs the permission form for an upcoming field trip and adds a check; both are put in the outside pocket of the backpack, a well-worked-out system. Julie gets a tight feeling in the pit of her stomach, remembering that she will not be able to be a parent chaperone on this trip. Her younger daughter, whom they still call "Boo"—from "Pooh Bear"—is now four and a half. She carries a few favorite objects in her backpack—Mr. Pooh and a soft piece of flannel from an old pair of pajamas—along with some extra clothing. Occasionally she brings a book to preschool, if it's her turn to choose a story for "reading circle." Julie has all the reading circle dates for the year marked on the kitchen calendar. Her fatigue is slightly mitigated by a sense that she is well organized.

Around 6:15, Julie goes back upstairs. She wakes up Peter and the girls. Sara dresses herself and needs only a little prodding. Boo is capable of dressing herself but pretends she is not, relishing one-on-one time with her mother. Julie gives in unless she has an early meeting. She helps the girls get ready while Peter showers. Before Peter heads downstairs, Julies reminds him what to make for breakfast, explaining to me, "He needs direction." In the kitchen, Peter toasts bagels and pours milk and juice for the girls. He drinks coffee, reads the morning paper, and ignores the dirty dishes in the sink. Julie quickly showers, dresses, and races downstairs to make sure that everyone is getting something to eat and the girls are not fighting. Her younger daughter has hardly eaten—Boo has perfected the art of dawdling, an expert at getting just a little more of her mother's attention than her big sister does. Julie leaves for work first, usually at 7:20 a.m.

Julie is a postdoctoral research scientist in her mid-thirties. She has a 45-minute commute from her suburban community to a biotech company just off of Route 128 near Boston, where there is a large concentration of high-tech companies. She is supposed to be in at 8:00, but she usually slips in a bit later, hoping none of the senior managers will see her arrive. She often makes a quick stop at the dry cleaner on her way, if there's time, and notes with exasperation, "Pete can never seem to remember to get his work shirts done." Peter waits at home with Sara until the school bus picks her up at 7:50; her school is on the other side of town, not on either parent's way to work. Then Peter drives Boo to childcare on his way to work, about a mile from home. A little after 8:00, he begins a one-hour drive to his workplace, a software company near downtown Boston.

Julie, a biologist, spends the day in her laboratory, usually not taking a real break at lunchtime. She leaves her experiments only briefly for family business, like calling the dentist to schedule appointments for the girls. She says triumphantly, "I got them both in on the same day!" Her thoughts keep drifting back to the field trip her daughter's second-grade class is taking tomorrow. She wishes she could get time off work to accompany them, but she can't leave her experiments in the middle of the day. Her supervisor is not sympathetic to school volunteerism during the workday, even though he has school-age children of his own. When she takes me on a tour of her floor, she points to the photos of his kids he has displayed on his desk, facing the door. With a meaningful look, Julie murmurs, "For public consumption." About 2:45 p.m., Julie begins to feel low-level anxiety. This is the time Sara finishes school and takes a bus to an after-school program at the childcare center she attended before kindergarten. Julie wishes that one or two days a week she could leave work at 2:00, pick up her daughter at school, and spend the afternoon with her. But she brushes away the anxious feeling, telling herself that she is lucky to live in a town that provides transportation to after-school programs. Julie wishes there were a program right in the school building, but then she would have two pick-ups rather than one at the end of the day. What would be better—less worry and two pick-ups, or more worry and one pick-up? Hard to say.

Julie has an important meeting at 3:00 that she hopes will help her focus on work rather than on her daughter. The research project she directs is nearing the stage of clinical trials. She and the other researchers in her project group must decide what is still needed to get the green light from the vice president for research to go to a Phase I.[2] She has been working toward this step for three and a half years, and explains to me, "If things go well on this project, I *maaaaaay* get a promotion." The length of "may" tells me Julie is not confident this will happen. The meeting goes well, but some colleagues raise issues she had not anticipated, and the discussion is longer than she expected. Julie's input is critical, but she needs to leave between 4:30 and 5:00 to pick up her daughters on time. She has to get to the childcare center before it closes at 5:45. If she leaves at 4:30, she feels a bit guilty about leaving work early, even though she has put in eight hours and worked through lunch. Leaving at 5:00 is more appropriate to her role as a senior scientist, but that may cut it too close, especially if there's heavy traffic. What would be better— putting in less time (interpreted as less commitment) at work and getting to childcare with time to spare, or putting in more time (interpreted as more commitment) at work and possibly being late at childcare? Hard to say.

Julie feels good the minute she sets foot in the childcare center: "I feel like they take care of me *and* the kids!" It is 5:35. She didn't cut it too close today. The center is a familiar, comfortable place, and despite a few predictable problems with "transitions" (a euphemism for weepy, clinging goodbyes in the morning), her girls have thrived there. Each girl was enrolled as an infant after Julie had taken a three-month maternity leave. They have had many gifted, loving teachers, and Julie is convinced that being in childcare has helped their development. She is very friendly with Phoebe, the director, who has been at the Apple Tree Child Care Center since the day Julie applied for her first child. First Julie lets Sara know she has arrived, because it takes her time to adjust to leaving, and the older children are required to help with clean-up. Then she pokes her head into Phoebe's office for a quick hello and is reminded about the pot-luck for families with children entering kindergarten next fall—yes, she'll be there; yes, she's bringing a main course. Julie is on a parent-teacher committee at the center, and the more involved parents do real cooking for pot-lucks, while those less involved bring drinks or prepared food. If she's pressed for time, she can ask her neighbor, Susannah, who lives down the street and works part-time, to make the dish. Julie doesn't know what she'd do without parents like Susannah to back her up. Peter will work late that night; he doesn't like to come to social events at the center. As Julie succinctly puts it, "He's not a joiner." Julie's tone indicates that she has more to say on this topic, but she simply adds, "Enough said." Then she goes to Boo's classroom, always unsure whether this will be a "dawdle day" or a "hug day." It's a hug day—Julie feels good about herself as a mother. On the days when she's late and the children dawdle, whining and not hugging, she feels like a bad mother. Is she a good mother or a bad mother—who can say?

By the time the backpacks are ready and goodbyes said to teachers and friends, Julie is feeling rushed. She has two or three more stops before home. First, the supermarket; they've run out of milk. Second, a quick stop at the drugstore to pick up a card for her elderly aunt, who is recovering from surgery. It would be easier if the girls would stay in the car; Julie feels they are old enough and it's safe. But Boo always wants to come in, and Julie doesn't want to leave Sara in the car alone, so both girls come into both stores. Boo begs for Oreos at the grocery store; "Mommy, Mommy, just this time." A delicate negotiation ensues, with the promise of "an after-dinner treat." At the drugstore, Sara needs a glue stick for a project, but remembers this only after they've already been through the checkout line. Another negotiation: When is the project due? Does she really need it tonight? By the time they get home, it's 6:45 and everyone is exhausted. Julie had been hoping to swing by her church to gather some materials she needs to prepare for Sunday school teaching over the weekend, but that will have to wait for tomorrow. Her church is nearby, but one more stop will push both girls over the edge. By the time they reach their front door, Julie herself is on edge—but the edge of what? She can't really say.

Still on Julie's "TO DO" list for the evening: dinner, baths, homework help, bedtime stories, dishes, laundry, and a long-distance call to her ailing mother in Pennsylvania, which always takes at least a half an hour. The only thing that can wait is laundry, and maybe the pots and pans that don't go in the dishwasher—they can soak overnight. Peter is working late, so she doesn't know what on her list she could assign him. Sometimes it's easier to just do it herself—or as she puts it, "I am the engine."

THE MISSING PIECE OF THE WORK-FAMILY PUZZLE: CARING COMMUNITIES

Julie's story has a familiar ring. Have we heard it before? Yes and no. Yes, Julie is one of 58 million mothers of children under eighteen years of age in the U.S. workforce.[3] She has an advanced degree and a good professional job, but she often feels that her education and ambition to rise in her company are more personally draining than professionally fulfilling. She relies on people other than herself and her husband to care for their young children, and she worries about whether she is spending enough time with them. She monitors the care of her elderly mother through long-distance phone calls and wishes she could be more directly involved in it. Her husband earns a good salary and does more to help with the children than men of the previous genera-tion, but their marriage feels more like "ships passing in the night" than a real partnership. Yes, Julie is pressed for time—the thoughtfully described, ever-present "time bind"—as she drives from home to work to childcare and home again each day.[4]

But Julie is not only trying to work and care for her immediate and extended family—the usual story of work-family conflict—she is also trying to "care for" her community. She defines *community* in several different ways and is an active member of several communities she identifies as important to her and her family. At her daughters' childcare center, Julie is a founding member and regular volunteer on the Parents Committee. She organizes social events for families, including fundraisers and discussions of curriculum and teachers' professional development. Julie attends church services regu-larly and is a volunteer teacher in the church's Sunday school, attending train-ing sessions with other lay teachers and the religious education director. At Sara's school, Julie wants to be a classroom volunteer, but she cannot get off work in the middle of the day. In each of these institutions that share in the care and education of her children, Julie is building relationships with pro-fessional staff and with other parents, most of whom also work.

Julie's volunteer activities, as well as the informal relationships she nur-tures with childcare workers, teachers, clergy, and other parents, are all part of what I call "community care work." Julie has built a social support network, based in and around the suburban community where she lives, that makes it possible for her to work and care for her family. Nurturing these relationships takes a lot of skill, time, and effort, and is a largely unrecognized and under-valued form of unpaid work—much like family care work. This kind of care work is different from traditional family care because it takes place outside the home, outside the "private sphere" long viewed as women's domain. Community care work involves people outside the family, often takes place in public institutions, and is required to knit families and communities together in long-term sustainable relationships. These ties create a sense of community and social support that makes work-life and family-life possible. Without them, families suffer on both practical and emotional levels. Community care work offers working families the sense that they are not alone, and that collective action outside the home is a viable way to solve work-family problems. I believe it is the missing piece of the work-family puzzle.

For too long, work-family researchers have overlooked community institutions and community care work. They tend to focus largely on the void that was created when women, the traditional family caregivers, joined the paid workforce, but they do not fundamentally challenge ideas about who should be responsible for family care, given this shift. They correctly point to inadequate, low-quality care arrangements for children and elders. But they look largely to the workplace and employer policies as the solution to family care problems, rather than seeking community partners and community resources. Community care work has also been misunderstood by researchers who study volunteerism and associational life in the United States. They claim that voluntary organizations are in decline and community life is fragmented, basing this conclusion on surveys of membership in organizations that began in the 19th and 20th centuries but barely exist today.[5] The extent and importance of the informal, grassroots activities of millions of working parents is often minimized or overlooked. These parents may not be formal dues-paying members of any organization, but they are doing the daily work of building and sustaining key community institutions on which working families depend.

This book challenges these oversights and omissions by putting community in the center of contemporary American life, not on its margin. I will explore the many meanings of community for working families today, and highlight both the successes and the difficulties of working, caring for family, *and* caring for community. I do not want to minimize the difficulties that working parents encounter if they choose to become involved in their communities. In fact, I will argue that we need to make many changes in public-sector and private-sector policies if we are to see community life and volunteerism flourish. However, I think that the seeds of a movement for strengthening the quality of community life have already been planted.[6] I hope that by telling the stories of workers who do community care work—and the stories of workers who *want* to but can't—I can offer some insights that will help this movement grow. The need for change in the lives of working families can seem overwhelming at times, but history teaches that large-scale social change is often brought about by the actions of small groups of people doing what they see as right. This book is like mining gold from gray rock: it is about unearthing the small acts of ordinary people and understanding their value.

WHAT FUELS THE ENGINE?

Julie describes herself as "the engine" of her family, a strikingly mechanical and work-oriented metaphor for explaining the multiple caregiving roles she plays. She works hard at her paid job, carrying significant responsibilities in her company's research and development efforts. She works hard at home, doing most of the childcare and housework. And she struggles to be involved in her community, though she minimizes what she has done and worries about what she is not doing. Next year, both girls will be in elementary school, making involvement in their school even more compelling, although Julie does not know how she is going to get the time off work to volunteer.

Julie is not a poster child for community involvement. As I see it, she does a good deal; but in her own words, "It is difficult and it is not enough." She feels she is not doing enough at Sara's school, and is frustrated that she can help with Sara's Brownie troop only on weekends. She says in a matter-of-fact manner, as if reporting on weather conditions beyond her control, "Tired is not the word for it, I am constantly exhausted." Her work—paid and unpaid—comes at a cost that is hard to measure and not always visible. So why does she volunteer in her community? And what makes it so difficult for her, and for many of her co-workers, to do this kind of work?

Julie is a community caregiver for two reasons. First, there is a history of community participation in her family. Her mother was involved in the public school Julie and her siblings attended, as well as in their church. Her father volunteered for the first aid squad and fire department in their town, and "He even drove us to Girl Scouts because Mother did not drive." The example of both of her parents instilled a belief that being active in one's community was "just something good folks did." This expresses a certain kind of moral imperative, but there is little moralizing as Julie tries to explain her second reason. Although her job is often stressful, and her children and marriage bring their own set of stressors, community work helps her feel connected with others in similar predicaments. It affirms her sense of "what is important." Through relationships with other parents, she gets support and understanding about the problems of working and caring for young children. Through relationships with childcare teachers, she gets advice on issues with her girls. She learns that some of the things she is worried about are "developmentally appropriate," even if irritating and disruptive to family life. When there are genuine problems with her girls, there are other adults to whom she can turn for help. Through her church, she feels connections with people who share a common faith and value orientation, and teaching in the Sunday school makes her a part of her daughters' religious education. Sometimes the sermons help her "put things in perspective," and sometimes not. Sometimes she prays, sometimes she cannot—but either way, she draws strength for the work week from the quiet spaces in the service.

ASSETS AND IMPEDIMENTS

The organizations Julie belongs to see her as an asset. The director of the Apple Tree and the director of religious education at her church plaintively wish for "more people like her." Julie has constructed a web of relationships that benefit all involved—her family, her childcare center, her church, and herself. If Julie's community care work helps her family and is needed by the community-based institutions she relies on, then why is it so difficult to do? As I talked with Julie and many others, three factors emerged as impediments to community involvement: (1) most companies have limited work-family or "work/life" policies; (2) families remain largely structured around traditional gender roles; and (3) communities of residence are distant from the places where most people work, and deficient in the support services most working families need.

Despite the good intentions of some employers, many family-friendly policies are too narrowly focused on the needs of the workplace: getting people there, keeping them there, and getting the work done. The reluctance of other employers to implement even minimal work-family policies means that these supports are still scarce, especially for those who work for small employers or who are low-wage, hourly workers.[7] Both these responses from the employers are making it difficult for workers to get time away from work to be involved in their communities. Many employers still believe in the existence of an "ideal worker," an unencumbered male with no caregiving responsibilities.[8] Basic questions about how families should be cared for, how work should be organized, how careers should unfold, and how many hours it is reasonable to work remain largely unchanged despite 20 years of work-family initiatives.

In addition, I believe there is a *stalled gender revolution* in the family that perpetuates the traditional gendered division of labor in the home, with women as the primary family caretakers and men as the primary bread-winners. This is not to underestimate the gains that women have made in the workplace and the importance of their economic contributions to their families, nor is it meant to underestimate the family care and housework that some men are doing.[9] Nonetheless, within most families, gender roles have not changed all that much. Most women are still working two jobs—one at home and one in the workplace—and most men still focus on paid work. Too few working women or men have time to care for the community institutions on which their families rely so heavily. Women cannot be expected to do all the community care work, or even some of it, unless men do their part at home. And men are still not doing their part in their families, no less in their communities.

Finally, the distance between home and work—a daily pattern of long commutes for many workers—and the lack of community-based supports for working families further impedes community involvement. Efforts to address "suburban sprawl," which has received much-needed public attention in recent years, have focused on preserving open space and challenging ill-designed development schemes.[10] These are important issues affecting the quality of our physical environment, but sprawl also affects the quality of our social environment, separating homes from jobs and separating people from one another. Sprawl can adversely affect the development of family-friendly communities in which children are safe, support services are affordable and accessible, and the spaces between homes, schools, and other important community institutions are designed to facilitate human interaction. The design of communities can shape, for better or for worse, the way working families relate to their neighbors, neighborhoods, and community groups.

It is not hard to see how each of these impediments to community involvement plays out in Julie's life. Her biotech company has some work-family policies in place, such as flextime. She can leave early to take her daughters to the pediatrician or dentist *if* she comes in early that day or the next. She can attend Parents Committee meetings at her younger daughter's childcare center *if* they are held the evening. But if Julie wants to volunteer at her older daughter's elementary school during the workday, she can't get the time off. She says she could use vacation days to do this volunteer work, but that would cut into precious time with her husband and children, and visits to her elderly parents several states away. She is faced with what seem to be unreasonable choices between greater involvement in her child's public school and time with her immediate and extended family. Julie has considered pushing this issue with her boss, but she feels that she may jeopardize her promotion if she challenges him, a senior manager known to be unsympathetic to "all that family stuff." Her wish to reduce her hours a couple of afternoons a week to pick up Sara at school is not something she would even consider proposing. When I ask her why, she is emphatic: "Someone at my level is expected to work full-time."

In her marriage, Julie faces a dilemma fairly common among professional women of her generation. Peter does do more than men of his father's generation. He waits with Sara for the school bus and drives Boo to childcare in the morning, but does little else to take care of the girls during the week. He does yard work on the weekend, but little housework. He often misses dinner during the week, and he takes no part in scheduling doctor's appointments or play dates for the girls. He never does the long-term planning for birthdays, vacations, or other special family events. Julie feels that Peter needs constant reminders to check the family calendar and to do his agreed-upon "share." She feels torn between being grateful for the help he does provide, and angry at the long hours he puts in at work that "takes away from the family." She hates sounding like she is "keeping a time sheet" at home, but she can't help counting when she feels he is not doing his part. Peter treats community volunteering as "optional," whereas for Julie it's essential. When Julie says tersely, "He's not a joiner," she is not making a statement about Peter's character, but acknowledging a fundamental difference in their ideas about who is really responsible for taking care of the girls and connecting their family to their community.

Finally, the location of the community where Julie and Peter live means a significant daily commute for each of them. Julie's travel between her suburban home and suburban workplace is not quite as long as her husband's, but she makes many more stops between the childcare center and home. Julie's concern about the distance between home and work is not about equity in her marriage, though; it's about the safety of her children and the difficulty of volunteering. She thinks if she worked closer to home, she could volunteer more and worry less. Julie is also concerned about the paucity of community-based services, especially for school-age children. She has to work hard to make all the separate pieces fit together in a way that meets the needs of her family.

CONSTRUCTING NEW SYSTEMS AND SUPPORTS

These impediments are formidable, but they are not fixed in stone. They are a product of cultural practices, norms, and beliefs created in an earlier historical period, and therefore they can be changed by people. Three key institutions in our society are in flux—work, family, and community—and each needs to undergo further transformation to support working families like Julie's.

The system of paid employment was created when most workers were men with no family care responsibilities. Now that the workforce has changed, the workplace must change too. The system of family care was created when most women were in the home and could devote themselves to caring for young children, the sick, and the elderly. Now that most traditional caregivers are not at home, the family—and gender roles within it—must change too. The social organization of communities reflects the old system of paid work and family care in a time when there was less need for community-based family support services, and women could more readily volunteer. Given the changes in work and family, we need new community-based services to support working families and new models of community volunteerism. What will it take to reconstruct and redesign work, family, and community? What will it take to create new cultural practices, norms, and beliefs? These questions motivated the writing of this book. The pages that follow contain strategies to catalyze this reconstruction process, as well as the stories of workers like Julie Taylor who are key actors driving this process of social change.

PART I

Work, Family, and Community in the New Economy

CHAPTER ONE

NEW TERRAIN FOR WORK AND FAMILY

MAKING THE COMMUNITY CONNECTION

Working families like Julie Taylor's are at the heart of this book. I hope to portray their lives in a way that does justice to the daily challenges they face—captured in their full complexity and messiness—and Julie's unwashed pots and pans are the least of it. These families have been significant contributors to this book. The stories that unfold use their narratives and their categories, so the book may at times seem more like a documentary film than social science research. Trained as a social anthropologist, and being a middle-class working mother myself, I walk a thin line between "observing" and "participating" in the worlds of these families—two cornerstones in the practice of ethnography.[1] I draw an important distinction, however, between what is particular and what is universal in the lives of these families.

This book is based on the lives of 40 middle-class working families in which at least one wage earner works in the biotechnology industry.[2] I first met these families as a member of a two-year team project on work and family issues in the biotechnology industry sponsored by the Radcliffe Public Policy Institute.[3] My own part of the project was a study of the lives of biotech workers *outside* work, in their families and, most important, in their communities. In my view, discussions of work and family have given too little attention to community, either as a focus of research or as a matter for employer policy and public policy. I structured my investigation around three aspects of community: how biotech workers view the quality of life in their communities of residence; how they understand, create, and participate in "communities" beyond the physical ones where they live, such as networks of neighbors or friends; and what the factors are shaping their involvement as volunteers in community-based groups and organizations. I am particulary interested in this third aspect of community as a measure of shared social responsibility that can change institutional policy and practice to benefit the common good. These concerns place my project squarely at the intersection of two current debates: the debate on work and family, which is essentially a debate about gender roles and the benefits of women's working outside the home; and debates about the health of our civil society. Let me begin by saying where I stand in this intersection.

THE PERSONAL IS INTELLECTUAL . . . AND POLITICAL

There is little agreement about which institutions in our society are responsible for the care of families and communities. Some say that it is the private responsibility of individual families, and particularly the job of women in those families, excusing both the public and private sectors from investing needed resources. Others say it is the job of employers or the government to provide what families need, with special attention to the needs of the poor, but with little thought to creating sustainable resources. Still others say that local, intermediary institutions—secular and religious nonprofit organizations—are the answer, despite the fact that it may be difficult to determine the larger social good from the particular needs of particular communities. Most agree that no one sector can do it all, but few have articulated how to bring together the resources of multiple sectors to enhance the quality of work, family, and community life.

My previous engagement with work-family issues as a researcher and an advocate for workplace change and women's equality has shaped my perspective on gender roles and the health of our civil society. I am not satisfied with the positions of conservatives, old-style liberals, or neo-liberal communitarians, which were briefly captured above. I do not agree with the way they frame the problem or with their solutions. Although I find some value in each perspective, I think that all three models perpetuate a false distinction between the private sphere and public sphere. This distinction—sometimes called the "separate spheres" model—perpetuates the division between male breadwinners and female caregivers, and re-creates the conditions for women to remain as the primary family-care providers.[4] In addition, this dualistic framework, with business and market institutions on one side and non market institutions on the other, places community outside the sphere of business concerns with adverse consequences for increasing social responsibility for famile well-being.

As Julie's story clearly demonstrates, the solution to work-family problems is inextricably bound up with issues of family care and gender equality, and many of Julie's strategies are dependent on relationships with neighbors and community institutions. But many discussions of resolving work-family conflict leave out community, and many discussions on civil society seem to leave the family on the sidelines. This reinforces the false claim that familial relationships are private, and that families can "make it" on their own without some kind of community support. Even in the emerging movement for civic renewal (which goes to some lengths to learn from the patterns of civic participation among women's movement activists),[5] the issue of family care is not adequately addressed.[6] If we leave the family out of "public problem solving" and civic engagement, then we are essentially leaving out the voices, needs, and interest of women.

I have worked for many years on the project of creating a society in which we recognize women's voices, workers' voices, and the interconnection between our personal and public lives. I have worked on expanding educational opportunities for women, on public policies that support children and families, and on raising workers' wages and expanding benefits crucial to their economic security. I have done this as a labor union organizer, as an activist in state and local politics, as a policy maker at the U.S. Department of Labor's Women's Bureau, and as a teacher and scholar in higher education. I have also promoted these issues as a working mother and as a volunteer in community agencies that serve low-income families, in my own children's childcare programs and schools, and in our synagogue. It is my experience that creating change on issues such as quality childcare, good schools, safe neighborhoods, decent wages, and family-friendly benefits is *not* something that families can do alone. Solutions require the resources of many institutions— we need responsible government, no matter what its size, and responsible businesses. Solutions require mobilizing the human and material resources of community-based nonprofit groups, both secular and religious. Solutions also require the ideas and participation of women and men mobilized at the grassroots level.[7] I believe that it is only by coordinating the resources and strategies of institutional and individual players that the needs of employers, working families, and communities will be met.

The present debate on the health of civil society does not acknowledge the extent of change in work and family life, nor the inadequate response of our basic institutions to this change. The question "Are volunteerism and community involvement today rising or falling?" is misleading. It is an "apples and oranges" question, because it compares two historical moments when work and family life looked totally different. Changing conditions call for changing concepts and definitions. I see several problems with the work of scholars who have emphasized declining voluntary groups and community involvement. These accounts privilege participation in membership organizations over other forms of association and informal networks. Some downplay the impact on civil society of the dramatic rise in the number of working women over the past thirty years, while others blame women's entrance into the workforce for the decline in volunteerism. Although some studies have shown that employed women are more involved than women who are housewives, because they have more skills and education,[8] these studies seem to misunderstand that many "housewives" either were formerly members of the workforce or are currently part-time workers, and both make substantial volunteer contributions. In my view, the volunteerism of both employed women and men is misunderstood, and its value minimized, because it looks different from what existed in the 1920s or 1950s.[9]

Much of the community involvement I have found among biotechnology workers and their families seems invisible because it is not associated with organizational memberships or leadership positions; it often eludes counting and large-scale surveys. I am certainly not the first person to suggest that we need to extend our definition of what constitutes community participation, particularly if we are interested in what women do,[10] but I am suggesting that an expanded definition should focus on the informal connections formed to assist with family care, broadly defined. This type of community involvement is not clearly visible to those building a movement for civic renewal because their definition of "public problems" downplays the personal and familial dimension. The way we currently take care of children, elders, the sick, and the disabled—some of which happens in public spaces, and some in the private space of the home—is a public problem. The community involvement of the workers described in this book crosses this public/private boundary every day of the week, at least twice a day, and any viable movement for a stronger civil society will have to learn to cross this boundary too.

The meaning and scope of community involvement among working families can be understood only by acknowledging the enormous changes that have occurred in the social and economic roles of American women. The very foundations of family and gender roles have been shaken over the last three decades, and the dust has not yet settled. Women are in the workforce to stay, but neither the private sector nor the public sector has responded adequately. Most employers have not changed or added to their benefits, and government has not changed public policy to address these new realities. This lack of responsiveness has created an enormous work-family challenge to all major sectors of our society. This state of affairs is undermining the productivity, the flexibility, and ultimately the competitiveness of U.S. firms in a global economy. It poses a significant threat to the care of our children and our elders. It also threatens the quality of life in our communities.

Working parents are relying on community-based institutions and services to help them raise their families, so we as a society need to allocate to these institutions the material resources and volunteer labor they need to remain afloat. Working parents also rely on their employers—who are often left out of the "civil society" debates—to recognize and support their efforts to work and care for their families. We need employers to understand that the care and education of the next generation is increasingly taking place outside the home, in the community, and that ensuring the quality of this care and education will require some volunteer involvement from the working adults they employ, and some investment from private sector companies.

This book offers an alternative framework for thinking about the state of our civil society. The focus on "decline" in certain kinds of membership associations, like the Elks or the PTA obscures the growth of other kinds of community involvement. New forms of engagement have been catalyzed by the entrance of large numbers of women into the paid labor force, and the consequent changes in traditional family care arrangements have created a new set of conditions for building and sustaining community. There is now a strong imperative coming from outside the family toward more social responsibility for families, and new connections are being born out of this new reality. New forms of "social capital"—just as important as money in the bank—are developing among working families in both urban and suburban environments.[11] These new relationships are binding us together and reshaping our communities in a literal and social sense.

PAID WORK AND COMMUNITY INVOLVEMENT

This book presents a multifaceted picture of community involvement among contemporary working families. In the chapters that follow, you will meet working parents who are involved with their communities and those who want to be involved but can't be. Lily Huang, a research scientist, wants to volunteer in her four-year-old son's preschool classroom one afternoon a week, but her supervisor says that someone with Lily's level of training and responsibility cannot take time off during the work day. Mike Hallowell, a biotech production worker, manages his son's Little League team and leads a Cub Scout troop, but since his promotion and his company's relocation to a facility farther from the city where he lives, he has difficulty getting home in time to continue volunteering in neighborhood after-school programs. Helen Rafferty, a middle manager, has recently started volunteering in her children's school; previously, her long work hours made this impossible, but when her company instituted an alternative work schedule, she became able to volunteer in the library and classrooms.[12]

Each of these stories raises an important challenge to the current structure of paid work. Each suggests a change in the workplace that could have positive results for family and community. For example, if Lily's employer were more flexible about work schedule and location, then she could find a few hours a week for her son's preschool. If Mike's employer would consider restructuring the production process, perhaps starting runs earlier in the morning, then Mike could get home in time to coach. These stories open a discussion about whether it is incumbent on employers to change their policies, or redesign the organization of work in their firms, to facilitate the community involvement of their employees. Helen's story prompts an examination of work schedules in particular, and whether alternative work schedules—including part-time work—can create conditions for increased community involvement.

These vignettes cannot do justice to the lives of the individuals involved, nor can they illustrate fully the difficult choices that working families face every day. However, when one considers that these stories are replicated in the lives of millions of working families, 365 days a year, one begins to grasp how the current work-family system is adversely affecting the quality of life in our families and communities. Individual stories are particularly useful for what they reveal about the systemic patterns and underlying structures in our society. And it is the way in which those patterns and structures shape our individual and social relationships that lies at the heart of two interconnected debates described earlier: the debate about work and family, and the debate about civil society.

WHEN WOMEN LEFT THE KITCHEN AND THE CRADLE: DEBATES ON WORK AND FAMILY

In the early 1970s, when women's labor-force participation was starting to rise, there was alarm in many quarters. Even though women had made a major contribution to the war effort during World War II by working in many defense-related jobs, and the country had not fallen apart in the process, twenty years later when more women started to work, they were blamed for a variety of social ills.[13] They were blamed for juvenile delinquency, rising drug use and other problems affecting children, as well as the rising divorce rate and other manifestations of marital dissatisfaction. It was not culturally appropriate even back then to say that women should "just get back in the kitchen," but some people thought that would be the best solution to the family turmoil they could not understand. In the meantime, women themselves were going to college in unprecedented numbers, entering the professions, and trying to rise through the ranks of corporate America.[14] Life wasn't easy for them at work or at home, but they persisted—some because of economic necessity, and others out of their desire for fulfilling careers. Many fought for their right to a life outside the home and some degree of financial independence.

As it has become clear that working women are not going back into the home, the terms of the debate about women's "proper place" have shifted. Some of those previously uncomfortable with women in the workplace have now declared that women are equal to men, and that no problems produced by this major change in the workforce remain to be addressed. Some have even declared that there is no remaining gender gap in wages,[15] though others argue that women still make 78 cents for every dollar a man makes.[16] Some oppose pay for family and medical leave and increases in funding for preschool and school-age childcare, while others argue for paid leave and an expansion of government-supported childcare programs. Perhaps the most convoluted and disturbing manifestation of the debate recently has been about the work and family issues of poor women. Some support public policies that require poor women to take low-paying jobs rather than staying home to care for their children and receiving a decent government subsidy. Others say that all women should have the choice of whether to work or stay home, and that if poor women have to work, they should at least be given access to subsidized childcare and decent-paying jobs. Recently, another round of "let's blame working mothers" appeared in the media.[17] A 2002 study showing that children whose mothers worked 30 hours a week while they were infants got lower "reading readiness" scores than children whose mothers stayed home was used (despite the way its authors interpreted the data) to cast doubt on the benefits of mothers' working outside the home.[18] Have the arguments changed, or have they stayed the same?

There is also a national debate among those who support women's participation in the workforce. These researchers, policy makers, and practitioners want to solve the dilemmas created by the withdrawal of women's unpaid caregiving work in the home, but they don't agree about what to do. Their differences date back to the early 20th century, when arguments raged between "equality feminists" and "difference feminists."[19] In those days, the debate centered on the merits of "protective legislation" giving women shorter hours, better working conditions, and maternity leave. In the late 20th century, we had our own version of this debate. Some argued for equal opportunity and the importance of opening up all jobs and careers to women. They championed women who tried to break the "glass ceiling" and enter the highest positions in corporate America. Others disagreed, saying that the focus on equal opportunity leads to adopting a "male model" of work and ignoring the ways in which women are different and have different needs than men.

Probably the best-known contemporary version of the "difference" position was articulated by Felice Schwartz, founder and former president of Catalyst, a nonprofit research and advisory organization working to advance women in business.[20] Her idea was that, if women are working and still doing most family care, then companies should acknowledge this and create a special set of benefits and career options that acknowledge and accommodate their caregiving responsibilities. A public debate ensued in response to Schwart's article in the *Harvard Business Review*, and the phrase "mommy track" (not her term) became common parlance.[21] Her proposals brought a wave of protest. Why should women have to give up equality and advancement in order to get flexibility and dependent care support? Why indeed?

A few scholars, notably Mona Harrington, have tried to bridge the gap between equality feminism and difference feminism.[22] Harrington has argued that we should put "the need for new systems of family care together with meaningful support for women's equality."[23] She writes compellingly that, as a society, we do *not* have to choose between taking care of our families and advancing gender equality, but she warns that doing both is a complex task. Harrington, trained as a lawyer and political scientist, proposes a two-pronged approach. First, she says, we need to focus on "the ideas, belief systems and particularly the ideology defining public and private functions" and bring people together in "a public discussion about different sets of ideas and values and priorities."[24] Only then can we move on to the long-term project of actually designing new policies. Harrington's work poses a bold challenge to those who wish to maintain the status quo, and a conceptual breakthrough for those working to weave paid work and unpaid family care work into a system that will be good for children, women, and families.

While some scholars and practitioners approach work-family issues by addressing problems with the family care system, many others have focused on problems in the workplace. The development of policies to make the workplace family-friendly has its own history, too complex to fully elaborate.[25] One catalyst for these new policies was a widely discussed Labor Department report, *Workforce 2000*, which warned the business community that the increasing number of women and minorities was going to change the dynamics of recruitment and retention.[26] The changing demographics of the workforce spurred the development of on-site childcare centers, services to help parents locate childcare providers, as well as back-up and emergency care options.[27] After an initial surge of interest in these policies, there was increasing documentation of the gap between policy and practice, and a low untilization rate of existing policies.[28] This led to a focus on the "culture of the workplace," with training sessions for middle managers on how to be more supportive of empoyees' needs. A shift to "work-life" policies, rather than work-family policies, soon followed in an effort to signal management's support for all aspects of personal life outside of work. Although the emphasis on exercise and stress management were positive for employee health, the implication that time to go to the gym has the same social value as time to care for family members was an unfortunate byproduct of this change.

A recent phase of work-family policy has developed calling for work redesign as an arena for intervention to alleviate work-family conflict. Rhona Rapoport, a sociologist, and Lotte Bailyn, a professor of organization studies at MIT's Sloan School of Management, were among the first to examine the basic assumptions underlying the way work is organized in most U.S. firms.[29] Drawing on her research inside corporations, Bailyn urges us to reexamine outmoded assumptions for structuring work and create new models for careers, for time worked in relationship to job performance, and for management based on trust among co-workers and respect for diversity.[30] Rapoport, Bailyn, and their colleagues argue that if companies restructured workplaces according to these new models, and adopted a "Dual Agenda," then it would improve the performance of firms and advance gender equality and the ability of women and men to have their personal lives taken into account by their employers.[31]

Whether the focus is on redesigning family care systems or workplace norms and policies, the need to address work-family problems *and* gender inequality simultaneously has emerged as critically important. New models of work organization, work schedules, and careers will be effective tools for resolving work-family conflict only if women's roles in the family and the workplace also change. If women's equality becomes a shared social value, then the entrance of women into the workplace will be seen as a boon to individual companies and the economy as a whole, not just as a drain on families.

The idea of bringing gender equality into discussions of work and family has gained increasing adherents. However, the omission of community continues to limit both research and praxis on these issues.[32] To the extent that community has been considered in relationship to work-family, there have been some attempts to connect community to family, but few attempts to connect community to work.[33] It is almost as though workplaces and families are floating in space, not grounded in real places. By confining the discussion to two spheres, women and men are either doing paid work in the "public sphere" or family care in the "private sphere." Our understanding of how these spheres interact has grown more complex;[34] a "spillover" effect is being named and research is showing how the arrows of cause and effect move in both directions.[35] But spillover is still discussed in terms of only two spheres. Something is still missing: another potentially mediating public realm, the community.

BRINGING IN THE COMMUNITY: A NEW LOOK AT THE BACKYARD

In this book, I will show the importance of seeing both workplaces and families as connected to—in fact, embedded in—communities. Community creates the physical and social context within which the battle to make a better work-family system is being waged. The communities of these working families are diverse in character, size, and composition; some are urban, some suburban, some rural. All these communities, however, have a social structure and organization that shapes the relationships of those who live and work in them and must be taken into account.

One issue that has undoubtedly made it difficult to integrate community into the work-family discussion is another cultural debate, this one about the nature of "community." Do we still have community in America? For some, community is equated with tightly knit, family-based units in ethnically and/or religiously homogeneous neighborhoods; social scientists in the period after World War II argued that this kind of community had been truly "lost." In the 1960s a new perspective emerged, arguing that community still existed, had been "saved," as it were. Certain forms of social organization were shown to be persistent, though perhaps somewhat altered, types of community, usually based on common social, political, or economic interest groups. More recently, this view has been replaced by the notion that we still have communities, but they are "liberated," loosely organized, sparsely distributed, and set free from normative constraints.[36] Barry Wellman, a sociologist, has argued that these types of communities are equally valid "alternative structural models. Each model speaks to a different means of obtaining and retaining resources, and all three models are likely to be reflected in current realities to some extent."[37]

I am not interested here in abstract "structural models," but rather in how diverse forms of community actually operate in people's lives. The biotech workers whom I met and talked to participate in many different kinds of communities and have many different ideas about what the term *community* means. They live in residential communities that are constantly changing owing to the pressures of economic development, gentrification, and sprawl. They are "customers" or "clients" of community-based services and programs that help meet the needs of their families. They also participate in many types of communities that are independent of where they live and, in fact, have no physical boundary. These may be social in nature, such as a community of friends; instrumental, such as a community of parents with children of the same age; or communities that stem from membership in a common institution, such as a childcare center, school, or faith-based institution. In some cases, these relationships lead to volunteerism and engagement for the benefit of a larger community.

This latter definition of community suggests a willingness among these workers to look beyond self interest and individual family interests, despite media stories about NIMBYism.[38] These stories feature communities that resist locating facilities they see as undesirable in their own neighborhoods, even if the facility is needed. They have opposed half-way houses for the mentally ill, clinics for AIDS patients, even childcare centers.[39] This book presents a different neighborhood phenomenon, a process in which working families reach out to each other and to community-based programs to address difficult issues they all face. They are essentially creating solutions to work-family conflict in their own backyards. "Backyard" is not meant literally—in fact, a number of families in this book live in urban apartments without a patch of grass in sight. These backyards are metaphoric, representing the willingness of ordinary citizens to take responsibility for the quality

of life in society as a whole by creating new personal and institutional relationships in the communities where they live.

Given that most adults work, it is important to understand how their
relationship to their job affects their ability to build meaningful connections
to people and organizations that give them a "sense of community." It is also
important to examine how paid employment outside the home affects their
ability to volunteer for community groups and institutions. Given that most
women work and are still the primary family caregivers, it is important to
explore how gender affects the extent of community involvement in working
families. These issues must be raised with an awareness of differences among
industries, jobs, and families. By paying attention to diversity, we can capture
the particular meaning of community in different kinds of families and workplaces. By paying attention to common problems that cut across industries
and socio-economic groups, we can better understand why we all have a stake
in the quality of our social environment, which some call "civil society."

WHAT WOULD DE TOCQUEVILLE SAY NOW? DEBATES ON CIVIL SOCIETY

Ever since Alexis de Tocqueville published *Democracy in America*,[40] the practices of American citizens and the health of civil institutions in American
communities have been a subject of scrutiny. In the past 15 years, the topic of
"civil society" has become contested terrain among both scholars and politicians. Many agree that we need to strengthen civil society because we need a
sector of social life independent of the state and the market, but there is little agreement about how to do this. Conservatives, who want to reduce the
role of government, argue that we need a strong civil society to shoulder
many of the roles and functions that have been carried out by government in
the past. They call on individual families to help in this effort through established charities. Liberals, who want to rebuild and reform government, argue
that we need to strengthen civil society as a means to rejuvenate each citizen's
relationship to government, and to revitalize its core functions. They believe
individual families, especially poor families, should be the beneficiaries of
government policies. The relationship of civil society to government has
received more attention from both camps than its relationship to the market.
Few say that strengthening civil society is the also the job of employers—a
position I will explore—or ask how changes in our economy that produce low
job security and frequent job changes may be affecting civil life.

As contemporary pundits and social scientists have assessed the current condition of civil society, their debate has focused on whether civic participation and membership in voluntary associations is falling or rising. On the one hand, in such influential works as Robert Bellah's *Habits of the Heart*[41] and Robert Putnam's *Bowling Alone*,[42] Americans are viewed as suffering from a profound sense of disconnection. Parents are working longer and longer hours and spending less and less time with children, and children are spending too much time alone. Simultaneously, adults in a variety of jobs and family situations are spending less and less time in voluntary associations. Although there is disagreement about whether the causes are structural, cultural, or moral, these scholars stress that one of the most precious of modern commodities—social capital—is in decline. That is, people-to-people connections are frayed in our society, participation in voluntary associations is down, and we are all suffering the negative consequences.

Some scholars, on the other hand, emphasize change rather than decline. The sociologist Alan Wolfe has argued that the drop in volunteer group membership may be quantitatively exaggerated, and the quality of social ties misunderstood. His interviews with middle-class Americans give evidence of continued civic and religious involvement.[43] Theda Skocpol, whose work integrates sociology and political science, has documented the depth and breadth of trans-local voluntary associations in the United States from the mid-19th to the mid-20th century. In her study of contemporary patterns of civic participation, she sees a shift in the nature of voluntary associations, which are now dominated by staff-led advocacy groups and professional associations.[44] A somewhat different but complementary perspective is advanced by the sociologist Robert Wuthnow, who argues that Americans are involved in their communities, but the nature of their involvement has become more short-term, project specific, and oriented to self-help as a result of the "porous" nature of contemporary social institutions and the impact of information technology.[45] In his recent writing, Wuthnow argues that to the extent that social capital is declining, this is occurring in marginalized groups whose members live so far outside the mainstream that they do not feel entitled to participate in voluntary associations. He urges more attention to the socio-economic divide in American society for understanding the shifts in civil society.[46]

Another strand of thinking that makes a more optimistic assessment about civil society is found among self-identified "communitarians." Rooted in a critique of individualism and liberalism, communitarianism has urged a realignment—or better balance—between individual rights and communal responsibilities.[47] Adherents of this school promote personal responsibility while also advancing the role of public institutions in caring for families and communities. They have tried to stake out a middle ground between political liberals and conservatives on questions of family values, the proper role of the federal government, and the place of local initiatives. There are many strands within this movement, and divergent views among political scientists and philosophers about the merits of communitarianism as a route to a stronger civil society.[48]

In the mid-1990s, concern about evidence of civic disengagement prompted the formation of the National Commission on Civic Renewal. By the time the commission issued its final report, "A Nation of Spectators,"[49] it recognized that "a nascent movement for civic renewal" was already under way. An updated report shows modest improvement in selected areas, such as falling crime rates and a decline in teenage pregnancy, lending credence to their claim that civic health is on the upswing in America.[50] This has been corroborated by the journalist E. J. Dionne, who points to the work of nonprofit organizations and faith-based institutions that are solving problems where government has failed.[51] Recently, Robert Putnam's "Bowling Together: The United State of America" suggests a revision or modification of the main conclusions of his book, *Bowling Alone*.[52] In the wake of the September 11, 2001, terrorist attacks, Putnam found that "the levels of political consciousness and engagement [among Americans] are substantially higher than a year ago." Using post-9/11 survey data, Putnam found that respondents expressed greater trust in government, in their neighbors, and among people of different ethnic groups. He also found that occasional volunteering was up slightly, but regular volunteering remained the same. He notes that there have been changes in attitude but not in behavior, and he warns, "Changes in attitude alone, no matter how promising, do not constitute civic renewal."[53] Putnam is guardedly optimistic about the potential for civic renewal since 9/11, saying, "Americans today are more open than ever to the idea that people of all backgrounds should be full members of our national community."

The best evidence for, and the best overview of, a national movement for civic renewal is found in *Civic Innovation in America* by Carmen Sirianni and Lewis Friedland.[54] Drawing on their participation in the Reinventing Citizenship Project and the Civic Practices Network, as well as interviews with people they call "innovative civic practitioners," Sirianni and Friedland argue that during the 1990s, "a broader civic renewal movement has begun to emerge, with a common language, shared practices and networked relationships across a variety of arenas."[55] The particular arenas of civic innovation they highlight are urban and community development, civic environmental-ism, healthy communities, and civic journalism. They do not count civic involvement as such unless people are directly involved in "public problem solving." This is setting a high standard for what constitutes community engagement and, as they acknowledge, leaves out many forms of "social cap-ital."[56] They believe that this is warranted because "the organizational forms and strategies for mobilizing social capital matter." Ultimately their project is nothing less than "revitalizing democracy for the 21st century," but the process they propose is grounded in the work of grassroots organizations. They provide clear evidence of the need "to build relationships across differ-ent associational networks and policy arenas, to further cultivate common language, and to catalyze mutual learning."[57] In this way, Sirianni and Friedland contribute important ideas about how citizens can create change on a wide variety of issues, and how people can work together across divides that often seem unbridgeable—just as the families in this book are building bridges between their workplaces, families, and communities.

WORKING FAMILIES IN THE NEW ECONOMY

The families profiled here are part of the "new economy."[58] They participate in a global economic system, experience the unremitting pace of technolog-ical change, and understand at first hand that job security has all but disap-peared for American workers, white-collar or blue-collar. By focusing on one segment of the new economy's workforce—knowledge workers in the biotechnology industry—we can get a first-hand look at one of the major shifts occurring in our country: the shift from an industrial economy to a service-based, information-oriented one.[59] Given significant recent develop-ments in the life sciences, such as the mapping of the human genome, this industry promises to be vital to our economic competitiveness as a nation in the 21st century—one reason I was interested in studying this group of workers.

Biotech workplaces are on the frontier of scientific research and infor-mation technology, and the competitive pressure to do cutting edge research and discover new drugs is relentless. This makes biotech an exciting work environment, but also an insecure one. Although this book is in one sense an in-depth case study of several workplaces within one industry, I believe the challenges of work, family life, and community involvement among biotech workers resonate in many respects with the challenges affecting middle-class working families in other sectors. Understanding the lives of biotech workers also provides a window into several issues that will affect families and businesses in the decades to come: the need for a scientifically literate workforce, changes in the employer-employee relationship, and the instability of many firms in a competitive global economy.

INTRODUCING THE COMPANIES

When I began this project, I had only minimal knowledge of the biotechnology industry. I immersed myself in reading industry trade publications, studying industry trends, and visiting biotechnology companies in the greater Boston area. Eventually the research team of which I was a part found three companies with CEOs and human resource directors sympathetic to our interest in studying work and family issues in biotech.[60] These individuals and other senior managers were very important in the early stages of the project. They recounted the history of their companies, described their formal benefits and work-family policies, and gave us tours of their facilities so that we could observe the work process. Ultimately, they gave us access to employees in their firms.[61]

The biotechnology industry in Massachusetts operates in the eastern half of the state. It is unevenly divided across three bands in a region sometimes referred to as the "greater Boston metropolitan area." The majority of firms—over 60 percent—clusters close to Boston generally, and in the city of Cambridge in particular. A smaller group of firms are housed between routes 128 and 495, two major commuting highways that encircle Boston, and represent about one-quarter of all biotech companies in the state. Finally, about 10 percent of firms lie to the west of Route 495, in and around the city of Worcester, site of a struggling biotechnology industrial park. Proximity to the large universities, prestigious teaching hospitals, and high-powered research laboratories in and adjacent to Boston is a magnet for biotech firms.[62]

I studied three firms in depth. The one I am calling "BioPrima" is a small company located in the western suburbs of Boston; "BioSegunda" is a medium-sized firm that has recently moved from a large city to a mixed-industry office park; and "BioTertia," the largest, is located close to downtown Boston. I will give more details on each company's unique characteristics in chapter 2, but for now I want to emphasize what they have in common—constant change. All three firms experienced a high degree of disruption during the four years I studied them. All three changed their names after acquisition, a merger, or a major internal restructuring of divisions. All three have had significant personnel changes at the vice-presidential and/or CEO level. To work in biotech is to work in a constantly shifting environment in which there is a premium placed on innovation. At the same time, biotech operates in a highly regulated environment in which the actions of the federal Food and Drug Administration (FDA) can assure of destroy the viability of individual firms. This means that job insecurity is a constant presence in the day–to-day world of these workers.

INTRODUCING THE FAMILIES

My first contact with each family was through meeting a family member who worked in one of the three firms described above. I then followed people into their homes and communities, as appropriate. In most cases, workers introduced me to people whom they defined as key members of their work-family support networks. This led to spending time with extended family members and friends, and took me into childcare centers, family childcare homes, after-school programs, schools, and faith-based institutions.[63]

The employees I got to know work in every part of the industry as high-level managers, postdoctoral research scientists, middle managers, professionals in quality control and regulatory affairs, and production and production support workers. Approximately one-third of these employees works directly in scientific research, creating the basis for the development of new products. A little over 40 percent hold non-research professional and managerial positions, and the remaining 25 percent manufacture biotech products and provide operational support to the production process. The education and training level among these workers is high relative to the workforce as a whole, but typical of new-economy workers.[64] Fifteen percent hold doctoral degrees in one of the life sciences, a little over 20 percent hold master's degrees, and approximately 40 percent hold a bachelor's degree in a management or scientific field. The remaining 20 percent have a high school degree and/or biotechnology certificate. Their wages and salaries vary accordingly, with production and technical workers making roughly half of what the associate scientists and middle managers earn. Senior scientists and high-level managers earn a good deal more.[65]

One of the defining features of the industry is the high proportion of women at all educational levels and in most occupational categories, almost half of the workforce,[66] and this is true in the companies I studied as well.

Although the industry is quite balanced in terms of gender, this is not true of race and ethnicity: there are few people of color in the biotech workforce,[67] and they comprise less than 10 percent of the families in this book. Of those families, each is part of a first-generation immigrant family from Asia, the Caribbean, or the Middle East.

These self-identified "middle-class" working families have substantial material and social privileges compared to poor members of rural and inner-city communities,[68] yet they themselves are socio-economically diverse.[69] About one-quarter of the workers I met hold "blue-collar" and "pink-collar" jobs, the kind of jobs some would call "working-class." They struggle financially with childcare and buying their own homes, and they have little or no savings to send their children to college or to fund their own retirement. Other families are more comfortable financially. They have professional and managerial jobs and make either a little, or in a few cases a lot, more than most American families. They can afford to engage in "domestic outsourcing"—that is, they can purchase the childcare, summer camp, elder care, and other family care and household services that make working and caring more manageable.[70] But they have their own financial issues: They may be able to afford quality childcare and own their own homes, but they tend to spend everything that they earn, or more. They are often overextended with credit card debt, need financial aid to pay college tuition for their children, and have difficulty saving for retirement.

Biotech is a relatively new industry and is attracting a young workforce. Most of the workers I met and interviewed are in their thirties and forties, a few are in their twenties, and a few are in their fifties or near retirement. Most of the families are married dual-earner families; approximately 20 percent are single-earner families in which the parent is separated, divorced, or never married. Of those families with children, approximately 40 percent of the children are in preschool; 50 percent are in elementary, middle, or high school; and about 10 percent are in college or living on their own. The demographics of the biotech workforce at present, with a large number of women in a variety of jobs, many families with children living at home, and many families dealing with elder care, make it an exceptionally good laboratory for examining the relationship among work, family care, and community involvement.

CHAPTER TWO

HOW FRIENDLY IS THE "FAMILY-FRIENDLY" WORKPLACE?

A VIEW FROM THE BIOTECH INDUSTRY

Jessica Bromfield is a professional biotech employee. When I met her she had just started working part-time in a job share position at BioSegunda. With several years of research already completed, I was well aware that part-time work is not easy for women to get in biotech, and job shares are almost unheard of, so I was expecting to hear a tale of sensitive managers supporting time for family care. But that was not what I heard.

JESSICA'S STORY

Jessica is in her late thirties and has 15 years' experience in the biotechnology industry. She has a B.S. degree in biology and has worked in the quality assurance departments of several biotech companies. This work involves constant communication with the Food and Drug Administration (FDA), and she enjoys the challenge of getting government approval for drugs and products that will improve the quality of life for people who are ill. In the mid-1990s, she was hired as a senior associate in quality assurance at BioTertia; she has worked her way up to supervisor of a small group.

Several years ago Jessica became the mother of twin girls and took 12 weeks' leave. When her leave was up, she did not want to return to the workplace on a full-time basis, although she was willing to do full-time work. She proposed to her boss that she work half-time at home and half-time at the workplace. Jessica explains:

I would love to stay home, but we just can't afford it. I mean this is the third company that my husband has shut down. He's in biotech as well. You have to have some kind of stability. . . . I had a very good relationship with my boss, and so I talked to him. . . . I had my computer set up. I had a laptop and dialing capabilities, everything is pretty much on our document system. They said, "Fine."

At first she worked three days a week at home and two in the office, and her mother-in-law provided childcare for the twins. On her home days, Jessica figured out how to do eight hours of work and take care of the twins herself. She started work at 6:00 a.m., putting in two hours before the twins woke up—a good time to call her European clients. She got in another two hours of work during the day at naptimes and worked four hours after the girls went to bed. Jessica was doing paid work and childcare for more than 16 hours a day. As she says, "I was very cognizant of being there for the phone, and being there for my e-mail. And in my mind, I thought I was doing a very good job keeping contact with everyone." But her boss thought otherwise, he asked her to start coming into the office three days a week.

This was the point when "things started to unravel," Jessica told me. Her mother-in-law could not take the twins for three days, so Jessica had to find a childcare center with two three-day openings. Her boss knew that she was unhappy with this arrangement and gave her a promotion—in Jessica's words, "to placate me." However, this supervisory role brought new difficulties. Jessica says:

> One guy would—started complaining, you know, that I was not always there for him . . . so my boss said, "Maybe we should think about one more day." And now I'm thinking, "It's one day after another, after another, after another. . . . This is it."

She scheduled a meeting with her boss; he canceled it. She went on a previously scheduled vacation; he called her at home and told her she had to work four days in the office. When she refused, she was told she had to write a formal request to the human resources (HR) department about continuing her schedule of three days in the office and two days at home. Jessica had never been asked to do this, but she wrote up what she wanted, and a formal meeting with HR was scheduled.

One day before the meeting, Jessica received a call from a former colleague at another biotech company, BioSegunda, asking if she would be interested in a job-share position. Jessica thought it was an "interesting offer," even though it was part-time, with less pay and no management responsibility. It was a permanent three-days-a-week position with full health insurance and other benefits on a prorated basis. Knowing about this offer made Jessica feel less trapped: "I felt I had something in my back pocket, so to speak." At the meeting with HR, Jessica was told she had four options: She could work 40 hours a week and come into the office five days a week; she could work four ten-hour days in the office and keep her title; she could go down to 32 hours a week and lose her manager title; or she could become an "independent contributor" (the company's term for independent contractor) and work three days a week, but lose all her benefits and her title. None of these were options that Jessica had put before management. She felt betrayed, and was shocked to find out that her boss was angry with her:

> And my boss said *he* felt betrayed by *my* suggestions. He felt that he had given me a way to make it on my terms, but that I gave him no room to wiggle, which . . . told him it had nothing to do with him, or wiggle, or playing games. I said to him, "I just told you what I could live with at this point in my life."

Jessica asked why they did not think her flex-place arrangement was working out. Her old boss mentioned the man she supervised who had complained about her "unavailability." He said, "People didn't like talking to [her] on the phone, because they could hear babies in the background." At that point, Jessica knew she had lost the battle. Close to tears, she said:

> There were times that I would shut myself in the bedroom when I was on the phone with a client, and I could . . . hear them crying . . . It's an awful feeling, because you never quite feel like, you're doing enough for the work, and you don't quite feel like you're doing enough for the kids.

She was given a few days to decide. Her offer letter from the other company came that Monday. On Tuesday, she announced to her supervisor that she was leaving. Everyone was stunned. Her old boss said, "I hope you didn't think those were your only options . . . we can work this out." Jessica told me, still in utter disbelief, "He actually said that to me!"

Jessica gave up full-time work, a supervisor's title, and five years of seniority to work part-time at a company where she felt there was support for flexible scheduling. Her new workplace is not perfect either; the workplace for working parents never is. Although Jessica feels that her new job is a big improvement, she and her job-share partner have to fend off subtle negative feedback from some colleagues. One male co-worker, a senior manager, started complaining to a vice president in the company. The VP asked him whether there was something that was not getting done, or if he was getting inconsistent answers from the two job sharers. He replied "No" to both questions, adding "I'm just confused." It is confusing to men and other workers who are used to traditional work roles and schedules to see people working differently. But for Jessica and other working parents, this new way of working is not confusing; it is the only thing that makes sense when one is trying to be both a responsible worker and a good parent.

The real question for worker-parents like Jessica is, "How open is biotech to designing work differently so that the needs of working families are fully recognized and accomodated? To answer this question, a better understanding of the biotech industry—its resources and constraints—is needed.

BIOTECH: A KNOWLEDGE INDUSTRY IN THE NEW ECONOMY

Biotechnology is emerging as a key industrial sector in the U.S. economy of the 21st century.[1] Potentially, biotech companies will make billions of dollars for shareholders and at the same time advance public health, improve agriculture, and protect the environment. Biotechnology combines an exciting area of scientific research, biology, with the dynamic and catalytic possibilities of electronic information technology.[2] The word "biotech" conjures up breakthrough drugs that will cure cancer and prevent or reverse Alzheimer's disease. One imagines scientists hard at work discovering the basis of life-threatening diseases or decoding genetic predispositions. The basis for advances in biotechnology dates back to the discovery of DNA in the 1950s, but as an industry biotech has only passed through its infancy in the 1990s; its maturation is occurring before our eyes. By the late 1990s, there were more than 1,200 biotech companies nationwide, with annual revenues of $15.2 billion and a workforce of more than 150,000 people.[3]

BIOTECH IN MASSACHUSETTS

The operative word for biotech in Massachusetts is "growth," despite some slowing as a result of the national economic downturn that began late in

2001.[4] The San Francisco Bay area had been the leading U.S. site for biotech companies during most of the 1990s, but by 1999 Massachusetts had the largest number in the country. Many factors make the greater Boston metropolitan region a fertile ground for the development of biotech. Most important is the existence of several major universities and medical schools that are graduating top-notch life and computer scientists. Tied to these institutions are teaching hospitals and laboratories where highly trained scientists can experiment and innovate. There have also been beneficial partnerships between state agencies and the industry's trade association, the Massachusetts Biotech Council.[5] Finally, there is a substantial supply of venture capital that—combined with a highly skilled workforce—has produced a "natural entrepreneurial engine."[6]

As the number of biotech companies in Massachusetts has grown, so has the workforce. In 1991, the Mass Biotech Council (MBC) represented 88 companies with a combined workforce of about 7,500; by the year 2000, there were nearly 250 companies with almost 25,000 employees, an increase of over 200 percent.[7] Another shift has been growth in company size. Like any industry that relies heavily on research and development, many biotech companies in the early and mid-1990s had fewer than 50 employees. As some of these companies moved products out of the research and development phase to approval by the FDA, they have grown. Many have added production facilities, quality assurance departments, and marketing divisions, and the MBC has stated recently that the industry could create as many as 150,000 new jobs by 2010.[8]

One of the most important new trends is that a number of the world's largest pharmaceutical companies have begun to establish a physical presence in the Boston metropolitan region.[9] The longstanding relationship between pharmaceuticals and biotech is often characterized as a parent-child relationship in which larger, wealthier pharmaceutical companies have entered into research collaborations with biotech start-ups. Sometimes this relationship has aided the growth and development of biotech; other times, it has meant a "brain drain" for biotech.[10] In either case, the increased presence of pharmaceutical companies signals the need for a highly skilled scientific workforce in Massachusetts. Although the new job opportunities are welcome, the MBC argues that this will only become a reality if state govenment works with local communities to speed the zoning and permitting process for biotech development. That story remains to be told.

IS THE MASSACHUSETTS BIOTECH INDUSTRY FAMILY-FRIENDLY?

A closer look at demographics makes clear the importance of family-friendly policies in these firms. As discussed earlier, the families I met are typical of the biotech workforce as a whole. Generally speaking, biotech workers are highly educated, about one-quarter hold Ph.D.s and over 80 percent have bachelor's degrees. The participation of men and women is roughly equivalent,[11] although there are fewer women in senior management positions. Most biotech workers are in their thirties and forties and have young children, as well as parents who are at the end of midlife, but not yet old and infirm. Approximately half the people in the workforce have one or more children living at home, and almost half of those children are of preschool age. This means that policies that address the care of preschool and school-age children—and, to some extent, support for elder care—are highly valued by the workforce. How responsive have Massachusetts biotech firms been in addressing these needs?

In 1997, the Human Resource Committee of the Massachusetts Biotechnology Council (MBC) and the Radcliffe Public Policy Institute jointly conducted a survey on human resource policies.[12] Its major focus was to learn more about the work environment in biotech, particularly for those with families. About one-third of the managers who responded to the survey stated that work-family issues are a drain on the morale of their employees, and two-thirds reported that childcare is "the most important work/family issue" for their employees.[13] Almost 60 percent of these managers believe that job insecurity and the uncertain futures of biotech companies have a significant negative impact on the morale of the biotech workforce,[14] and is more of a problem than the level of family-friendly policies.[15]

One of the most striking findings was that 95 percent of the employees surveyed worked full-time, and over one-third of the employees surveyed worked more than 40 hours a week; employees in senior management positions worked an average of 47 hours. Most firms that responded to the survey reported the availability of parental leave at the time of birth or adoption, and offered personal sick days.[16] However, these policies did not go beyond compliance with the Family and Medical Leave Act, a 1993 federal statute.[17] Very few companies reported offering job sharing, or on-site childcare, or leaves for community service.[18] Even though approximately 40 percent of the human resource managers stated that assisting parents to take time off when their children are sick is an important work-family benefit, few provided this as a formal policy.

A more recent benefits survey emphasized traditional benefits such as health insurance and retirement plans.[19] Two-thirds of employers surveyed provided Dependent Care Flexible Spending Accounts (DCAP) that allow workers to use pre-tax dollars to cover their family care expenses. Slightly over one-quarter of the firms provided childcare and elder care resource and referral services to assist employees in locating providers. Among these companies, almost three-quarters paid for this service, while the other quarter made it available for a fee. Only 5 percent of companies provided some type of backup or emergency care, and only one provided on-site childcare.

In terms of flexible work arrangements and leave policies, the benefits were modest, and only slightly over half of the companies had official flex-time policies. Most did not have a formal policy on part-time work and offered it rarely, on a case-by-case basis, at the discretion of individual managers. Benefits for part-time employees varied from adequate to limited. Less standard arrangements were not usually available.[20]

In sum, there is a discrepancy between what these biotech companies provide and the awareness, at least on the part of human resources managers, of the extent of work-family problems for many employees. Over half of these companies consider themselves "extremely" or "very" helpful with personal issues and work-family issues, but the array of family-friendly benefits is modest compared to the level of "best practices" in other industries.[21] Many companies stated that their small size makes it difficult to provide these benefits. In addition, the volatile environment in biotech—with frequent layoffs, rapid expansion, and new ownership—often cuts into the resources needed to expand work-family benefits.

CONSIDERING "COMMUNITY RELATIONS"

Massachusetts biotech has only recently begun to consider community issues, underscoring the relative immaturity of the industry.[22] There is not a great deal of data available yet as to how many companies are aware of or involved in community outreach, and whether they are trying to develop relationships with community-based organizations that could provide family support services to their employees. In 2000, the MBC initiated a new working group, the Community Outreach Committee. This committee began by conducting a benchmarking survey to determine "the current state of community relations and outreach programs being conducted by members of the MBC."[23] It is not surprising that none of the small firms—many of which are still in a start-up phase—had a community relations function and/or department. Even among the medium-sized and larger firms, only about a third had set up such a department. However, a number of the moderate and larger firms said they intended to establish such a function in the near future, indicating that their operating environment requires more attention to organizations in their communities.

Many firms have experienced pressure from local residents or advocacy groups who are questioning the nature of their biomedical research, often another example of NIMBYism ("not in my backyard").[24] A small number of companies are involved with cloning, but even those doing less controversial research may be under scrutiny about the focus and methods of their research and product development efforts. For this reason, biotech companies see a need to be sensitive and supportive to local community needs. Some companies surveyed report that community groups in cities and towns where their firms are located approach them for funds. In most instances, the CEO personally decides whether the company will respond, and if so, how generously. The survey concluded that most community relations programs "do not appear to be strategically driven," but rather "rely heavily on the interests, moods and inclinations of a single individual—the CEO or other key officer."

While most community relations efforts focus on charitable contributions, there are other forms of community involvement emerging in biotech. Out of a small number of responding companies, one-quarter of the firms have established employee volunteer programs, and about one-fifth have either set up scholarship programs or donated their products. Most charitable contributions are made in the areas of health and education, which is not surprising given that most companies are "intensely interested in promoting health care research and in having an educated well-trained workforce." Employee volunteerism is also modest: volunteers participate in once-a-year events such as walkathons or sports events; some are school volunteers; some donate time to work in soup kitchens or homeless shelters. One type of volunteerism is noticeable by its absence: work in an organization in the employee's own community or with a group significant to his or her own work-family needs. Usually, it is an organization chosen by the firm's CEO or community relations department that benefits from employee volunteerism.

The most significant finding of the survey is that although many biotech companies say they encourage their employees to do volunteer work, only 15 percent actually give their employees time off to volunteer.[25] For many biotech workers, paid time off is necessary to make this type of community involvement feasible. In recommendations drawn from the survey, the Community Outreach Committee suggested the development of a "tool kit" and other resources to help more biotech companies establish community relations departments. However, they never mention how the structures, policies, and pay arrangements of biotech firms may affect the ability of employees to make a volunteer commitment for more than one day or one event a year. If this were a company goal, coordination with the human resources department and the overall strategic plan of the company would be required. However, not even the largest biotech companies appear to be at that level of planning in their attempts to build community relationships.

THREE BIOTECH FIRMS

This book is based on an in-depth investigation of 40 families in which at least one member of each household is employed in one of three biotech firms in Massachusetts. A brief sketch of each company's history will give the reader an understanding of some of the external, industry-driven factors affecting the work-family lives of their employees.

BioPrima is a small, publicly owned biotechnology company located in a mixed-use industrial park. The company was founded in the mid-1980s, and in the late 1990s it merged with another small biotech company located in another state. Its corporate headquarters and major research and development facilities remain in Massachusetts, but it has some employees working at a Midwestern facility. The total workforce hovers around 60 employees in Massachusetts, and about 75 overall. During the company's entire history, it has been in a research and development mode, trying to develop products that will prevent or treat disease by tapping the resources of the immune system. Although the company had no products on the market by 2002, it had several products moving through the FDA's clinical trial process. Despite their lack of success in bringing a product to market, BioPrima has a number of long-service employees in both research and management who are highly committed to the company and confident that their research program will lead to success. There is a strong belief among the scientists that the company will be commercially successful in the long run, and that their products will replace existing products of lesser effectiveness.

BioSegunda is a medium-sized biotech company. When I first visited, it employed around 60 employees at one site; it now employs about 200 workers at three sites. The company has had four major incarnations, three different locations, and a period of bankruptcy. It began in a large city under one name, struggled financially, and filed under Chapter 11. The company then relocated, took a new name, and reduced its operating costs, but continued to struggle. In the late 1990s, it moved to a new industrial park close to Boston in hopes of recruiting more highly skilled workers. No sooner had it settled into the new location than the company was acquired by a medium-sized biotech company and changed its name again.[26] It has a small number of commercial products, including a vaccine and a patented adjuvant that is sold to a cohort of pharmaceutical partners for use in developing new drugs.[27] The company now faces many questions about its future owing to its location in three sites and the product development strategies of the new owner. It has laid off long-service personnel, including postdoctoral scientists, over the past few years. Most of its research and development work is consolidated at one site, and the new owner may consolidate the two production facilities, causing further personnel changes.

BioTertia is a large division of an even larger, publicly traded biotechnology company with more than 5,000 employees. It began as a separate company founded in the late 1980s, then changed its name when acquired by the parent company. The name changed again when the parent company went through a significant restructuring and combined several divisions into a new subsidiary. It has two viable commercial products that assist with the regeneration of specialized tissue groups, and several products in the research and development phase, including some in clinical trials. Despite its relative commercial success, there have been layoffs in recent years. This has created a climate of insecurity, and some valued employees have left rather than wait for their pink slips to arrive. The manufacturing component of this company is much larger than that of BioSegunda, and the workforce is much more diverse, including a higher proportion of employees with high school or associate diplomas. During my research, management instituted an alternative work week in the production department to accommodate specific clients' demands for two key products. While production and administration of this subdivision remain separate, the research and development department has now merged with that of the parent company.

The family-friendliness of these companies fits with the findings of the recent human resource surveys described above. The policies of the two smaller companies have remained modest, and accommodations to family needs are often handled on a case-by-case basis. They provide some flexibility, but this is more available to highly trained professional employees than to the less skilled sectors of the workforce.[28] Part-time work is rare—a particularly contested area—and some employees privately express their view that favoritism prevails when management is faced with requests for alternative work schedules. BioTertia, the largest of the three companies, has made work-family policies more formal and does provide free resource and referral services for dependent care. But the day-to-day culture of the workplace in BioTertia actually appears less family-friendly. The demands of their manufacturing departments put significant pressures and constraints on the lives of workers, whereas in the two smaller companies, flexibility regarding hours and schedules is sometimes possible through personal negotiation.

None of these companies has made significant investments in community programs or services for employees. In the two small biotech firms, there is no staff position focused on community relations, although the CEOs of both companies support in principle the concept of corporate community responsibility. In BioTertia there is a one-person community relations office and some community outreach work developing. The company has given scholarships to local students who want to pursue careers in the life sciences and some employees have participated in local charity fundraising. However, there are no policies to support employee community volunteerism, especially in a community organization of their own choosing.[29]

INSIDE THE BIOTECH WORKPLACE

Although some industries and occupations remain sex-segregated, since 1970 women have entered male-dominated fields in unprecedented numbers, especially in professional fields such as law and medicine.[30] In the biotechnology industry, rooted in research in biology, genetics, and biochemistry, the number of women is high. There are roughly equivalent numbers of women and men in the industry, with a high proportion of women in professional research and middle management jobs, but few women in senior management or CEO positions.[31] Judging by these numbers, women in biotech are doing well. They have jobs with decent wages and salaries, and career opportunities that exceed what would have been available to those who remained in the academy.[32] They are beneficiaries of a series of national legal, educational, and employment trends benefiting certain groups of women. But what does the picture look like when women biotech workers are mothers with family care responsibilities, and what happens to their male counterparts?

In these biotech workplaces, family-friendliness is a work in progress, as documented in the two Mass Biotech Council surveys of human resource policies. Some workers I spoke with told me that they have supportive supervisors who understand their need to leave early or stay home with a sick child. Others say their supervisors talk about the importance of family, but do not accommodate the family needs of those they supervise. The translation of formal policies into practice was not well developed in the three firms studied. Even though BioTertia has more extensive formal policies, the story of Jessica—the professional manager and mother of twins who could not get permission to work at home some days—illuminates what happens when policies on "full-time work" are subject to interpretation by an individual manager who is not willing to accommodate family needs. The stories of Crystal Carter, a production worker, and Beth Finley, a research scientist, give evidence that Jessica's frustrations are not uncommon.

CRYSTAL'S STORY

Crystal Carter is in her mid-twenties. She grew up in a small working-class city outside Boston, completed high school, and took some courses at a community college. She left college at nineteen for financial reasons. After a few years working in a medical office, she got a job as a "manufacturing associate" at BioTertia. This a position placed her in an environmentally controlled "clean room" where people work in special green suits that cover their street clothing and shoes, nets that cover their hair, and latex gloves. Crystal's work involved preparing the glassware in the laboratory area and providing sterilized materials for the production area. She enjoyed her job and saw it as a continuation of her interest in medicine. After working for approximately one year, Crystal left to have her second child and took 12 weeks' unpaid maternity leave. When she returned, she and her husband decided that he would work days and she would work evenings. This arrangement meant that they would not have to use childcare—which they could ill afford—and the children would always be with a parent. On Crystal's first day back, she was shocked to find that she was not going back to her old job, but rather was assigned to janitorial duties. Crystal explains:

> I started having to "biodecontaminate"—as they call it—basically I had to wash the ceilings, wash walls, wash floors, all night. And that's all I did. And I literally worked out of the janitor's closet . . . I didn't like it. It wasn't some-

thing that I had ever anticipated seeing when I applied for the job. And it's something that I wouldn't have applied for. And so when they had done this to me, without my say—I was repulsed by it. I think I worked under those conditions for maybe a month and a half, maybe two months. And then I just couldn't take it any more, because I got those looks, those hierarchy looks from the people. "Oh, that's just the janitor, don't worry." Literally carrying trash out of the "clean room." And it was not what I wanted to do for myself.

Crystal quit her job. She tried to talk to her supervisor who had previously praised her performance but he was not helpful. When she left for maternity leave, Crystal was led to believe she would have a "comparable job" in terms of pay, responsibilities, and working conditions. This is, in fact, legally mandated by the Family and Medical Leave Act of 1993. She even had reason to hope that she might get promoted. But instead of a promotion, she felt she had been demoted. Her supervisor told her that she had nothing to complain about, but Crystal felt differently:

And that was their big thing. "They're being paid the same, so why are they complaining?" . . . It's not a matter of pay. It's matter of what we applied for in a job, and what we have education for. I've got a lot of medical experience in my past. I don't need to scrub walls and ceilings.

After quitting her job, Crystal stayed home full-time with her two children and became pregnant again. Though she enjoyed the time at home, she felt she had been treated unfairly—that she had in some sense been punished for taking time off to have a baby. Not only were the janitorial duties demeaning to her, but other biotech workers seemed to hold her and her cleaning work in low regard. The experience left Crystal feeling bad about herself as both mother and worker.

As I sit with Crystal sits in her kitchen, she is in constant motion—jumping up to check her infant son while he napped, moving laundry from the washer to the dryer, taking hamburger out of the freezer to defrost for dinner. In between tasks, she reflects on her decision to leave biotech. She says, "I mean, actually, BioTertia, I really did enjoy. And like I said, I do regret the fact that I am not with them any more."

As she speaks, a sense of loss clouds her voice. In checking on her date of hire, I found out that Crystal had worked at the company a little less than one year at the time of her maternity leave, so technically the company did not violate the FMLA because Crystal was not covered by the act, which requires one year's seniority as an eligibility requirement for leave. However, the company did violate the spirit of the law, defeating its purpose that workers should not have to choose between job and family.

BETH'S STORY

Beth is a postdoctoral research scientist in her late thirties. She has worked at BioSegunda almost ten years and is the mother of two school-age children. When her children were still in family daycare, Beth's husband got a one-year position out of state that would advance his career. Beth was reluctant to separate from him for a year and did not think she could handle working full-time and taking care of their two children by herself, so she asked her company if she could take a leave of absence. She proposed working for part of the year in a laboratory with ties to her biotech firm that was located in the state where her husband would be doing his postdoctoral work. This would enable her family to be together for seven months of the twelve. Her request was approved, and Beth initially felt the company had been flexible in accommodating her family needs.

When Beth came back to work, however, she began to feel resentment about her leave among senior managers. This was conveyed in both subtle and not-so-subtle ways. It surprised her because there had been a precedent for this kind of leave of absence: a male scientist had gone out of the country for six months to accompany his wife on her sabbatical. The year after Beth returned, she received two disappointing decisions about her position in her firm. First, she did not receive a raise she expected. Then she was asked to take on more management responsibilities but did not get the promotion she thought went along with them. She said nothing, worried that if she complained she would never get them. Beth explains, "I mean it [the leave] showed a certain amount of flexibility on their part . . . although I really do believe that it hurt me in terms of salary and management advancement in the long run." Beth did eventually get a senior management position two years later, but she believes her request for a family-related leave delayed the process. She says:

> I think I would have gotten promoted sooner. I only got promoted last year,
> even though I had been managing staff for more than that, and I got a decent
> salary increase last year, but you know I didn't get it when I first started assuming responsibilities.

Beth believes that the company's decision to grant her a leave was filled with mixed messages. When her leave request was approved, she thought senior management supported her desire to keep her family together. When she returned, she realized that the leave was seen unfavorably, and she was in some sense "punished" for taking it. The company's foot-dragging on her pay and promotion was particularly irritating to Beth because the male scientist who had taken a similar leave was immediately promoted to senior vice president upon his return. The company seemed to be saying that it was fine for men to take leaves, but not for women—especially when they made family the explicit reason.

While the stories of these two women are unique in their details, they reveal a pattern of problems experienced by women in biotech, but not by their male counterparts. None of the men I interviewed told any stories of this kind, although many of them have families. They uniformly report that supervisors are understanding about parental leaves and the occasional need to leave early for soccer practice or to come in late from a parent-teacher conference. These men rarely took advantage of family-friendly policies. For example, none had taken more than a week's leave at the time of their children's birth or adoption—usually calling it "sick time" or "vacation time"— and only one man reported taking FMLA leave.[33] Men did not complain about impeded advancement or raises that came late. They did not ask for family accommodation, keeping their public profile well within that of the "ideal worker"—a primary breadwinner with no family responsibilities— regardless of their situation at home and the extent they helped with family care.

Some women, in contrast, did take advantage of existing family-friendly policies. Some employees, like Jessica, tried to create new policies to accommodate their needs. Most of the women who took parental leave and returned to full-time work did not have problems as significant as Crystal's. On the other hand, those who returned to work and wanted a different kind of schedule—either reducing the total number of hours worked per week, or working some hours at home and some in the workplace—did experience problems. Some, like Jessica, were forced to quit and find a company that would accept alternative work arrangements. For women who tried to return to their prechildren work style, there were great costs to their families and themselves: stress, fatigue, and burnout. For women who were allowed different work schedules after childbirth, there were other costs, including negative messages from co-workers and managers, and more serious consequences such as loss of promotion opportunities and, ultimately, job loss. Women like Beth, who already had their children and needed leave for family reasons, were caught in a double bind; they were given what they asked for, but when they took it, they paid a price.

FROM PERSONNEL MANUAL TO PRACTICE

These stories illustrate the gap between what policies are officially available to employees at the three firms, and what happens in practice.[34] Sometimes policies do not exist, as in the case of Jessica's working at home. Even when policies exist, requests to use them may be denied. In my conversations with workers, I probed to learn how managers interpret formal policy, how they create informal policies when none are provided, and how employees feel about using them.

PARENTAL LEAVE: AFFORDABILITY AND ATTACHMENT

Many of the workers I interviewed had taken time off from work after the birth or adoption of a baby. Although mothers and fathers take leaves in comparable numbers, the leaves of mothers were much longer and were always taken as "parental leave." At BioTertia, the common practice is for new mothers to take three months off, two months paid and the third month unpaid. The company allows up to five months' leave, but no one interviewed had taken that long. The stories of two other employees show that, across occupations, there are many issues following maternity leave.

For some workers, such as Maria Cabral, affordability is the major issue. Maria is from a large first-generation immigrant family and has two children of preschool age. Now in her late twenties, she was one of the first children in her family to get an American high school diploma. She started at BioTertia as a production worker but changed to a less strenuous production support job after her second child was born. Her husband does construction work that is sporadic and unpredictable, so the family relies on Maria's steady, albeit modest, income. She said, "I couldn't stay home for months and not get paid. I couldn't live that way unless I was rich."

Laurie Pratt is a middle manager in her late thirties who supervises a department of production workers. Her husband has a full-time professional job, so she says she could afford to have taken more than a three-month leave when her first child was born, but she did not do so because she felt her supervisor would disapprove. Laurie says that if she has a second child, she plans to take more time off and finance the leave with savings and vacation time. She would also like to request a gradual return to work and work part-time for a while. She says the company allowed one other woman in her department to do that, and she hopes that her supervisory status will not be an obstacle. She seems unaware of Jessica's difficulties at the same company.

The feelings of new mothers about the length of their leave time are difficult to discern. Just as new parents are reluctant to discuss problems with their childcare arrangements, they seem equally reluctant to voice displeasure with their leaves. There is a kind of pat, cheery quality to their responses about the adequacy of their leave time that belies a complex set of issues about their attachment to their newborns, and uncertainty about whether it is a good idea to leave a three-month-old baby in another's care. Maria, for example, joked about how boring it was to do housework while on leave, but kept mentioning how strongly attached her first son, Anthony, is to her:

> And he was very, very hard to adapt to other people. If I walked into one room, he would cry. I couldn't even take a shower without him crying. He was like too attached.

Anthony's difficulty adapting to others becomes transposed into Maria's difficulty with his starting out-of-home childcare. She says, "Even still today, he still wants me . . . he's still my little boy . . . in the morning, I have to always hold him." In speaking of this daily embrace, Maria seems to be communicating her distress about their daily separation.

Laurie's ambivalence about leaving her baby is expressed through a protracted process of deliberation about her schedule ever since she returned to work from her maternity leave. She worries that she has not been spending enough time with her baby. She has arranged for her husband to care for their son one day (Sunday) of her four-day work week, but she confides that she is going to ask her supervisor if she can reduce her ten-hour days by working four nine-hour days. Laurie really wants a work week of 30 to 35 hours, but is reluctant to request this because it does not conform to company norms about the time supervisors are supposed to be at work. This parallels her reluctance to request additional leave when her child was born. Informal workplace norms seem to supersede the policies in the personnel manual.

Although Maria and Laurie are in different financial situations, they share a common ambivalence about leaving infants in the care of others. By publicly discussing how attached their children are to them, Maria and Laurie may also be conveying to others (and perhaps themselves) that they are "good mothers" even though they are working. The new fathers I spoke to did not seem to need to prove their attachment to newborns, nor do they express anxiety about being away from home. Their willingness to return to work quickly and work steadily—to be good breadwinners—is the culturally sanctioned way for fathers to show their commitment to their newborn children.

Leave at the time of adoption follows a similarly gendered pattern. Two parents among the 40 families I met, one man and one woman, had adopted children. Mike, an associate scientist at BioPrima, kept working and stayed at home with an older child while his wife, Lisa, left the country with her sister to go and pick up their newly adopted son. When the baby came home, Lisa was given a maternity leave of six weeks, and Mike took the same amount of paternity leave he had taken with their first biological child—one week. Lisa went back to work part-time after her leave, but she did not feel comfortable being away from her new son and soon quit her job. She and Mike agreed that one parent needed to be home, and that it should be Lisa. So the leave Mike took was seen as appropriate, and the issues of separation, attachment, and anxiety about out-of-home care were only expressed by his wife.

The second adoption, by Rachel Warren, a single mother who holds a professional position at BioTertia, was also cross-cultural but went much less smoothly. When Rachel adopted her daughter, she was working not at BioTertia but at another biotech company. Her supervisors would not give her any leave, even when she offered to use up all of her accumulated vacation time. In fact, they told her directly that if she left to go get her daughter, then she would lose her job. Luckily, she obtained a position at another biotech company where the head of human resources offered her an eight-week paid adoption leave: five weeks in China, and three getting her daughter settled back home.[35] Rachel did not feel that she had adequate time with her new daughter, but as a single parent, she could not afford the luxury of a longer unpaid leave.

CARING FOR SICK CHILDREN: NOT A DAY OFF

Although new mothers take much more time off than new fathers for birth or adoption, staying home with sick children is fairly equally shared by married biotech employees who are part of families where both parents work.

Which parent stays home is related to the nature of the work done by each spouse, the amount of travel they do for work, and their companies' policies to cover this kind of situation. For example, Mike, the adoptive father described above, reports that he usually stays home with his kids because he has more sick days and more overall flexibility on his job than his wife does; she has now returned to work. If they split a day, Mike will leave at 5:00 a.m., work from 6:00 to 10:00 a.m., and return home by 11:00 a.m., and then Lisa goes to work for the afternoon.

Helen Rafferty, a middle manager at BioTertia, says she is usually the one who stays home with her children when they are sick because her husband, a self-employed insurance salesman, cannot cancel appointments with clients and is frequently on the road. Helen is allowed to use her own sick days, and her supervisor has assured her that if she needs more, "We'll work it out." Helen believes that her supervisor's experiences as a working mother herself have made the difference on this issue. Asked how her workload is affected when she stays home with a sick child, Helen answers, "Well, what I do is that I have a computer hookup at home, and I bring stuff home with me."

For Helen, as for other professional biotech employees, a day with a sick child is *not* a "day off." There are phone calls from work, time on the computer, and pulls in multiple directions. Several workers expressed reservations about this situation. The arrangement may work with a school-age child, but it is less likely to work with a preschool child. It may be feasible with a mildly ill child, but not for a seriously ill child; and even a mildly sick child of any age wants parental time, making work at home difficult. Most workers say that their supervisor understands the need to stay home with a sick child and does not penalize them for taking time off, but there are not-so-subtle messages about making the day "productive." Caring for a sick child is not viewed as "real work."

The situation of single parents with sick children is especially stressful. Most single parents interviewed mentioned their fear of not having enough sick time to cover their children's needs, and their fear that they will not be found in an emergency. There does seem to be some recognition on the part of supervisors that single parents face particular challenges, but they have the same number of sick days as those who are married. Malika Shaheed is a single mother and laboratory specialist at BioTertia. She explains the difficulties of not having enough sick days to care for her children:

> I don't use my vacation time. My vacation time here, and my sick time here, and my personal holiday times here, I save for when the children get sick. Because I have three [boys] and when one gets sick, it takes about three weeks to get back on your feet, so I need all the time as possible that I can . . . [because I] have to keep getting paid.

The problem with this strategy is obvious: a lack of family vacation time. This year, Malika says, her boys were not ill very much, and she has accumulated enough vacation time to take their first family trip. At Christmas, they are going to the West Indies to visit her great-grandmother. Malika says, "She's really ill, so I want [my sons] to get there before it's too late. So that's a big goal for me this year." The tradeoffs—time to care for sick children versus time for vacation, time to care for sick children versus time to visit an elderly relative—seem unfair, but they are often the tradeoffs a single working mother must make.

FLEXIBILITY FOR WHOM?

Within the Massachusetts biotech industry, scheduling options vary greatly by company and by occupation. At BioPrima, where there is no production facility, most people are on some variant of a 9-to-5 schedule. The company appears to have no problem with employees using flextime options such as coming in early and leaving early. However, the company has had conflicts with employees who have proposed part-time work schedules. One employee was dismissed after requesting this type of arrangement.[36] Ultimately, she was able to renegotiate her job to a contract position that provides part-time hours but no benefits—a major tradeoff. In contrast, Colleen McCarthy, an associate scientist, has worked out a 20-hour/two-day work week to maximize time to care for her preschool sons. Flexibility is available for some employees at BioPrima but not for others, and requests are handled on a case-by-case basis. It seems to depend on the supervisor's orientation, and how much pressure project teams are under in the clinical trial process.

At BioTertia, which houses a significant production facility, scheduling issues are complex and volatile. During my first year interviewing workers at this company, major scheduling changes were announced. These changes were welcomed by some but not by all. The shift to a ten-hour day, four days a week was viewed very positively by Bill Kopell, a production worker in his mid-twenties. He works Sunday through Wednesday, goes to college in the evenings, and uses Thursday to do course work. The new schedule enables him to have a two-day weekend with his wife and daughter and still have time for his education. However, Ralph Carter, another production worker in his twenties, has mixed feelings about the four-day schedule. It allows him to take courses at a community college near his home for his associate's degree and help his wife at home on weekdays. The couple has two preschool children and a baby on the way. He also likes the extra pay that he receives for working Saturdays and Sundays. On the other hand, Ralph says regretfully, "I can't go to any family events." He will miss summer barbecues and other extended-family get-togethers. We first spoke in July, and Ralph was already worrying about the Christmas holidays.

The supervisors, scientists, and other biotech professionals at BioTertia are more positive about the schedule changes. These employees have the option of working four ten-hour days but are not required to do so. As described earlier, professionals like Laurie Pratt and Helen Rafferty like the four-day work week because it helps them manage their family care needs. It gives Laurie more time at home with her son and reduces the impact of Helen's long commute. In both cases, there is another parent at home who can be with the children on weekend days. In contrast, all the single mothers with professional jobs at BioTertia have maintained their Monday-through-Friday, 9-to-5 schedules. They say it would be an enormous hardship for them to do otherwise: those who live alone have little weekend backup, and weekend childcare is expensive and hard to find.

Diverse family situations and other factors affect whether changes in work schedule produce greater or lesser flexibility for particular workers. A "one-size-fits-all" model is bound to affect some adversely. A company that adopts a model based on multiple flexible schedules is optimal, and the small biotech firms seemed more able than larger companies to take that approach to flexibility.

"FAMILY VALUES" OR VALUING FAMILIES

The culture of the workplace is a complex reality, constantly being constructed and reconstructed by formal policies, informal practices, and a shared language of sanctioned ways to talk about work-family issues. There are employees at all three companies who speak positively, even effusively, about the attitudes of supervisors and the overall responsiveness of their companies to work-family issues. This includes employees at all levels in a variety of occupations. For example, a female scientist says of BioPrima: "It is a company that is very supportive of families. Partly because of the general attitude of the company, partly the attitude of my boss . . . he is very involved with his own kids." A male production worker at BioSegunda comments: "Supervisors understand that a job isn't your whole life. And you're not going to stay on the job if they insist that it is your whole life." A female manager at BioTertia says: "Ted's motto is 'Family comes first.' . . . I do my best to minimize the interruption, but when I have to go, I go."

Biotech employees learn about workplace norms from the words of their supervisor, and about workplace realities from the behavior of their supervisor. Many employees say they must "go the extra mile" to get the full support of a supervisor—for example, one woman worked up to the day before going into labor, another worked at home during a pregnancy with medical complications, rather than taking time off. The relationship between supervisor and employee is not static; there is constant negotiation. Laurie Pratt says that if she were to advise an expectant first-time mother, she would say:

> Build up the relationship with your supervisor ahead of time. Like I knew that if I did a good job working at home when I was pregnant, that would bode well for me if I wanted to stay home if and when the child was sick. So I started looking forward in that way.

The motto "Family comes first" provides a framework of shared language that makes both employees and managers feel comfortable, but the pressure to "get the job done" is constant. The way work is organized in biotech—with round-the-clock care of research animals, tight production schedules that rely on fragile human tissue, constant pressure on researchers to complete experiments that might lead to new drugs before their competitors—often means that workers are away from their families on weekend days or unable to participate in family holidays. "Family comes first"—except when work must come first.

CREATING A FAMILY-FRIENDLY WORKPLACE: A SHARED PROJECT

Even though many workers I spoke with value the family-friendly policies at their companies, formal policies are quite limited, especially at the smaller firms; their use is uneven, and the consequences of using them remain unpredictable. Women use these policies more frequently and for longer periods of time than men, and that is not always advantageous for their careers. The depth of support for employees' work and family lives is in part limited by the fact that many biotechnology companies are still struggling to establish commercially viable products. While companies are still in a "start-up" phase, it may be difficult to invest significant resources in family-friendly policies. The conditions of economic downturn in 2002–2003 do not bode well for an expansion of these policies in the near term.

Several factors that I noticed at all three companies limit efforts to create a family-responsive work environment. First, there are significant pressures to work full-time, or more. The majority of employees work at home on weekday evenings; others work at home when their children are sick and when they are disabled because of pregnancy. They are not encouraged to take leave at the time of birth or adoption that goes beyond what is mandated by law, and when they return from parental leave, they are pressed to work full-time. It is difficult to negotiate a gradual return to work that would allow a limited period of part-time work, and permanent part-time positions are rare. These pressures combine to devalue the importance of family caregiving work relative to paid work.

Second, although some research and management employees have flexibility in their schedules and in the place they do their work, production and clerical workers have little access to flexible work arrangements. This not only puts those at the lower end of the occupational hierarchy at a disadvantage; it also creates a climate of preferential treatment and lack of equity within each firm. Jessica's story shows that managers also face flexibility problems, despite their supervisory status.

Finally, the low level of job security in the biotech industry as a whole, and the fragility of particular companies—especially small companies like BioPrima and BioSegunda—casts a shadow over the attempt to provide supportive work-family policies. Even high levels of education do not create job security. More retraining programs that build on the transferability of biotech knowledge to other industries, cross-industry transfer policies, and portable benefits might mitigate this situation in the future. In the meantime, layoffs and low profits mean that families are constantly worrying about the viability of their firms and the stability of their jobs.

Biotech in Massachusetts is a young industry in transition. Management is neither blind to the family needs of its workforce nor consistently responsive to them. This is not so much a question of insensitivity as a reflection of the intense competition in the industry, especially among less established firms, and the constant struggle to bring new products to market. Work-family policies are modest, and often viewed as just one more piece of the employees benefits package. This model of developing a family-friendly workplace is flawed in two ways. It does not address the way work is organized inside biotech firms, thereby thwarting efforts at work redesign that might lead to significant alternative work arrangements. It does not address the crisis of caregiving in families by contributing to childcare or elder care services, leaving families to fend more or less for themselves. Creating work-family policies that would facilitate greater resources for community-based family support programs, or policies that promote community volunteerism, are not even on the agenda yet for the vast majority of firms. As biotech comes of age as an industry, its ability to address the work, family, and community needs of its workforce will be as vital to its success as breakthroughs in scientific research. In fact, the ability of biotech firms to recruit scientifically trained workers at all levels may rest on the expansion of work-family policies.

Family is still viewed as a private matter by most managers in biotech reflecting attitudes and values deeply entrenched in our culture. In this way, the work-family policies that do exist reproduce the traditional division between the public world of work and the private world of family. Until these divisions are reduced or dramatically realigned, family care will remain the exclusive concern of individual biotech workers and their families, and not the shared concern of families and biotech firms. Perhaps if employers invested more in the community institutions—in programs that are based neither at home nor at work—then a process of realignment could begin. And if biotech employers facilitated greater employee volunteerism in community organizations, the task of building work-family support systems would become a shared project with many players that redefines both the public and private spheres.

CHAPTER THREE

ALL IN THE FAMILY

IT'S NOT A PRIVATE AFFAIR

It is 6:00 a.m. at the Steinbergs'. Fran, who works full-time as a biotech manager, and Philip, a full-time software engineer, get up at the same time. Fran uses the treadmill first because she has to leave for an early meeting. According to their much-discussed childcare arrangements, Philip will take their seven-year-old daughter, Rebecca, to the bus this morning, and Fran will pick Rebecca up around 6:30 at her mother's. Their careers are equally important, so they try to share childcare equally: whoever has to leave first in the morning does the evening pickup, they've agreed this is fair. Even though Fran must leave by 7:00, she manages to get a load of laundry going and iron her daughter's favorite outfit before she goes. Fran dresses quickly and goes into Rebecca's room at 6:50. She kisses Rebecca and whispers that she is leaving in ten minutes. Rebecca begins a sleepy protest. Fran, having anticipated this, tells Rebecca that her favorite outfit is ready to wear. Rebecca pulls her down on the bed with a wordless hug.

As Fran says goodbye, Rebecca calls out, "Tell Daddy I can't be late . . . okay?" Fran, not wanting to take sides on this issue, answers, "Have a great day, sweetie. I'll see you at Bubbie's." Fran is grateful that her mother, Estelle, can take care of Rebecca after school. Estelle helps Rebecca with homework and cooks her dinner, so Rebecca doesn't have to wait for a late dinner, and Estelle doesn't have to eat alone. Fran leaves her house in an upscale section of a large city, hoping traffic will be light and she won't be late for the senior managers' meeting. If she has time, she'll check in with her mother at 8:00; if not, she'll call later. They usually speak twice a day now—once in the morning to see how her mother is feeling (she is having health problems), and once in the afternoon to see what Rachel and Estelle are up to.

In the meantime, Philip has gotten dressed, and made himself a cup of coffee, and is on the computer doing e-mail. Rebecca wanders into the study 20 minutes later, saying, "You're supposed to get me up." Philip answers, "I thought Mommy got you up. Go get dressed and I'll make you a bagel." Rebecca leaves, gets dressed, and heads for the kitchen. "Where's my bagel?" she calls out to her father, still on his computer. "It's all ready, honey . . . it's in the toaster oven." Rebecca eats breakfast by herself. "We have to go," she calls to her father in the study. "I know, Becca," Philip replies. "I'm just finishing this e-mail, and I'll be right there." At 8:30, they leave the house for a five-minute walk to an 8:40 bus. "See," says Philip when they get to the bus stop, "plenty of time." Two minutes later, the bus arrives. Rebecca gives her Dad a wordless hug and climbs on board.

It is 6:00 a.m. at the Strattons'. George, who works full-time as a biotech research scientist, gets up first. His wife, Elizabeth, who quit her full-time job in advertising a year ago to stay home with the kids, is still asleep. Both children are sleeping and don't need to get up until 7:00. George showers, dresses quickly, and tiptoes downstairs to make breakfast for himself. The house is quiet. He brings his briefcase into the kitchen and pulls out some journal articles he is supposed to review. He was going to do this the night before but was too tired. He's glad for a little extra time this morning. After ten minutes, his son appears in the kitchen. No one ever has to get Stephen up; he's got a built-in alarm clock and more energy than the rest of the family put together. He starts asking his Dad one question after the other about last night's Red Sox game. George answers, "I haven't had time to look at the paper . . . I don't know what the final score was," trying to get to the gist of the article he's reading before he has to leave for work. George gives brief answers to Stephen's questions and continues to read. Stephen picks up on his father's ambivalence and bounds back upstairs to get dressed.

Promptly at 7:00, Elizabeth appears in the kitchen. She is dressed and has already made a preliminary attempt to get Allie, their younger child, out of bed. She tells George that Allie is not feeling well and may be running a low-grade fever. No response. "Do you think I should call the pediatrician?" George looks up momentarily, "Whatever you think is best, honey." Elizabeth looks slightly annoyed and announces she's going upstairs to take Allie's temperature. George keeps reading, looks at his watch; he's got five more minutes. Stephen comes downstairs—two at a time—and starts bombarding his father with questions about his softball game that afternoon. "Do you think the coach will let me pitch? Do you think you'll be able to make the game?" George gets up, packs up his briefcase, and starts heading out the door—it's 7:30. "I'll try, buddy. I'll really try. I've got a late afternoon meeting and I'm not sure what time I'll be able to get out of there." Stephen looks away. George adds brightly, "But Mom will be there." Stephen mutters something like, "She doesn't even like baseball," and leaves the kitchen. George is halfway out the door when Elizabeth reappears. "She's got 99.4, should I keep her home?" George looks trapped, "I'm going to be late, honey. Whatever you think. Call the pediatrician." He leaves.

Elizabeth sighs and starts breakfast for the kids. She carries Allie downstairs, installs her and her comforter on the couch, and puts *The Little Mermaid* in the VCR. She rushes to make Stephen's lunch and asks if he has his glove for the afternoon game. She grabs her purse and says to Allie, "I'll be back in five." She smiles, waves an encouraging goodbye, and leaves to drive Stephen to school. She's happy she can keep Allie home—something that would have been much harder if she were still working—but she has so much to do. She'll have to call school, tell them that Allie is sick, and let them know she can't make the Curriculum Committee meeting at 10:00. If Allie naps, she might have time to make plane reservations for the family to visit George's mother on the occasion of her seventy-fifth birthday. She says to me, "I don't know how I ever worked."

This "tale of two families" is really a tale of the stalled gender revolution. Observing the morning routines of the Steinbergs and the Strattons, one might ask, "Is this the 1990s or the 1950s?" When Elizabeth and George both held full-time professional jobs, the daily routines of these families probably looked quite similar, however, the Strattons felt their lives were spinning out of control. The decision for Elizabeth to leave her professional job is filled with tradeoffs. There is much less weekday stress in the family, but Elizabeth has put her career on hold and is doing virtually all the childcare, housework, and community volunteer work. Is becoming a "housewife" the only way for women to regain their sanity—and some sleep?

BEYOND THE TIME DEFICIT

Much of the current discussion about work-family conflict and work-family balance targets time as a major problem. The argument goes something like this. The 40-hour work week is a myth of the past. Workers in the United

States are working longer and longer hours.[1] Even when workers are not in the workplace, many are still working, because computer technology, e-mail, voice mail, and beepers allow our employers, clients, and co-workers to track us down at home, in the evenings, on weekends, and even on vacation. Between the lengthening work day and the dissolving boundary between home and work, there is little time for family. There is a great deal of truth in these formulations and most working parents will tell you they lack enough time to get everything done. This situation has been referred to as the "time bind" or "time deficit."

However, a review of research on time and working families reveals a more complex picture.[2] On the one hand, there are lawyers, physicians, and various categories of managerial and professional workers who are burdened by too many hours of work. On the other, there are low-wage, semiskilled workers looking for full-time rather than part-time jobs, seeking overtime, or needing a second or third job to help make ends meet. The way time is organized at work and at home is a social construct—it is "man-made." Work time and family time could be organized differently if employers were willing to reshape the work day. As described in chapter 2, some employers offer flextime and other alternative work schedules, part-time work, and working in spaces other than the workplace. If these time-related experiments were more widespread and were available to working parents in a variety of jobs and family situations, we might begin to see some easing of work-family conflicts, and the time deficit might be seen more accurately as a symptom of the problems that working families are having, not the cause.

There are three interrelated factors shaping family life that combine to aggravate work-family conflict. First, most marriages are not equal partnerships. Even though some men are doing more unpaid work in the home than their fathers did, the primary responsibility for domestic work and caregiving still lies with women.[3] Second, the number of family-friendly workplaces is still relatively small. The lack of flexibility and the emphasis on full-time work has created family strategies that reproduce traditional gender roles within marriage. Third, there are many cultural messages telling families that the problems they face are private or individual, and they should solve these problems by themselves.

This chapter will examine each of these problems in turn, emphasizing that the stalled gender revolution inside families can be understood only by examining the pressures and forces outside the family. This is not an indictment of the family, or of the young fathers who are sharing family care and housework and breadwinning with their wives. It is rather an effort to understand how the lack of change in the way work is organized, and the lack of support for working families in communities, are making it very difficult to expand gender equality inside families. An ideology of privatization impedes the process of turning to people and institutions outside the family for the support needed to handle work-family issues.

WORKING AGAINST THE ODDS

The fact that there is still gender inequality in marriage is not exactly news, although the contemporary women's movement began calling for change by 1970.[4] Now we have a society in which most men and women are married, some are not, and most women are employed, regardless of their marital status. Women are contributing their talents to the world outside the home in business, government, and the nonprofit sector. But what does the world inside the home look like? First, the good news: There is more gender equality in marriages where both parents are working. Second, the bad news: employed women do more housework and childcare than employed men, and in marriages where one parent is working full-time and one is at home, women do virtually all the family care work. In the families I got to know with a stay-at-home parent, women were doing over 90 percent of the housework and family caregiving; in single-parent families, usually headed by women, the mothers do it all. We are told by scholars that marriage is good for husbands, wives, and children.[5] Most children raised in families with two married parents do better materially, academically, and emotionally than children raised in families with a single parent. Men and women who are married fare better economically, are healthier, and live longer than those who are not. If this is true, then why are working parents having so much trouble?

Through the experiences of biotech employees, I will take a detailed look at the strategies and choices of married couples and single parents. Their stories reveal both how families cope, and the tensions inherent in daily work schedules and domestic routines. Their strategies are shaped by the lag between the new realities of family care and by outdated public and private policies.[6] Some workers devise private solutions as a response to this institutional and policy lag, while others struggle to devise collective solutions by creating new social ties and community connections.

THE DAILY WORK-FAMILY ROUTINE

During the work week, the daily routine for married biotech workers is hectic. Time with children and spouses is limited. Most of the workers I interviewed have only half an hour in the morning to see their immediate family members, unless they take the children to school or childcare. In the evening, depending upon the ages and bedtimes of the children, they have two to three hours after they get home from work, and this time is crowded with many activities, only some of which involve family time. Gender differences among these workers are significant. More women than men transport children to and from school, extended-day programs, and childcare, especially in the afternoons. This fact puts more women home in the late afternoon, responsible for grocery shopping, other errands, dinner preparation, and homework help. The most common care task for men is taking children to childcare or school in the morning, and the most common housework task for men is cleaning up after dinner; some see the weekend as time off from work *and* family. Women do some portion of these tasks plus a wide array of others on a daily basis, and they do not have a day off from caregiving or housework.

SHARING TASKS VERSUS SHARING RESPONSIBILITY

In dual-earner families, the degree of sharing is a constant subject of negotiation. Fran and Philip Steinberg have a system. They check their weekly schedules on Sunday evening; whoever leaves first in the morning is the person responsible for picking up their daughter in the afternoon. While this sounds fairly equitable, difficulties surface when both have an early meeting, or when the one who has to leave early also has to stay late. When these issues arise, it is Fran who arranges backup care. Fran's role as the person who organizes Rebecca's care, and makes alternative plans when work pressures are mounting on both parents, is a common pattern in these dual-earner marriages.

Housework also is shared to some extent, with Fran doing most of the tidying tasks and Philip doing approximately half the dinner preparation. Tidying tasks are discretionary and take longer than dinner preparation; while dinner can be either cooked or take-out. Fran's standard of neatness propels her to spend a number of hours cleaning during the evening and on weekends. She is lucky to have a cleaning person who comes every other week, but by week two she finds herself doing more and more housework.

Fran feels that after-dinner time is the most fairly shared part of the day. She and Philip have limited evening commitments during the week—an occasional meeting or a class of short-term duration. They both help Rebecca with homework and spend "downtime" with her in the evening.

Another method of sharing between two parents with full-time jobs is to divide each day on a regular basis. This works fairly well for Mike and Lisa gets up every day at 5:00 a.m. and leaves the house by 6:00 without seeing their two children. Lisa takes care of breakfast for both children, dresses the baby, and drives one child to family childcare and one to school. By getting to work early, Mike is able to leave work early, at 4:00 p.m., so he picks up his daughter every day from her after-school program and starts dinner. He doesn't make "fancy dinners—it's usually spaghetti," and one night a week they order pizza. This dual-earner family is one of the few I met in which the husband rather than the wife is home in the late afternoon.

In most of these dual-earner couples, there is sharing of tasks without real sharing of responsibility. Peter Taylor, Julie's husband, prepares breakfast in the morning but requires her direction about what to make. He drops off one child in the morning; Julie picks up both children in the afternoon, runs errands, makes dinner. Most evenings, she has to remind him to clean up. Over the years, Julie has developed minimal standards about how much "family work" she needs her husband to do to make life in their two-career family function, but there are many tasks she does not try to delegate. She keeps the family calendar and is in charge of remembering special occasions: "I get birthday cards for my mother, and I get birthday cards for *his* mother!"

Some married dual-earner couples handle work-family stress by having one parent work full-time and one part-time. This arrangement has been called the "neo-traditional family."[7] About 20 percent of the dual-earner couples in the biotech firms I studied have tried this approach. In each family, it is the wife who is working part-time. These women were working full-time but cut back their hours and took on additional childcare, housework, and volunteer work. The circumstances triggering this change varied: sometimes it coincided with the birth of a second child; sometimes the cumulative exhaustion of having two parents work full-time prompted a search for alternative work schedules. Usually, men's higher earnings are the reason given for why it was the wife who cut back her hours, but the pull of traditional gender roles was also a factor—even if unstated. The result of this change invariably led to the wife assuming more tasks *and* more responsibility.

DECIDING TO HAVE ONE PARENT (MOM) STAY HOME

In biotech families where the husband and wife have made a decision for the
wife to "stay at home,"[8] a traditional gender-based division of labor exists that
is reminiscent of, but not entirely the same as, the model of one male breadwinner and one female homemaker. The daily routine of George and
Elizabeth Stratton is not unique to them; in other couples who tried to live
a life of shared work and shared care, the reality proved so stressful for both
partners that they now prefer a less egalitarian marital relationship.

THE MYTH OF THE STAY-AT-HOME MOM

In the families who have chosen to have one parent stay at home, both members of the couple seem comfortable with the ideology of the husband as primary breadwinner and the wife as primary caregiver,[9] but this ideology masks
an important and little-discussed reality. In these families, the full-time stay-
at-home mom is not only doing a great deal of unpaid work, she is also doing
paid work. For example, Elizabeth Stratton began working part-time doing
small projects for her old employer when her daughter started kindergarten,
although from 11:30 a.m. on she is completely absorbed with her children's
activities. She reports that doing even a few hours of paid work a day re-creates
the feelings of stress that she associates with her former life. Among the other
stay-at-home moms, one teaches aerobics several mornings a week at a health
club, another works as a part-time writer on health issues, and two other
women run family childcare services. Most but not all of these mothers work
out of their houses, where they can move back and forth, mentally and physically, between family work and paid work during the day.

The 1950s model of the stay-at-home mom has all but disappeared. The
21st century stay-at-home mom is a member of the *contingent* workforce.
That is, she is either self-employed, an independent contractor, or a part-time
worker, and in each case has no benefits. Some of these women aspire to have
professional careers and some do not, but they all expressed a desire to
increase their earnings. The need for two incomes does not disappear when
couples decide to have one parent stay home.

Interestingly, many of these women think of themselves as "out of the
labor force," and some are defensive about "not working." Sally Kopell, who
is married to a production worker at BioTertia, works as a part-time family
childcare provider. She is proud that her earnings allow her family to buy

things they otherwise could not afford, like a VCR, but Sally does not think of herself as an early childhood teacher with career opportunities. She takes a self-deprecating stance, saying, "I'll never be a rocket scientist . . . I don't think I could be a career person and a mom too." Sally is living one reality—part-time worker and full-time mother—while clinging to an image and an ideology of full-time, stay-at-home motherhood.

BEING MOM AND DAD WHEN YOU'RE JUST MOM

With only one adult to do it all, the challenges of housework, caregiving, and family time are particularly challenging for biotech workers who are single parents. There are two approaches to working and caring taken by the single parents I met. Malika Shaheed, who works as a regulatory affairs specialist at BioTertia, is an Afro-Caribbean single parent of three boys under age twelve. She reports on a typical morning at her house:

> I am up between 5:00 and 5:30. I'm usually fixing lunches, getting breakfasts, tying up anything from the night before. For example, ironing clothes that need ironing, anything like that. Then the boys get up. I feed them; we all sit and eat. Making sure that everybody has everything they need for school. All papers, everything is signed, mom stuff. Then I get dressed and I bring the boys, drop off two at school, or sometimes they walk depending on the weather. Then I have to drop the baby off, my youngest, to daycare. And then I am usually here [at work] about 8:00.

Malika has done three hours of unpaid work before her paid job begins. When her marriage broke up, she moved to Massachusetts to be near her father and get help with backup or emergency childcare, but she manages her daily routine solo.

The situation of Barbara Feldman, a methods validation specialist and divorced single mother of two, is different. She moved in with her parents and relies on them to help care for her son and daughter. On a typical morning, Barbara gets up at 6:30 a.m. with her kids, makes them breakfast, and eats with them. She needs to leave the house by 7:30, so her mother, Shirley, makes sure her granddaughter leaves the house on time to walk to school and drives her grandson to preschool. Shirley picks up her grandson at 11:30 a.m. from his half-day preschool program, then drives him to his afternoon babysitter. She also drives her granddaughter to after-school activities such as soccer practice and ice-skating. Shirley's driving provides the missing infra-structure of a fragmented childcare delivery system.

The pattern of activities at the end of the day is also different for Malika and Barbara. Veronica, again, does it all—picking up her youngest at child-care, making dinner for the boys, helping the older two with homework, doing housework. She says a "good night" is when she can go to bed at 9:00 p.m., and a "bad night" is when she has to stay up until 11:00 to get everything done. Barbara, on the other hand, gets home around 6:00; her mother usually makes dinner while Barbara assists her daughter with home-work. Barbara takes care of baths and bedtime stories and rarely goes out in the evenings, except to take the kids to an occasional family-oriented com-munity event or attend a school-related meeting. This is not to say that life is easy for Barbara—both she and Malika complain that they do not have any personal life as single mothers—but sharing a household with her parents gives Barbara a kind of support that Malika lacks.

EXTENDED FAMILY TIME: EASING THE BURDEN?

Many workers live closer to their extended family than they do to work. There are both positives and negatives to this proximity. For Mike, there are many pos-itives to living close to his wife's family. They get help from his wife's sister and brother-in-law with childcare pick-up at the end of the day and weekend babysitting. In addition, these two families and other relatives have cottages and trailers in a rural family compound and these relationship form the core of their social life. Mike uses terms like "old home week" and "kids central" to describe the feeling and excitement of three-day holiday weekends "at camp" with extended family.

For others, the social obligations involved in belonging to a large extended family can be burdensome. Maria Cabral, who holds a production support job at BioTertia, is a second-generation member of a large Portuguese-American family. She is one of three children and her husband, also Portuguese-American, is one of eight. Her father has four siblings and her mother has five. Everyone lives locally. She says:

> My family is so big. It's like every month there's something. Sometimes it's like every week there's something. It gets annoying in a way, 'cause that's like more money to be spent. . . . It's like a wedding this month, a birthday next week, and that stuff adds up.

Maria and her husband lived with her parents for a while when they were first married but now live in an apartment complex 20 minutes north of the city where they were raised. There are still expectations that she will visit relatives often over the weekend, particularly her grandmothers. She says, "It's just kind of hard in a way. To go to someone's house just for a visit. . . . That's another mission, you know what I mean?" Yet Maria, like many other biotech workers with extended family in the area, relies heavily on her family for help with childcare. The burdensome family visits on the weekend and the costly gift purchases are part of a complex network of relationships that entail extensive reciprocity.

THE UNRESPONSIVE WORKPLACE

The stalled gender revolution inside the family is being slowed by the lack of workplace-based transformation. Two workplace issues in particular affect the quality of life inside families: work spillover and traditional full-time work schedules.

WORK SPILLOVER: OR "JUST A MINUTE, I'M FINISHING MY E-MAIL"

Family time during the week is often dictated by how much work employees have to bring home with them. On one end of the occupational spectrum, the responsibilities of production and technical workers are confined to the work day and the workplace. Bill Kopell, a production technician, says he never does job-related work in the evening, and his wife, Sally, agrees. In contrast, all the managers interviewed indicated that they spend some time working at home—not every night, but every week. Checking e-mail from home is common. Maureen Stendall, who directs client services at BioTertia, puts in two to three hours of work most evenings after her four-year-old daughter, Kristin, goes to sleep. If she needs to work on the weekend, her husband takes Kristin out to a playground or for a hike so she can get some work done. Maureen says her husband enjoys the time alone with their daughter and does not seem upset by the number of hours she works during a typical weekend.

Some spouses do mind when their spouses work at home, though. Scott Porter, a senior manager of manufacturing at BioTertia, says he brings work home every week, including paperwork and phone calls, and estimates that it takes one hour a week. His wife, Jackie, estimates that Scott works two or three nights a week for an hour or longer. If phone calls are included, Jackie thinks Scott spends about eight hours a week working at home in the evenings—a radically different estimate from Scott's. Jackie finds the phone calls intrusive, but she says the family has adjusted and things are better than when Scott worked every other weekend. Scott used to work six or seven days a week, and Jackie says, "Home was just where he slept . . . [the] family gave him a hard time about it." Now he is on a beeper and works one out of every five weekends. Scott regrets the way work cut into family time in the past. Although his children are now in college, Scott tells the following story as if it happened recently:

> I missed seeing them on Halloween one year because I was working late. I should have literally dropped what I was doing and walked out—if I had to do it again. But I had stayed late to take care of a problem that had occurred at work. Even to this day, they occasionally remind me of it. . . . They do it kiddingly. To them, it's kidding. To me, it's not.

The reduction of family time owing to work pressures can be significant, and the effects can be long-lasting for parents and children.

For many biotech employess, work also spills over into the weekend. Lester Brown, a quality control supervisor at BioTertia, and his wife, Nancy, both hold demanding, full-time professional jobs, and both feel shortchanged by the weekend. Lester comments:

> I think we've sort of fallen into this mentality where we just sort of look for the weekends. . . . But with my position, we have to try to serve [clients] every day, seven days a week, so our busiest times are actually Saturdays and Sundays.

Lester works one weekend a month. Nancy works in retail and travels about one week out of each month, often traveling over a weekend day. This leaves them little playtime with their two-and-a-half-year-old son, who attends a childcare center full-time during the week. Sundays when Lester is not working and Nancy is not traveling are usually spent going to church in the morning and visiting with family in the afternoon. They prefer to socialize with Nancy's brother and sister-in-law because they "can schedule it at the last minute," whereas getting together with friends requires advance planning, which weekend work demands make difficult.

Some employees live in such tight economic circumstances that there is no such thing as family time on the weekend. Malika Shaheed, one of the single mothers introduced earlier, works five eight-hour days a week, Sunday through Thursday. But her paycheck from her biotech job is not enough to support her three sons. So she works in a department store on Fridays and Saturdays to make ends meet. When asked how she handles arrangements for her children on the weekends, she replies:

> Saturday is my worst day because I don't get to do the family things with them that they really want, biking and different things like that. But what I've done is I've tried to schedule myself [at her second job] for times later in the afternoon [so] at least I could eat breakfast with them. And I cook them a big breakfast, like pancakes, and really do it up.

Malika tries to see her father and her aunt on the weekends, but often there is no time. Weekends are not a family affair for all biotech employees.

"I'D LIKE TO WORK PART-TIME, BUT . . . "

Many biotech workers complain about their full-time work schedules. They say they need two full-time incomes to pay the bills and try to save for college for their chilcren. They resent the extent to which full-time work dominates their lives, but very few workers I interviewed work part-time.[10] For those few I spoke to who pursued part-time options, a lengthy process of self-doubt, struggle, and indecision preceded the decision. After that, a process of negotiation at work ensued: some supervisors were supportive, others were not. Part-time work is not advertised or encouraged in the biotech firms studied, but this fact masks an unexpressed desire on the part of a number of full-time workers, especially women, to reduce their hours of paid work.

One group of women who express an interest in part-time work are mothers of infants and preschool-age children, like Jessica Bromfield, the mother of twins. Another group are mothers of school-age children. Connie Porcini works as a senior research scientist and has managerial responsibilities at BioSegunda. She is married to a man who is self-employed, and they have one daughter in first grade. Connie mentions several times during our interview how tired she is. She says she fantasizes about taking a couple of months off "because I'm getting burned out there." But this is not feasible according to company policies, and she recognizes that it would be only a short-term solution. When asked what might be a long-term solution, Connie says, "I would maybe ask for an hour less a day," explaining, "I think

I'd be a lot more rested. My day would be a lot less hectic. And I'd have more time for my daughter."

Connie immediately stops short of playing out this option in her mind, however, declaring it impossible. She says her company would not accept her leaving early each day, given her supervisory responsibilities. Reduced work hours and supervision of other workers are viewed as mutually exclusive. In addition, she carries the health insurance and other benefits for her family and worries that working less than full-time might entail prorating her benefits. Even though it would help her feel less tired and have more time for family, the potential negative consequences of raising it with her supervisor convinces her not even to try.[11]

Jessica and Connie have children of different ages, but they share a common desire for less time in the workplace and more time with their children. Although they work at different-sized companies, they both believe that their supervisors would not look favorably on reduced hours. They worry that they will be seen as less committed, serious, and loyal than their male colleagues. The privileging of full-time work over part-time shows how problems at work contribute to the stalled gender revolution at home. This is demonstrated in two ways: none of the men interviewed raised the option of part-time work as desirable for himself; and women seemed to feel that if someone were going to cut back, it should be them. The residual strength of the "ideal worker" norm means that women are more likely than men to seek ways of accommodating work to family caregiving.

FAMILY STRATEGIES: THE FIRST LINE OF DEFENSE

The strategies most families use to manage paid work and family care are centered on their immediate households, extended families, or both. These strategies do not represent the totality of their approach, but they do have a significant impact on gender relations within the family. The workers I met are clear that—workplaces and public policies being what they are—members of their family are their first line of defense in the battle to manage work and family. This said, there are some interesting differences in how these workers utilize family resources, and each has different implications for gender equality in the family and for the likelihood of using community resources. I noticed three different family-based strategies.

The first is the "super-mom" strategy, for lack of a better term. It has two key variants: the married-mother version, and the single-mother version.

Almost half of the families I met employ this strategy, not necessarily as a conscious choice (in the way some families choose to have a stay-at-home parent), but more as a product of necessity. This is due to the lack of involvement, or passivity, of husbands in married-couple families, and the absence of husbands or other partners in single-parent families. Mothers are "the engine" that drives the daily routine and links the family to the larger community. This strategy is costly: these mothers somehow find time to volunteer in their communities and build successful careers, but the toll on their health and well-being is palpable. They complain of being constantly tired; they fear burnout and not being attentive to their children. One biotech manager said, "Work uses me up, and I don't know where to go for a refill." The "super-moms" are in a sense pioneers, because they are using community solutions to solve work-family problems.

In the second strategy—the "extended family" strategy—relatives provide significant dependent care assistance and financial resources. About a third of the families I met are using this strategy quite successfully. It centers on close intergenerational relationships in which the older generation helps with childcare, the middle generation agrees to take on elder care responsibilities now or later, and the children gain a sense that many adults are invested in their future. This strategy also strengthens family ties to community groups, for example, when grandparents facilitate participation in after-school programs or religious school.

However, this strategy does not come without some strains in family relations, especially where there is shared household space. There is also the issue of the health of the older generation and how long they will be able to help with childcare. Thus, this strategy is not static in duration or configuration. In addition, the extended family strategy—in which the family is defined as multiple households rather than a single nuclear-family household—in some sense lets employers off the hook. Employers are providing few supports for family care, while the family, broadly defined, is doing a huge amount of unpaid work so that some members can get paid to work. Moreover, this strategy is not available to all workers, particularly those whose extended families live far away.[12]

The third strategy—the "stay-at-home mom" strategy—is built around traditional gender roles with the husband as primary breadwinner and the wife as primary caretaker. One-fifth of families I met use this strategy. On the positive side, this strategy seems to facilitate a high level of parental time and involvement with children, and significant involvement in community-based institutions outside the family. On the negative side, it re-creates a traditional division of labor within the family in which women do all the caregiving and housework. But the fact that some families move in and out of using this strategy, depending upon the ages of their children and other factors, suggests that some of its drawbacks may be temporary.

Although having one parent stay home brings some financial savings, particularly in the area of childcare expense, it also has some financial cost. The family as a whole loses income, and women may lose retirement funds and career opportunities. Some families who make this choice say that the non-financial benefits for children and community far outweigh both the material and personal costs, but there is one cost that is difficult to measure, and not auspicious for the overall family equation: the lack of an egalitarian division of labor between spouses at home.

GENDER INEQUALITY IN THE FAMILY, REVISITED

In discussions with biotech workers, I was told repeatedly that spouses are critical in managing the demands of work and family, but whether couples choose to fulfill or challenge traditional role expectations varies enormously. In assessing the three strategies described above, husbands and wives have the greatest degree of equality when they employ an extended family strategy. When relatives help in the care of young children, husbands and wives have less stress in their daily routine and seem less likely to fall back on traditional gender roles.

This is evident in the story of the Steinbergs. Both Fran and Philip can advance in their careers, and both can work late if need be, because they have Fran's mother to rely on for after-school care. When they get home from work, they can devote themselves to Rebecca. They do not have to worry about preparing dinner right away; Rebecca has already been fed by her grandmother. Two common sources of daily tension—getting to a childcare center or extended day program on time for pick-up, and getting food and fixing dinner—have been removed. But there is an unknown factor in this family care equation—Estelle's health; should it decline, they will need a new strategy.

The super-mom strategy is usually adopted because of a lack of involvement by husband or other partner. Julie Taylor's story is a perfect example of the pros and cons of this strategy. She gets some help from her husband, Peter, with daily childcare, but little help with housework. She is the one who does all the "community care" work, building ties and a support system with other parents, volunteering at the childcare center, and teaching Sunday school. The result is that there is little gender equality in Julie's marriage, and little time in her work week for rest. Coming home from work one day, she wonders aloud, "I'm not sure how long I can keep running in this marathon." The super-mom strategy is probably viable only on a short-term basis.

Finally, gender equality in families using the stay-at-home mom strategy is complicated to evaluate. On the one hand, these families appear to be replicating the old male breadwinner/female homemaker model. On the other hand, many of these women are actually working for pay—usually a small number of hours at home—and as contributors to the household budget, their role in the family and in their marriages is not as traditional as it may appear. Given the fact that they are part-time workers, full-time caregivers, and usually highly involved in community groups, they could be called a new kind of super-mom. They are living either the best of both worlds or the worst, depending on your point of view.

The story of the Stratton family typifies the contradictions inherent in the stay-at-home mom strategy. George brings home the paycheck, and Elizabeth cleans the house, prepares the meals, takes Stephen and Allie to their after-school activities, and volunteers in her children's elementary school. Although the Strattons appear to have a very traditional marriage, the legacy of Elizabeth's professional training and career and her recent full-time employment alters the dynamic between them and their expectations for the future. The fact that Elizabeth and George made a joint decision for her to leave the workforce makes her current role in the family a matter of choice. Of course, the reasons that they chose for Elizabeth to stay home, rather than George, have everything to do with traditional gender roles: Elizabeth was bringing home less income, and she is seen as the "more appropriate" parent to invest all her time in childcare and community work.

BEYOND PRIVATE SOLUTIONS

Gender roles and gender equality are in flux in the Stratton family, as they are in the Steinberg and Taylor families. The tensions inherent in each strategy means that each is subject to change, and the viability of traditional gender roles is being constantly challenged. Over time, families' strategies might shift, with differential consequences for work, careers, marriage, time with children, and time for community involvement.

The path to greater gender equality in the family, in my view, lies neither with the old male breadwinner/female homemaker model, nor with the model of two parents (or a single parent) working full-time, full-year, year after year. Paid work cannot be the sole basis of gender equality because, right now, the structures and design of the workplace do not support that goal. Paying women to do family care work and housework is not a viable solution because it perpetuates the consignment of women to the domestic sphere. The idea of men and women doing exactly the same amount of paid work and the same amount of care work seems—at this point in history—to be a recipe for equal exhaustion, not genuine equality. Restructuring work and care roles inside nuclear families is important, but unless it is accompanied by new employer policies, new public policies, and enhanced community support, it will remain a private solution.[13]

A major shift in gender relations will come about only via a profound cultural change in attitudes about who is responsible for the well-being of families. If family care remains the private problem of individual families, gender inequality will persist. On the other hand, if families can reach out into their communities—to other families, neighbors, and the community institutions that provide care, education, recreation, and spiritual nourishment—there is hope that that work-family problems will become our collective social responsibility. In the chapters that follow, I will explore how workers feel about the cities and suburbs where they live and what they have achieved through various forms of community engagement. I will follow workers into their neighborhoods, into the childcare programs and schools they use, and into the faith-based institutions where they worship. Each domain reveals both the promise and the difficulty of building meaningful connections in a society that currently devalues family caregiving and the care of our communities.

PART II

FROM FAMILY CONNECTIONS TO COMMUNITY INVOLVEMENT

CHAPTER FOUR

COMMUNITY AS A STARTING POINT

PLACE AND PARTICIPATION

The usual starting point for designing solutions to work-family problems is the workplace. Those willing to take on the challenge usually ask: "Is the employer providing the needed policies and supports to make it possible for people to both work and care for their families?" In this book, my starting point is the community. I question the effectiveness of past efforts to create work-family policies because most companies use the workforce attachment of individual workers as a starting point for eligibility. Employers ignore the families of which workers are members and the communities where workers live. They do not take into account the employment, or lack thereof, of other adults in the worker's household. Perhaps most important, they do not assess the resources that exist in the communities where the company is located and where workers live. I think we need a new model that takes a worker's community of residence as a starting point for addressing work-family problems, and builds collaborations between employers and community groups to create solutions. These partnerships could develop a community-based infrastructure of work-family support that would withstand the ups and downs of individual companies and provide a buffer for families against the uncertainty of the new economy.

I learned that for many biotech workers, "community" is their starting point as well. Not only is it literally the place where they start their work day, but it is also the place where many of their work-family supports are located. Networks of parents who help each other with transportation and backup care, services and programs for childcare and elder care, and institutions like schools and religious congregations are most often found in workers' community of residence. This is not to say that other forms of community are not important, but rather that the physical place where people live is a significant dimension of community that often creates the foundation for other kinds of support and connection. I learned a particularly vivid lesson about the power of place, and the centrality of residential communities for this group of workers, in the spring of 1998, about a year after I started work on this project.

COMPANIES MOVE, BUT FAMILIES DON'T ALWAYS FOLLOW

As I began to learn my way around the three biotech companies chosen for my research, I found that the only thing I could count on was change. Personnel, scientific projects—even whether the work week starts on Monday—were in a constant state of flux. For example, I met with the director of human resources at BioTertia, and when I called the following week to start setting up interviews, I learned this man had taken a job elsewhere. I attended a science meeting at BioPrima, carefully noting who was present. When I contacted one of the women scientists from the meeting several weeks later to see how work on the project was affecting her family time, I found out the entire project had been discontinued—two years of research and development work, and several million dollars, down the drain.

One of the most dramatic changes that occurred was BioSegunda's decision to move all its operations to a new office park about 20 miles away. One day when I was out at the company, I overheard snatches of conversation in the lunchroom from disgruntled employees about how the move would increase their commuting time. It occurred to me that the move was prompting many BioSegunda workers to rethink how they felt about their commutes—a major factor in how families manage their work and family lives. I started to understand the impending move not only as a major transition for the company, but also as an opportunity to get to the heart of the matter of this book—the relationship between life at work and the quality of community life.

I approached the vice president of human resources (HR) at BioSegunda and asked if I could talk with him about the move. I told him that I wanted to learn more about why and how the company had made the decision. "No problem," answered Bob Redding, a person of unusual and consistent good cheer, "I think I have just the information you need." Bob had been with BioSegunda six years, first as the director of HR and then promoted to vice president. An important member of the senior management team, he had been unfailingly helpful since I first began visiting the company. On the wall of his office, there was a large map of the eastern half of Massachusetts, covered with multicolored pushpins. It had been the job of Bob's staff literally to map the distance between each worker's community of residence and the current location of the company and compare that to the distance between their homes and the company's new location.

Bob quickly assured me that after making these calculations, they had become convinced that the move was a wise one for the company. He acknowledged that it would increase the commute time of some workers, but "not an unreasonable amount." As I probed further about the move toward Cambridge and Boston, a key strategic factor emerged that had nothing to do with the equity of commutes. Bob said, as if revealing nothing terribly important, that the CEO felt strongly that moving would bring the company closer to the pool of highly skilled scientists so important to a biotech company's competitiveness. Bob said, "A lot of people just don't want to live out here," without saying which "people" he was talking about. Another thing that Bob did not say—but that was obvious from the color-coded pushpins—was that the senior managers would have shorter commutes after the move, but most other employees, including production workers, scientists, and middle managers, would have longer commutes.

I asked Bob if I could hold two employee meetings without supervisors about the move: one with workers who held production jobs, and another with workers who held research and research support positions. Bob agreed, and the meetings were held at lunchtime with food provided by our research team. I wondered if anyone would come, hoping the food would be an incentive, and the sensitivity of the topic not too great a disincentive. At the first meeting, everyone from the production department attended; the group was one-third women and two-thirds men. Nervous banter began, with in-jokes I could not decode. The group seemed close-knit, and several people had worked together over five years. One man, Mike Hallowell, seemed to be the informal but acknowledged leader. People watched to see how participatory he would be in the session, and when he began talking openly and at length of his own feelings about the move, others soon followed suit.

A couple of people in the production group lived right in Westville, where BioSegunda was located; others lived anywhere from 20 to 50 minutes away and were already dealing with a significant commute. After going around the table once, it was clear that everyone's commute was going to be longer after the move, and everyone was upset about it. Steve Lombardi, a married father in his early thirties with two young children, summed up the feelings of many of his co-workers:

> I'm comfortable with the commute now, but I am not looking forward to an hour and twenty minute commute. I'm not looking forward to doubling my gas. Plus I'll be away from my family—an extra ten hours a week.

As people talked, their concerns about time were translated into financial terms. They would have to pay more for gas and tolls, their cars would depreciate, and the company was not going to compensate them for these added expenses.[1] When I asked if this concern had been brought to management's attention, they answered that it had, but it "has just been refused across the board." Hank Bartholet, a man in his early fifties, recounted the story of a company-wide meeting a year earlier where he raised the issue directly with the CEO. He took the tack that wage scales are higher the closer you get to Boston, so, he asked the company president, "Shouldn't our wages go up correspondingly with the move east?" I asked how the CEO handled the question. Hank said:

> [He] spent probably three to five minutes beating around the bush, saying [that] the wage scale where we're going is very similar to where we are . . . and when he got done, I said, "So the answer to my question is no?" "Yes," he said. He never had to say "no."

Everyone snickered around the table. And one woman added, "Even if you get a raise, that's not going to pull you up even with where you were." Heads nodded silently around the table.

The discussion moved back to non-financial concerns as I asked how the move was going to affect their family time and the possibility of being involved in their communities. Hank, who has a grown daughter with two little boys of her own, said he doesn't have enough time with his grandsons as it is, and his wife was not going to like his getting home later. Steve Lombardi, whose wife is at home full-time taking care of their children, mentioned that she likes him to get home by 5:30, so she can have a break from taking care of the kids and prepare dinner. If he gets home later, their early evening routine will be disrupted. It was not just his immediate family that was going to be disrupted:

Plus I'm involved with the community—I'm on the Board of Health in [Adamsville]. I'm also active in my church in [Adamsville]. . . . Even now I have a hard time being with my family and doing the things I do. Something will have to give.

Steve was not the only one who talked about how the move would negatively affect community involvement. Mike Hallowell, a married father with a twelve-year-old, was worried about how he would continue his involvement with his son's after-school activities.

My son has been into everything, Little League, and football, and Cub Scouts, and I've led everything that he's been in, because it's been doable. Considering the time it takes me to get to and from work, I can get to practice for five o'clock from here without a problem . . . but Bridgeton? [the new location] It's going to seriously curtail my community service activities. That I'm quite concerned about.

I asked whether anyone was considering moving closer to the new location. I received an immediate round of negative responses, with several people talking at once. They said the price of homes is higher closer to Boston, and that there is little stability in their industry. As one woman put it, "You wouldn't want to sell your house and move, because we are in the biotech field . . . all it takes is one bad trial and the company goes under." Two men said they had built their own homes and would never leave them. Betty Carson, a single mother in her late forties with a teenage son, had already talked about how a longer commute would increase the difficulty of managing a household alone. She simply added, "All my friends and all my activities take place minutes from my house." And Mike said with quiet intensity:

My wife and I are both life-long Westville residents. We are living on the street that she grew up on, where her parents lived for 25 years . . . I really don't see myself moving east for *this* job.

Mike's comments were followed by uneasy laughter from the group, a laughter that acknowledged the limitations and occasional humiliations of "this job," a laughter that affirmed Mike's allegiance to Westville.

All these workers are aware of their lack of job security, and Bob Redding's mention of the skilled workforce closer to Boston was no secret.

As Betty put it, "Technicians at our level, [a] dime a dozen." The instability of biotech and their position in their company is one reason they are reluctant to leave their communities. But even more important are the family, neighborhood, friendship, and volunteer service ties within those communities. All these relationships bind these workers strongly to their homes and hometowns. Their communities, not their jobs, are the anchors in their lives.

A week later, it was time to meet with some members of the research and development department at BioSegunda. The catered lunch was set up as people entered the conference room. I entered with my own set of expectations. I expected that occupational differences, as a marker of class, would affect people's response to the move. I expected that people in the second group would put up with longer commutes because they held more prestigious, better-paying jobs. I expected they would consider moving closer to BioSegunda's new location because the primary attachment in their lives would be their professional jobs. I was wrong on all counts. The reactions of the professional workers were remarkably close to those of the production and technical workers. A slightly larger group came to this meeting, mainly women. In their initial comments, they expressed unhappiness about the move because it would increase their commuting time. There was less discussion about how the cost of gas and tolls would cut into their paychecks, and more talk about how longer commutes would mean less time for family. Their emphasis was a bit different, but the themes were the same.

When I asked about moving closer to the new location, I got another round of negative responses. Lily Huang, a research scientist with a four-year-old son, said she would not consider moving. She and her husband recently bought a new house on a cul-de-sac. Most of their new neighbors are also working families with young children, and they like this. Lily also does not want to move because she has a good childcare center for her son near their house. He is very attached to his teachers, and Lily does not want to disrupt that. When I asked if she would consider moving her son's childcare closer to the new location—mentioning the childcare center that was scheduled to open in the new industrial park—she quickly answered "No." Having childcare near home was a preference voiced by many parents of young children. Lily also raised another issue: her desire to spend a few hours one afternoon a week volunteering in her son's center. She has occasionally used "sick days" to do this, but can not get her supervisor to give her a flexible schedule which would make a regular comittment possible. She said sadly, "That [longer commute] is going to stop the discussion [on that request]—close it once and for all."

Another family care issue was raised by Sylvia Harris, a single woman in her mid-forties who lives a significant distance from the company. She and her mother, who also works, share responsibility for her elderly grandmother and disabled uncle. They split taking time off for doctor's appointments and other family needs. Sylvia fears that a longer commute to her company's new location may hurt her ability to take time off for her elder care responsibilities. Her job, which involves work with animals, does not have a lot of flexibility:

> And animals don't know holidays, don't know vacations. The research we're getting involved in is very specific, very labor-intensive. And there are going to be times when it's hard to schedule, it's hard to work around this. They [other researchers] can set their stuff aside and walk away from it. But we can't.

Sylvia and her mother rely on a number of community-based elder care services in their town—Meals on Wheels for lunch, and transportation services that take people to the doctor when their relatives cannot. Sylvia explained that if she moved closer to the new company location, she and her mother would have to find services all over again, and the providers would be strangers to her grandmother and uncle. Sylvia said simply, "It just wouldn't be worth it."

Other professional employees voiced concern that the additional commute would curtail their volunteer activities. A mid-level manager involved in supporting his daughter's ballet school expressed worry that he would not be able to help out with dance recitals. A woman biologist with a strong interest in environmental issues said she would have to give up her work at a local recycling center. Another scientist said the longer commute makes it unlikely that she can keep volunteering at a local soup kitchen. She said, "I feel that people like me, who have so many privileges, should give back. But there's only so many hours in the day, and I just don't know how to fit it in once we move."

WHEN MAJOR DECISIONS ARE NOT NEGOTIATED

Each worker in these lunch group discussions had his or her reasons for being distressed about BioSegunda's relocation. Part of their distress was caused by management's lack of consultation with workers in any department. The decision was made behind closed doors and then announced to the workers as a *fait accompli*. Only the CEO and senior managers at the vice-president level had any real input. Also distressing were the increased time of daily commutes and the way that would cut into precious family time. The production workers, in particular, voiced concern about the depreciation on their cars and the expense of extra gas and tolls.

In addition, the workers' distress reflected their attachment to their communities of residence. For some, it reflected the strength of family and neighborhood ties; for others, it centered on the nature of their family care arrangements; for still others, it was based on their volunteer commitments to community organizations. There was one reason that they all shared: whether they were low-paid production workers or better-paid research scientists and professionals, the fragility of companies in the biotech industry was affecting their lives. Like many workers in the new economy, they have come to understand that they have little or no job security, and that their employer feels little sense of long-term responsibility to them. As one production worker put it, "They look at us as . . . expendable, everybody can be replaced." Given the uncertain future of their biotech company, these workers responded by looking to their communities as a source of stability and support. They say they cannot count on their jobs, but they can count on the people and institutions where they live. The pressures that new economy is bringing to bear on working families are making the creation of strong communities more important than ever.

WHAT IS COMMUNITY?

One of the first tasks in trying to understand how community fits within a work-family framework is to adopt an inclusive definition of the term *community*. Just as *family* has to be reconceptualized to discard the mythic "Ozzie and Harriet" two-parent, married, heterosexual family as the prototype for all families and embrace the diversity of real families,[2] so must we go beyond narrow or outmoded definitions of *community*.

Many dimensions of community will be discussed in this book, but I want to begin with workers' definitions of the term. I asked what they would consider a "dictionary definition" of the word *community*, and here are some of their responses:

Colleen McCarthy, an associate scientist at BioPrima: "The symbiosis of all the places and organizations within a defined geographic area."

Hank Bartholet, a production worker at BioSegunda: "People living in relative proximity to one another, working together for the common benefit of all."

Beth Finley, a postdoctoral research scientist and manager at BioSegunda: "A group of people united for a common purpose living in close proximity."

Each definition incorporates a spatial dimension. Though people have somewhat different ways of specifying activities that bring people (or institutions) together, the idea of physical proximity unites all three formulations.

The definition of community that first comes to most people's minds is a geographically bounded space—the physical spaces where we live, the areas where we buy or rent homes, the places we park our cars at night, the places where we do our grocery shopping and take our dry cleaning. From this perspective, community can take many shapes and sizes; it can be a block, a neighborhood, a suburban town, or an entire city. Individuals can be members of one or all of these geographical units; they are not mutually exclusive. The area covered by a public school district, a voting precinct, or the parish of a church can shape the physical boundaries of a community.

The term *community* also refers to the social relationships and connections between individuals and institutions.[3] These can be based on regular affiliation with or participation in a workplace, a school, a college, or a religious institution. Alternatively, the relationships may be based on membership in a group of similar institutions, although the claim of "community" may express the desire for common value more than the reality, and it can cover up important aspects of diversity within an institution. For example, assertions such as "We belong to the Jewish community" may cover up important differences among Reform, Conservative, and Orthodox Jews. When relationships are based on intermittent affiliation or membership, such as belonging to a health club or professional association, the experience of social connection is less intense. There is often minimal face-to-face interaction or direct knowledge of other members of the group.

Community is sometimes used as a synonym for *social network*.[4] This type of community is a highly voluntary and self-selected enterprise including people you choose to spend time with: your friends, your self-help group, or your book club. This variant may be is based on the educational, recreational, and employment histories of the person at the center of the network. It does not depend on physical proximity but is rather based on the frequency and intensity of contact between members. The members of one person's "community," in this case, may be completely unknown to one another, though some networks have members who do know each other.

There are also communities based on commonalities of race, ethnicity, sexual orientation, or physical ability. This type of community is based on shared history or common memory and is sometimes associated with the development of social movements based on "identity politics."[5] There is often a political rationale for asserting the existence of a community of common interests, even if in fact there are significant differences among the members. For example, candidates for elective office may claim that they have the support of the "African American community," when in fact members of this community may vote Democratic, Republican, or independent, and some may not even be registered to vote. It is not uncommon to hear political interest groups referred to in these terms, such as the "gay community," the "Latino community," and so on.

A new type of community has emerged since the advent of computer technology. This "virtual community" is defined by electronically generated connections and is not dependent on any kind of physical proximity. Although it bears some relationship to communities based in social networks, ties are created solely by information technology, and people are connected through chat rooms and e-mail. Some of these communities are based on list-serve groups with a common hobby, like amateur astronomers, or nonprofit advocacy organizations, like the Sierra Club, most of whose members may never know one another in the traditional sense.

The geographic-physical community and the virtual community lie at opposite ends of a spectrum. Some argue that virtual communities are replacing geographical communities,[6] but this position seems to be a gross overstatement of the power of computer technology in our lives. The biotech workers in this book participate in both, but I found no evidence that virtual community is predominant or even very common for them. In between lie a variety of ways that people come together on the basis of common employment relationships, religious commitments, educational goals, professional connections, and personal relationships. These kinds of communities are not mutually exclusive; I met workers who consider themselves members of communities based on many kinds of sharing and reciprocity, be it a profession, a faith tradition, or having children the same age. Many see community as a coping strategy and support system that allows members to link their personal, economic, and social goals to the goals of others with whom they have something in common—in this case, the enormous challenge of integrating work and family. Finally, some of the workers I met view "community" as a desirable state of being that emphasizes a commonality of purpose, that transcends individual needs. In this view, workplaces, families, and the communities where people live are part of a greater "community"—the community that crosses the boundaries between cities and suburbs, between regions and states—the community that shares common assets and common problems. Recognition of this larger community is essential to moving family care and family well-being out of individual households and into the public domain.

THE EMPIRICAL COMMUNITY

While some have struggled to define the term *community*, others have worked to document the diversity of real communities in the United States and around the world. As the scholarly effort to understand American communities unfolded during the 20th century, one of the classic studies was *Middletown*, written by the sociologists Robert and Helen Lynd in the 1920s,[7] drawing on the methods of social anthropology. The Lynds lived in a small Midwestern city and presented an analysis of its intersecting spheres of work, family, school, recreation, religious observance, and civic engagement. Their acute ability to observe daily life and put their findings in a social and historical context provided the first in-depth look at the lives of middle-class Americans. In the post-World War II period, community studies diverged in two directions: some continued to investigate the middle class, following families into suburban communities to learn how the postwar economic boom was shaping both work and domestic life; others shifted their focus to the work, family, and community lives of the poor in inner-city neighborhoods. In the 1960s, these studies highlighted the problems that plague poor communities, such as family dysfunction, gang violence, or teen pregnancy. Most of the studies of poor urban neighborhoods used a "deficit" approach in their analyses. Researchers were preoccupied with documenting social deterioration, lack of social cohesion, rising crime rates, and lack of neighborliness, bolstering a "blame the victim" perspective on the poor.

Some researchers took issue with this approach. The noted sociologist Herbert Gans, in his study of an Italian-American tenement community destroyed to build luxury housing, insisted that the social decay in this neighborhood was caused by poverty, not the character or habits of its residents.[8]

More recently, the sociologist William Julius Wilson has pointed to macro-economic, structural issues, such as the lack of employment opportunities in inner city neighborhoods, as the source of inescapable poverty for their residents.[9] Although drug use and unemployment may be real, they exist alongside evidence of families struggling to survive in very adverse circumstances and building strong social ties to enable this survival. Documenting the "assets" of poor urban communities is epitomized in the work of the anthropologist Carol Stack. Her study of a neighborhood in a large city in the Midwest highlights the supportive, kin-based networks of caregiving and reciprocity that characterize an African American urban community.[10] Her approach shows the poor as active agents, not passive victims, with their own strategies for handling work and family issues. Stack's work, and other neighborhood studies within large metropolitan areas like New York City, has furthered the move away from the deficit approach toward a focus on the strengths of diverse urban neighborhoods.[11]

Suburban communities became a subject of research after World War II. Probably the earliest study is William Whyte's now classic depiction of the "organization man," documenting the friendships and social groups of white, male middle managers in the suburbs of the 1950s.[12] In the 1960s, several studies of suburban communities appeared,[13] with divergent assessments of suburban life. Some viewed suburbia as a cultural wasteland, the source of many of the social ills of that era, while others found positive opportunities for American families who lived in suburban areas. Recent studies of suburbia tend to take the more positive view.[14] Several examine the historical development of the suburbs,[15] and view suburban communities less as enclaves of white middle-class managers, and more as extensions of urban areas that have their own class and ethnic diversity. The social historians Roz Baxandall and Phyllis Ewen critique "anti-suburbia snobbery" and argue that suburban development was originally part of a vision of giving "ordinary people, not just the elite . . . access to affordable, attractive modern housing in communities with parks, gardens, recreation, stores and cooperative town meeting places."[16]

The work of geographers has added a unique perspective to our understanding of both urban and suburban communities.[17] They emphasize how a spatial perspective can bring a new dimension to debates about poverty, the underclass, and other socio-economic issues. Feminist geographers have begun to explore the diversity of women's experiences in cities to show how structures of inequality, including those based on gender, can shape life in urban areas.[18] Path-breaking contributions, such as the work of Susan Hanson and Geraldine Pratt, provide models of how the creative use of a spatial perspective can expose unseen interfaces between women's work, family, and community lives.[19] A spatial perspective is useful for understanding not only the "outside" space we inhabit, but also the "inside," and the ways in which the built environment structures our domestic lives. This perspective was introduced to contemporary audiences in the pioneering work of Delores Hayden,[20] who argues that our tenacious attachment to single-family homes, based on the nuclear family, perpetuates inequality in the family and the workplace.

PLACE MATTERS: EXPLORING THE COMMUNITY CONTEXT

The past half-century has seen two significant changes affecting communities at the local level in the United States. One is the growth and development of suburban communities and the consequent decline of population, schools, and services in urban areas. The second is the general movement of the population from the "Rust Belt," spanning the states from Northeast to Midwest, to the "Sun Belt" in the south and the west. The quality of life for families living in the large metropolitan areas of the Northeast has been greatly affected by declining urban centers and sprawling suburbs. In a recent study, Matthew Kahn argues that there are many social costs to suburban living, although there may be private benefits to suburban dwellers.[21] In particular, he cites the negative impact of long commutes and the high level of resource consumption of suburbanites versus urbanites, such as oil for cars and land for houses that decreases open space and land for agriculture. These trends, he suggests, should prompt a critical look at the physical design of suburban communities and a better balance between the resource consumption and needs of suburbanites and urbanites.

Such trends are visible in eastern Massachusetts, especially in the greater Boston metropolitan area where the biotechnology industry has taken root. This region has been the site of two varieties of sprawl. There is the usual kind of sprawl, meaning uncontrolled development taking over open space and farmland, with little thought given to its environmental or social impact. Since the mid-1970s, more than 70 percent of the region's economic growth has occurred in the suburbs, accompanied by the usual decline in urban population centers.[22] The second kind of sprawl is "job sprawl," in which more and more jobs have also left Boston and moved to the suburbs, especially

along the two interstate highways that ring Boston.[23] These twin sprawls have
created a familiar pattern of new housing, office parks, and malls accessible
only by car, and a general degradation of the historic character of small-town
New England. Perhaps the only positive aspect has been some loosening in
the historic pattern of segregation in greater Boston, with some minorities
also leaving the city to become suburban homeowners.[24]

The biotech employees profiled in this book live in a diverse range of
communities from the old urban centers and exclusive suburbs close to
Boston out to the newer suburbs and rural communities surrounding
Worcester in central Massachusetts. Over 55 percent live in the suburbs, a
quarter in cities, and about 15 percent in rural areas.[25] The 40 families I met
live in 34 communities in the eastern half of Massachusetts, and two communities in contiguous New England states. These statistics, however, do not
convey what it is like to live in these communities—the quality of social relationships and the vitality of public institutions—from the perspective of
working families. By exploring how workers themselves talk about the places
where they live, it is possible gain entrée into multiple aspects of their experience of community.

THE DEEP DIVIDE: THE DISTANCE BETWEEN HOME AND WORK

Following Julie Taylor and her husband, Peter, along their well-traveled
weekday paths, it is clear that many of the institutions, services, and individuals they rely on are clustered in or around their community of residence.
This place has great salience in their lives. Their older daughter Sara's school
is in their town, as is the childcare center that their younger daughter attends
all day, and that houses Sara's after-school program. The stores and restau-
rants they use are near their home—the places they go for groceries, take-out
food, medicine, school supplies, household goods, and dry cleaning. The
church they attend is one town away, a ten-minute drive. Their workplaces,
however, are 45 minutes to an hour from home, not counting extra time stuck
in traffic. Julie drives south and slightly east to an "edge city,"[26] and her husband drives directly east into a large city. There is too great a distance
between home and work for Julie or her husband to do any family errands or
community volunteer work during the day. It must all be done at the beginning or end of the work day, or on weekends.

The popular phrase "suburban sprawl" does not accurately convey the
spatial challenges facing working families. There is rather a deep divide, geo-

graphically speaking, between their community of residence and their places of employment that significantly shapes their lives and choices.[27] The most graphic expression of the deep divide between home and work is embodied in daily commuting. Some employees feel the commute is wasted time, but others say they look forward to a break from the pressures at home and at work. A short commute is less burdensome timewise, but a longer one allows for a more defined boundary between work and home. When Lester Brown, a manager at BioTertia, was asked if he could change one thing about his work situation that would make work-family issues easier, he replied:

> Move it [work] closer to home. . . . Commuting time is essentially wasted time. And when you figure that getting everything [his son's backpack, his briefcase] into the car and, getting to and from work, it's probably an hour on either end of the day for both of us.

I thought the direction of Lester's imaginary move was worthy of note because it departed in spirit from the sentiments expressed by workers at BioSegunda on the same topic. When I probed further about whether he and his wife—who also has a long commute—had ever discussed moving their home closer to work, Lester answered:

> We've thought about it, but we really both kind of like where we are living— whether it's just the community which is nice, [or] the proximity to the ocean. There is a lot to be said for having home not too close to work, too, because then when you're home, you're away from work.

There are miles traveled, and there are other kinds of distance. Given the impact of computer technology and the expectation that professional workers will do some work at home, perhaps the effort to maintain this boundary allows a greater focus on family and community.

All the workers I met drive to work, from five minutes to over an hour each way, with most people having substantial commutes of 35 to 45 minutes each way. Most employees calculate commuting time as part of their workday—as time when they cannot be with family or friends or do personal business. Commuting is an ongoing source of difficulty for workers who commute at least two hours a day. But distance between home and work does not appear to be a factor in most people's choice of where to work. In fact, it seems to work the other way around. Those with the longest commutes periodically wonder about whether they should move closer to work and usually decide against it, ultimately recommitting themselves to their communities of residence. The most prevalent attitude is that a short or long commute is something that comes with a job, and that one tries to figure out how to make the best of it.

An important and complicated set of questions related to gender and the distance between home and work has been addressed by the geographers Susan Hanson and Geraldine Pratt. They conducted a community-based study of Worcester, Massachusetts, in the 1980s and examined how spatial considerations have shaped both household relations and the employment of working women and men. They found that "generally those who have the heaviest domestic responsibilities do work closest to home."[28] They argue that occupational segregation—the concentration of many women in female-dominated occupations—can be explained partially by the women's continued responsibilities for home and family, which in turn shapes their desire to work close to home.

The experiences of the biotech workers I got to know tell a different story. First, there is no substantial difference between the commute times of male and female workers. In fact, some of those with the longest commutes are women. Second, there is no difference between women who are married and those who are not, or women who have some assistance from their spouses with household work and those who do not. This suggests that as more and more women have entered professional and technical jobs, rather than low-wage or low-skilled jobs, patterns of proximity between home and work have been changing. Women still bear major responsibility for household work, but their household responsibilities do not appear to be a major determinant in their decisions about where to work. These women appear to be motivated by a different set of issues than the women Hanson and Pratt describe.

The stories of three women who spend over two hours a day commuting demonstrate the complex factors that keep them tied to their communities. Fran Steinberg, a married biotech manager with one child, grew up in the community where she and her family now live. She has many ties to her hometown: her mother and sister live there; her synagogue is there, as well as her daughter's school and after-school provider. Similarly, many factors keep her tied to her present job. She has a senior position with an excellent salary, a great deal of responsibility, and long-term service, and her most important professional contacts are close to her workplace. Taking all these factors into account, Fran has no plans to change her home community or her job, so she chooses to maintain a long commute.

Rachel Warren, a lab specialist in her late thirties, has an hour-and-a-half commute each way. Fifteen years ago, she moved from a large city to a semi-rural suburb. She loves her house because it faces the woods, with no busy roads, it is quiet and serene. As a single mother, she appreciates the safety of her community and its good school system. She likes the fact that there are lots of activities offered for families with young children, such as puppet shows, story hours at the library, and concerts on the town green. On the other hand, every work day is a 12-hour day because of her commute. She leaves the house by 6:30 a.m. and does not get home until 6:30 p.m. Nevertheless, the good salary and benefits she gets from her biotech company, and the quality of life in her community for both her and her daughter, reinforce her conviction to stay put.

Helen Rafferty, a production supervisor, has lived in an upscale white-collar suburb for 14 years. She and her husband lived in a blue-collar suburb closer to her workplace when they first got married. Although she is now farther from work, she feels their decision to move away from an urban area enabled them to get "more for their money." She likes the fact that the houses are bigger and the lots are larger, despite her concerns about "suburban sprawl." She says the main factor in moving to this town was that it has excellent schools and is "very family-oriented." She knows a lot of people there, as do her children. However, she "hates" her commute. She has to get up at 5:00 a.m. every morning and does not see anyone in the family before she leaves at 6:00. Since she has decided against moving, her solution has been to take advantage of a new alternative schedule and work four ten-hour days, thereby eliminating one day of commuting.

These women's lives lend weight to an alternative "spatial story" than the one told by Hanson and Pratt: a new story based on women's employment in technical, professional, and managerial jobs in an industry that is gender-integrated rather than sex-segregated. This story does not discount the problems generated by the spatial divide between the workplace and the home, but it specifies them in new ways. In fact, I would argue that while women biotech workers have better jobs and benefits and more meaningful work than many women who work in sex-segregated occupations, their long commutes do add an impediment to fulfilling their family care responsibilities and to getting involved in their communities.

Strong ties to residential communities were expressed during the two meetings I held at BioSegunda, and similar sentiments were voiced by workers at the other companies. Employees at all three firms have constructed complex, multilayered networks of support in their communities over many years, and they are reluctant to abandon these. In fact, these community-based support networks appear to provide a sense of security and stability that employment in the biotech industry does not. These strong community attachments may be a conscious strategy for dealing with the low job security in biotech, or a more generalized desire for connection with others. In any case, the strength of community ties is being constantly tested as these workers experience restructuring, layoffs, and relocations.

CHOOSING A COMMUNITY OF RESIDENCE: OPPORTUNITIES AND CONSTRAINTS

The workers I met have choices about where they live and well-defined criteria for selecting a community of residence. Their three most important criteria are affordability, safety, and good schools. Affordability has taken some families quite far from the communities they find most desirable. Given the lack of job security in biotech, many are afraid to take on large mortgages. This has placed people in communities that may have been their third or fourth choice, but where their mortgage will be manageable if their company closes or they get laid off. Few people anticipate leaving employment in the industry, but they are uncertain how long they will remain with their current employer.

The desire for a safe neighborhood with a low crime rate has translated into a choice of suburban (and a few semi-rural) locations for many families. These workers, like many other Americans, equate cities with high crime rates, despite the fact that many suburbs also experience both property crimes and violent crimes. There is much interest in houses located on cul-de-sacs, properties that abut undeveloped land, or those on streets filled with other single-family homes. Most biotech workers do not want to live near large apartment buildings or publicly subsidized housing, although some do reside there. Although no one mentioned the issue of race, these preferences may be coded ways of expressing their desire to live in all-white neighborhoods.[29] The workers who are people of color—most of whom are first-generation immigrants—express similar preferences. Their class identity seems to shape their residential choices more than does affinity with their racial or ethnic group.

Finding a community whose school system has a reputation for excellence is a desire I heard from almost every parent I talked to, whether or not they had school-age children yet. Determining the quality of a community's school system is a challenge. Some workers dig deeply for information, calling PTA presidents, getting names of other parents in the community to call, and more recently, looking at MCAS (achievement test) scores published in newspapers and available on the internet. Other workers seem content to take the word of their real estate broker, and this is something on which realtors are now trained to provide information, especially to first-time home buyers and families with young children.

ONWARD AND UPWARD?

Upward mobility, as expressed in choices about where to live, is a strong theme in conversations with the workers about choosing a community. Many talked about growing up in a blue-collar city or suburban town and moving to a white-collar suburb. The majority of employees are homeowners, but most who are not expressed their desire to leave a rental unit and buy a house, preferably in a white-collar suburb.[30] Their primary rationales again involve perceptions of low crime and good schools. Proximity to extended family members was a key factor for almost half of those interviewed, and only one worker moved away from extended family to gain privacy.

Mike Sinclair and his wife, Lisa, and their two young children, recently moved to a community over an hour away from his biotech company, leaving a rental apartment in the blue-collar town where he and Lisa grew up and buying a home in a white-collar suburb. They considered buying a house in their hometown but decided that moving to a more affluent town would give them access to a better school system and a safer community. In addition, they are now a five-minute drive from his wife's sister and brother-in-law and their teenage children, with whom they have a very close relationship. Lisa's sister is their key person for backup and emergency childcare, and her nieces are important weekend babysitters. Although the move extends Mike's commute to work by 15 minutes each way, their new community is a visible affirmation of their success in achieving a solidly middle-class lifestyle.

Not every family I met has an upwardly mobile goal. Frank Parsons, a scientist and senior manager at BioPrima, and his wife, Natalie, decided to stay in the blue-collar city where they moved early in their marriage. Their decision was founded on both financial constraints and positive community connections. Making some sacrifices regarding their house and lifestyle enabled them to keep one parent at home while their children were growing up. The house they bought is in the same town—actually on the same street—where Frank grew up. Frank, now a graying man in his late forties, says it was "serendipity" that a house came on the market in his hometown just at the point that he and Natalie lost the rental apartment where they had been living while he was in graduate school. Their decision to buy this house was motivated primarily by their interest in being close to Frank's mother and old friends. In addition, Natalie's work with the local public school and their church have given them strong ties of their own to this community, making it truly their home.

Women who are single parents often are not upwardly mobile, and divorce is often accompanied by downward mobility.[31] Barbara Feldman is a single mother in her mid-thirties who works in a professional position at BioTertia. She had lived in a white-collar suburb with her husband and two children, but at the time of her separation, she moved back into her parents' home in the blue-collar city where she grew up. This gives her help with childcare as well as proximity to old friends and other family members, but she longs for a place of her own. However, the cost of even a rental apartment that could accommodate her children is out of reach. Another single mother Barbara knows at work has been able to continue living in a white-collar suburb since her separation, but she had to move from a house she owned into a rental apartment. Homeownership remains an unrealized dream for both women.

THE PASTURES OF SUBURBIA ARE NOT ALWAYS GREENER

Despite the fact that many workers I spoke to aspire to be homeowners in white-collar suburbs, and many achieve that goal, there is an interesting counterpoint to the upward mobility trend. A number of workers grew up in blue-collar urban and suburban communities, moved to white-collar suburbs, and now find they are missing what they left behind. Colleen McCarthy, an associate scientist, provides one of the clearest examples. She and her husband have recently moved to a white-collar suburb with their two young sons and bought their first house. Despite the fact that they have now accomplished a long-held goal of homeownership, Colleen does not feel part of her new community: other issues besides short-term residence are involved. Colleen describes at length the blue-collar urban community where they had been living, a community very similar to the one in which she grew up. In that town, she belonged to a playgroup with other mothers and young children that met every Thursday. When she went to the playground, she always saw people she knew. Community programs for young children were all on a drop-in, drop-by basis; if there was a show or a story hour at the library, she could go at the last minute. In her new community, Colleen finds that participating in programs for kids requires preregistration.

In her old community, Colleen was very involved in the local church parish and taught catechism classes. In her new community, there are two churches that serve families of her faith, but she does not know which to join; both project exclusivity and wealth. Colleen has heard that many members go on expensive ski weekends and trips to Ireland sponsored by the church, and she fears that she and her husband will not be able to participate in church social events owing to their limited financial resources.

Other workers who had made the move from a blue-collar city or suburb to a white-collar suburb spoke with conviction that their move represents something positive for their children's future, but they miss the people and institutions they grew up with. They seem to have underestimated both the effort needed to create meaningful connections in their new communities, and the value of their relationships in their old neighborhoods. Jessica Bromfield, the mother of twins described in chapter 2, now lives in a North Shore suburb. She and her husband chose this community because her husband was raised there, and his parents, who provide part of their regular childcare, also live there. But Jessica misses her life in her old neighborhood in a large city. She misses the "triple-decker" where she grew up, a multifamily dwelling where she and her siblings and cousins lived and played. She finds it hard to meet people where she lives now and takes her children to the street where her mother lives to go trick-or-treating on Halloween. She loves showing off her children in their costumes to the families she knows who still live in her old neighborhood. She says wistfully, "We follow my old route."

INSIDERS OR OUTSIDERS IN SUBURBIA: WHO BELONGS?

Biotech workers idealize suburbia—both those who live there and those who aspire to—but even the families who express enthusiasm about suburban life convey feelings of being outsiders when they speak at length about their experiences of living there. The "outsider" syndrome cuts across class lines, occupations, and family types. Two stories demonstrate the depth of these feelings.

Helen Rafferty, a biotech manager who likes having a big house and a big yard, appears enthusiastic about her upscale suburban community, saying, "Oh, it's great, I'm very happy here . . . I wouldn't want to move." Although she looks like other members of her suburb as a white, married mother of two, she has found living there hard because she is one of the few working mothers there. She tells about attending at week day evening event hosted by the Newcomers' Club in her community. At 9:00 p.m., she was exhausted and indicated that she had to leave. The other women tried to convince her to stay and drink wine with them. She declined because she had to get home to do laundry and confirm carpool arrangements to get her children to their after-school activities—"I mean I had stuff to do that I couldn't do the next day." The other women kept trying to convince her, until she finally blurted, "No, I am not a lady of leisure. I have to go to work in the morning." At that point they got angry with her, asking how she could call them "ladies of leisure" when they do housework and volunteer work. Helen retorted, "And I said, 'I have to do all that on about 50 hours a week less time.' And they just looked at me and said, 'Oh, you're right.' It was an amazing realization."

A different but in some respects parallel story comes from Malika Shaheed, an Afro-Caribbean single mother who lives in a rental apartment in an upscale suburb named Hilltop. She lives in this community because she was able to get a rent subsidy in public housing and because the town has an excellent public school system. But she does not want to stay there because

> It's a predominantly white neighborhood. It's a predominantly Jewish neigh-
> borhood. We're Black and we're Muslim. . . . There's no cultural organizations
> in Hilltop that focuses on [our] culture, [our] ethnic background. I'm from the
> islands. There's nothing in Hilltop that focuses on that.

Both Helen and Malika are minority members of their communities, Malika in the familiar sense, and both women share feelings of not belonging. Their stories and Colleen's reveal, by negative example, some of the ingredients that families need to feel connected to their communities of residence. Working families with children need to be able to connect with other families with children in a spontaneous, low-cost way. They need access to religious institutions, regardless of their income. They need to be able to find people in similar situations—whether according to work status, ethnic group, or religious affiliation—and have meeting places and times where there is an easy "cultural fit," where they will feel comfortable.

PLACES WHERE "EVERYONE KNOWS YOUR NAME"

"Neighborhood" is often viewed as a concept whose time has come and gone. The immigrant ethnic enclaves that characterized early-20th-century urban areas are dismissed as irrelevant to the lives of 21st-century families.[32] However, some of the families I met talked to me at length about their neighborhoods. They have close social ties to people they live near, and they describe these relationships as crucial elements of their work-family support systems.

Carl Mulligan, an associate scientist at BioSegunda, described a close-knit neighborhood in the small urban center where he lives. Carl is married and has one teenage daughter living at home, and two stepchildren from his wife's first marriage who live nearby. Carl's wife also holds a full-time job, and so they face challenges in the afternoon when their daughter comes home from school and they are still at work. Carl and his wife rely on neighbors to give them a sense of safety for their daughter while they are at work. Carl says, "I have good friends on the street. Yeah, they are good people and they are people who will always watch out for us."

Carl explains how the work schedules of families in the neighborhood complement one another. In the family two houses down the street, the father is a teacher and is off in the summer, "which is great because in the summertime [daughter] Megan's always down there." Help in caring for one another's children has created reciprocal bonds between Carl's family and other working families on the street:

> Sometimes they'll have Megan over, so Megan has a place to be, and we'll do the same with their kids. . . . So we're trying to watch out for each other's kids and give them a time out as well as a place, where instead of warming something up in the microwave, they can get a real good meal.

For Carl, these relationships go beyond "neighborliness"; he considers them friendships. In fact, he has a theory of how friendships for adults evolve over time:

> I think it happens to almost everybody who becomes a parent, you start meeting new friends through your kids. That's where we are now . . . the neighborhood kind of friends.

While this picture of neighborhood life seems to harken back to a bygone era, some neighborhoods change, and not always for the better. Some workers do not want to return to their old neighborhoods, like Mike Hallowell, who works at BioSegunda. Although he still lives in the same city where he grew up, he has moved to a new neighborhood. He says he doesn't go back much, and if he tried to attend Sunday services in his old church, he'd be seen as a "black sheep":

> It's just a different kind of environment from what is was 25 years ago when I was active in the church, when I was a kid. . . . It was always a working-class neighborhood . . . back when I was living there a lot of the original home-owners were still in the neighborhood and took good care of their properties. It has declined dramatically.

The loss of viable businesses that has affected many downtown urban areas has pushed longtime residents out of Mike's old neighborhood. The rates of homeownership are down, and new residents lack the kinds of jobs that would enable them to buy the old houses and fix them up. Mike feels a strong sense of connection with residents in his new neighborhood, a part of the city where his wife grew up and still has family, but there is sadness in his voice when he talks about his old church and what has happened to the street on which he was raised. By moving to a new neighborhood where he has family ties, he is able to re-create some of the old neighborhood feeling he lost.

THE PERSISTENCE OF "ROOTS"

When I interviewed Lily Huang, a scientist at BioSegunda, she talked about community in ethnic terms. A number of times she used the phrase "the Chinese community," referring to the neighborhood where her in-laws live or to neighborhoods in other cities that are home to people with a common national heritage. For Lily, this community exists in two large cities, and she lives in a suburb midway between. The geographical divide between these ethnic communities and her own community of residence provides a chal-lenge for Lily in handling her work-family issues. She makes regular trips into the "Chinatown" in one city and describes these as an important part of her family time on weekends:

> Then once a month we go to Chinatown to do the food shopping. So that's how we do the Saturday and the Sundays. Most time we bring Will [her older child] and everybody [her husband and in-laws] all together. We go to the

Chinese supermarket to buy the Chinese food. It takes about three hours back and forth, so it's a big plan.

Lily explains that she does not know anyone personally in "that Chinatown" but prefers to do her shopping there for certain food items she cannot get elsewhere. She does know people in "the other Chinatown" where her in-laws live. She visits frequently on weekends and sometimes drops her older child off there during the week to be cared for by his grandparents.

Lily would like to get involved with some of the groups for Chinese immigrants—both she and her husband were born in China—but she does not have the time. She was involved with these groups when she was a graduate student, she says, "but now I've got two kids stuck with me, so I just, you know, got lost with them, and I haven't gotten in touch with [these groups]." Lily is considering sending Will to Chinese Sunday school, a program in the "other Chinatown." This is not a religious school, but rather a group organized by Chinese-American parents for their children. They meet on Sundays to learn the Chinese language, Chinese dancing, and other aspects of Chinese culture. Lily says it is important to her and her husband that their children are bilingual, and they feel they need to make a special effort to ensure this exposure; in her words, "put him [her son] in a class, let him catch a little bit."

Lily and her husband do not have much contact with other young parents who are Chinese. They have a couple of Chinese friends who are also professional working parents with young children, but most of their friends are European-American. Their ties to China remain strong: Lily's parents still live in China, and come for long regular visits, and Lily goes back to China to visit her extended family. Her parents have no plans to move to the United States, nor do Lily and her husband have plans to return to China. She explains, "So right now we are not thinking about it, but I'm not sure when I'm getting old—when the kids go to college, maybe." Lily speaks about the "Chinese community" in Massachusetts with the same intensity that animates her voice when she speaks about her parents. Lily's work-family support system is not based solely in the place where she lives; it is also based in the "Chinese community," an important part of her identity.

POSSIBILITIES FOR CHANGE

For many of the "knowledge workers" in this book, employment in biotech has brought a fuller realization of a middle-class lifestyle than their parents had. Many have more education, larger incomes, and bigger houses in wealthier communities than their parents.[33] But as they acknowledge, their arrival in suburbia is often a mixed blessing. Their ability to own a home and be a resident of a moderate or upscale suburban community may be the fulfillment of a lifelong dream, but the reality of living there leaves some people with nostalgia for the communities where they grew up, and a sense of being outsiders.

The workers I met express a range of frustrations with community institutions—frustrations that could be a catalyst for change. What if Colleen convinced the library in her suburb to eliminate their formal preregistration policies and allow more children's programs to be accessed on a drop-in basis? What if Malika were successful in bringing materials on Afro-Caribbean life into her children's childcare center or school, so that the curriculum was more multicultural? What if Helen were able to find some other working mothers who could support each other and work together on creating after-school programs in their local school? A first step in the process of making their communities more responsive is assessing both community assets and community needs, and defining what would make a family-friendly environment.

DEFINING THE FAMILY-FRIENDLY COMMUNITY

The stories of biotech workers paint a less than rosy picture of work-family support at the community level. Several magazines devote an annual issue to the "Best Companies" for working women or working families[34]—and several others focus on which cities have the best "life style"—but there is no issue of a major magazine to my knowledge that assesses the family-friendliness of communities of residence.[35] How would one decide? What criteria should be used? Drawing on narratives of workers I met about the quality of life in their communities, as well as social, economic, and demographic data about the 34 cities and towns in Massachusetts where they live, I constructed a "Family-Friendly Community Index" for evaluating the environment for working families. (See Appendix 2 for details.) Building on the current interest in "social indicators" as a way to measure quality of life for families and children, the Index is composed of ten social indicators:[36] economic self-sufficiency and housing affordability; preschool child care programs; education in public schools; after-school programs; elder care services; public libraries; access to parks, recreational programs, and open space; access to public transportation systems; neighborhood safety and stability; and access to integrated health and family support services.[37]

If the final scores for each community were grades, there would be few cities and towns with stellar "report cards"—but that is not the point. The intention is to establish a baseline from which benchmarking goals can be set. Looking at the results as a whole, not surprisingly wealthier suburban communities tended to score higher, while cities and rural communities scored lower, (see Table 1.). If we disaggregate the indicators, we can take a more accurate snapshot of community strengths and community weaknesses. For example, the communities that score high on quality of education are usually those that score very poorly on housing affordability. This means that families are often forced to live in communities with inadequate school systems because they simply cannot afford to purchase a house where the schools are better. The majority of families I met fell somewhere in between: they end up with mortgages that are higher than what they can afford, and schools that are decent but not as good as they had hoped.

Looking at the relationships between other sets of indicators, communities that score well on transportation—the urban centers—usually score poorly on parks, recreation, and open space. Those that scored well on parks, open space, and housing affordability—usually rural communities—scored poorly on the quality of childcare, had no after-school programs, and moderate to poor schools. The communities that seemed to score fairly well on a variety of indicators are the "economically developed suburbs" clustered between two major interstate highways close to, but not in, the greater Boston area.[38] These are communities where housing costs are high but not outrageous, schools are good, and most family care services are accessible and high quality, but expensive. This is another way of restating the fact that families with higher incomes generally have access to better public schools and services, while lower-income families are stuck not only with low wages but also with inadequate supports and services. This has particularly serious consequences for the next generation, who need a high-quality education to qualify for higher-paying jobs and live in more affluent communities with better support services.

Two overall findings emerge from this assessment of community family-friendliness. First, most communities are not set up to accommodate working adults with multiple responsibilities to their employers, their children, their elders, their neighbors, and their community groups. Information about existing resources is often hard to find, services for families with children are not coordinated, and the quality of services is almost impossible to assess without in-person site visits. This situation requires time off work, and most employers do not provide leave time to research and visit five potential child-care centers. Second, almost all community-based programs and services strain the pocketbooks of middle-class working families and deplete the those of the working class. They are only "affordable" for families at opposite ends of the economic spectrum—low-income families who are eligible to receive subsidies for housing, childcare, and after-school programs (only 10 percent of families in this study), and upper-middle-class families with two professional incomes who live in affluent suburbs (about 15 percent). In the moderate-income suburbs, where most biotech workers and most middle-class families live, communities get little federal or state assistance for family support programs and do not have the tax base or budgets to create these pro-grams from scratch at the municipal level.

WHAT USE IS A COMMUNITY INDEX?

Creating this index turned out to be a far more challenging task than I orig-inally envisioned. The data needed to measure each parameter of family-friendliness are often hard to find. The state collects certain types of data but not others. Municipalities collect less data than state agencies and often use different categories and definitions as starting points, making available data sets difficult if not impossible to combine. But these problems are instructive in themselves. They underscore the fact that there is no systematic and coor-dinated tracking by states or town governments of the well-being of children, families, and communities that can give us a comprehensive view at the local level.[39] Without this information, it is difficult if not impossible for commu-nity members to identify problems and plan for change.

This index is intended as a pilot tool for communities to use to strengthen and coordinate existing services, and to plan for new ones. Each indicator could be expanded or reconstituted, and there may be other indi-cators that should be added. This is part of the grassroots process that is needed—to change or redefine indicators to meet specific community needs. Only a tool that is flexible and that can be adapted to reflect chang-ing conditions and the diverse needs of different communities will work. This Index has only been applied to 10 percent of the cities and towns in Massachusetts. Testing in more communities, and other states, can refine its measures and improve its usefulness.

QUALITY OF LIFE AND COMMUNITY RESOURCES: BUILDING RECIPROCITY

There is a commonly held preconception that most middle-class families do not need community-based family support programs—that they can purchase all the services they need, or take care of things themselves, without relying on institutions outside the family. The experiences of the families profiled in this book challenge these assumptions or misconceptions. Biotech workers and other new economy working families do need community-based programs to support their work and family lives, and many cannot afford the fee-for-service programs that are available.

As we will see in the chapters that follow, many middle-class families have created strategies to address their lack of access to family-friendly workplaces *and* family-friendly communities. Some of their strategies are family-based, as described in the previous chapter. While these may be an adaptive response, they are burdensome to families and society because they often depend on the lost income of one parent, interrupted careers, and diminished pensions. These strategies are risky because the same generation may need care themselves when they are still needed to be caregivers. These individualized family "solutions" underscore the need for more accessible, affordable community services.

Some of the strategies are community-based and hold great potential for bringing collective resources to bear on what are ultimately social, not personal, problems. But many difficult questions remain. How can community institutions become more responsive to the needs of working families? What role do employers have in building the capacity of communities to be responsive to working families? How can the time of working adults be freed to provide volunteer support to community-based services and programs? We need to build reciprocity into the fabric of our communities—a system where community programs support families and families give their time to build and sustain community institutions. As we will see, the lives of biotech workers are full of stories of reciprocity. Some of their efforts succeed, others fail, and lessons can be learned from both.

CHAPTER FIVE

More Than Roads and Bridges

Many biotech workers are searching for something in their lives beyond their jobs. They told me that their connections with others are what gets them through the work week. As one woman who works as a quality control specialist put it, "It's all those little things that other people do that keep me from crashing and burning!" Working families know they need more than roads and bridges to get to work. The physical infrastructure that connects cities and suburbs to workplaces is a necessary but hardly sufficient component of the daily work-family routine. What is needed is a social infrastructure that connects families, workplaces, and communities in a mutually beneficial system of support. Although these workers do not use words like "infrastructure" to describe what they need to manage paid work and family care, many are engaged every day in building just such a system. The work of constructing this support structure is critical to the survival of the families I met, but it is sometimes invisible—even to them. I wanted to understand how they make connections with others without imposing my own ideas about what they are or should be doing. To this end, I included a drawing component, which I call a "mapping exercise," as part of my initial interview with each worker.

MAPPING WORK-FAMILY-COMMUNITY CONNECTIONS

I asked workers to draw a map of the connections between themselves and others who made it possible for them to work and take care of their families.[1] The term "mapping" immediately brings to mind the discipline of geography and the age of exploration when Europeans discovered territories previously unknown to them. In this book, the term *mapping* has several related meanings and purposes. One is to describe social relationships of workers at home, at work, and in their communities, and their interconnections. Another is to describe the spatial relationships between different parts of a family's work-family support network. The concept of social mapping is not new, and there are no completely "unknown territories" in the social realm either. A valuable (if not unique) aspect of the approach in this book is the emphasis on having people create their own social maps. Many researchers who study social networks collect data on people's social relationships and create their own representation of social ties and social support.[2] My approach is to ask people to tell their own stories, and then draw pictures that map their own lives.

MAP CONSTRUCTION: PROCESS AND CONTENT

My request to draw a map elicited a wide range of reactions. No one refused to draw a map, but the ease or difficulty with which people approached the task was in itself revealing. Many workers seemed to feel lost at first, only to find their bearings once they put pen to paper. Some assumed it was a "test" with right and wrong answers. When assured that this was not the case, some became more unsure, while others felt freed to create their own unique images. On the whole, those with denser networks and more complex maps seemed to have an easier time making the maps. They seemed intuitively to see their lives as connected to others in a way that those with sparser maps did not.

The order in which workers drew individuals and institutions on their maps was also interesting: the strongest relationships were usually recorded first or second. The spatial layout of the maps usually had little to do with actual physical distance, but it conveyed information about the strength of a connection or the frequency of contact. Placing individuals and groups either in the center or on the periphery of the map was another way of depicting the quality of social relationships.

The narrative explanations that accompanied the drawing process were often helpful in decoding the schematic representations. Many people experienced a process of discovery in the map-making. As one worker said, "I've never done this before, this is interesting," explaining that the map itself provided a new way of looking at his own life, and that it taught him something about himself and his relationships. Discontinuities between the narrative and the figures on the map revealed new issues to explore, and sometimes information was conveyed during the mapping process that had never been mentioned. For example, when I asked one man about his parents during our first interview and whether he had any elder care responsibilities, he said his father had died and his elderly mother was healthy and lived independently quite far away. When he drew his mother on his map, however, he drew her close to his own family, with bold lines connecting her to his two school-age children. He then explained that she often comes to stay with them and care for her grandchildren, especially when his wife is away on business or needs to visit her own parents, one of whom is in a nursing home.

WHAT DO THE MAPS TELL US?

In this chapter, I will use some of the maps collected to discuss how biotech workers create systems of support to manage both paid work and family care, and the extent to which these systems include people and institutions outside the family.[3] I am particularly interested in whether families use resources located in the communities where they live and, if not, how they form other kinds of communities. Two particular approaches to mapping, social network analysis and "assets mapping," can help make sense of these maps.[4]

Social network analysis is useful for answering the question "How do people receive social support?"[5] One way to answer this question is to look at the structure of the network and things that can be counted. How many people are in the network? Who is connected to whom? How frequent is the contact? How many ties does one individual have? Another way to answer is to look at the value, intensity, and meaning of the relationships between people in the network, dimensions of connection that are not easily quantified. Are the ties durable over time? What is being given or exchanged? Are the ties reciprocal? This type of analysis focuses on how people experience being part of a network, how they maintain their network, and its significance in their lives. Taken together, these two components of social network analysis can connect the issue of resources and social support to the larger issue of community.[6]

Assets mapping is useful for answering two questions: What resources already exist in a community to support families? How can communities create change and access additional resources? Assets mapping comes from the fields of community development and community planning.[7] Practitioners begin by surveying the capabilities and skills found within a given community, first at the individual level, then at the level of citizen groups and non-profit organizations, and finally at the institutional level. By making an inventory of resources and accomplishments and mapping their locations, this approach can assist communities in building capacities, developing part-nerships, and creating environments that are responsive to the needs of all parties.

By looking at the map of Julie Taylor, whose story was described in the Introduction, we can learn a number of things about how she constructs her work-family support system (see Figure 1).

Julie's network is large and complex. It includes both individuals and institutions. She draws bold lines to indicate her major sources of support. The institutions she most relies on are the childcare center that cares for her preschool daughter and provides after-school care for her older daughter, and her church. The people she relies on include her own parents and other par-ents. Her map shows not only the importance of the support she receives from other parents, but also how certain groups of parents comprise impor-tant subgroups in her system. She creates one circle of parents who use the same childcare center and elementary school and are neighbors, and another circle of parents who use the same childcare center and attend the same church. These parent groups are important to Julie for two reasons: first, her husband, Peter, works long hours, does limited childcare, and does not vol-unteer in community institutions; and second, her extended family lives out of state and is not available to help care for her children. Many of the people in her network she sees daily, others at least once a week. The relationships revolve around the care and education of her children and are highly recipro-cal. Her childcare center provides care for her daughters, and she volunteers her time to work with teachers and helps run the center. Her church provides religious education for her children, and she volunteers as a teacher in the Sunday school. Many people in her support system know each other, making the network dense and reasonably durable.

It is interesting to specify the weak ties, as well as the strong ones, in Julie's network.[8] Her workplace is drawn farther from her and her children than her church, the childcare center, or the groups of parents and neighbors she relies on, and her description of her supervisor makes it clear that his support is often lacking. The tie to her daughter's elementary school seems particularly weak, as indicted by her dotted line and her comments about the guilt she feels over being unable to volunteer in her daughter's classroom. Finally, Peter's family and college friends are all at some remove, drawn on

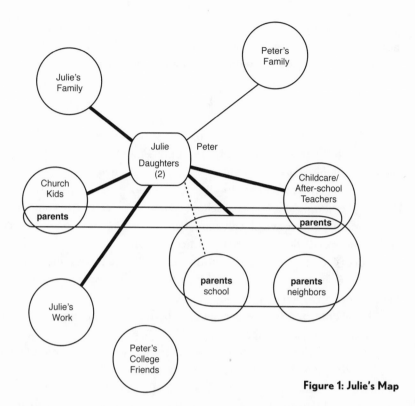

Figure 1: Julie's Map

the map and named but never mentioned during our conversations. Even Peter himself is added at the end of the drawing process. Julie started her map with a circle including herself and her daughters, so when she remembered—with some embarrassment—to add Peter, she literally draws him outside the immediate family.

Julie's map clearly shows the assets she has available to help her meet the challenge of managing work and family. Her childcare center has been a major asset since her eldest daughter was three months old. She is already experiencing a sense of loss, anticipating the time when both girls will be in elementary school and she will no longer see the center director and the girls' teachers regularly. Her church is significant, not only for the religious educa-tion it provides but also for the quiet time, spiritual guidance, and comfort Julie receives when listening to sermons and attending services. When we combine her map with the narrative of her interview, the parents of her chil-dren's friends stand out as a central asset, unifying the many institutions with which she is associated. They provide material assistance and emotional support, and she returns this in kind. She sees these relationships as critical to her now and in the future while her girls grow up. It is important to note that assets—and therefore, networks of support—are not static; membership comes and goes.[9] If Julie were to draw her map a couple of years from now, the childcare center would no longer appear, but her network of parents might have grown in size.

Julie's map can also be seen as a picture of what is missing, or what needs to change to increase support of her family. Potentially, her daughter's elementary school could be a source of support. Her map suggests that she is already connected to parents in the school, and that group may be a link between her family and her local school system. Her workplace could become a greater source of support by allowing her time off to volunteer in the school and more overall flexibility in her schedule. One thing that is striking on Julie's map is that no public institutions in her life are interconnected. A link between her employer and her public school, for example, could transform her network and increase her social support. Mapping community assets can reveal new opportunities for partnerships between community organizations and other key institutional players.

As Julie Taylor's map shows, "community" takes many different forms and may or may not have a physical location. Many workers say they belong to multiple communities that provide different types of social support. Most workers I spoke to emphasize one type of community that is particularly valued and meaningful in their lives. Four major "narratives of community" emerged during the interview and mapping process. While these groupings give salience to what some families have in common, there remains a degree of individual variability and unique meaning in each narrative, in each map.

THE EXTENDED FAMILY IS ALIVE AND WELL

It is often assumed that the extended family does not really exist these days, or at least that it does not play an important role, because people move around a great deal and do not live in multigeneration households any more. In fact, relocation only affects a small percent of the population in any given year, and some people do live in multigeneration households.[11] Second, even for those not sharing households, the sharing of human and financial resources is significant. It is hard to know how many of the workers in this book would "make it" without the labor, money, and emotional support they receive from their extended families. In fact, I would argue that the ability of many biotech families to achieve and maintain a middle-class lifestyle depends on these resources.

Ties with extended family are regular and intense. Many biotech employees see their extended family members once to three times during the work week, and regularly on weekends. Even without face-to-face contact, there are regular phone calls, among both people who live near extended family and those with close relatives out of state. The size of these extended family networks varies quite a bit, from a few people up to almost 90 people. People within these networks tend to know one another and interact with some regularity. Spending time with extended family is the fourth most common type of activity among workers I met, after work, housework, and errands. The majority of the employees interviewed have extended family living nearby. Those whose extended family live out of state often spend their vacation time visiting with these relatives. This is challenging for married couples with parents in two different parts of the country, but they make these visits regularly, at least once a year.

The role of grandparents and siblings is particularly important in the dependent care strategies of families with children still at home. There are many less tangible benefits shared by extended family members, including positive feelings of support, interdependence, and resilience. Extended family members play a particularly important role in the lives of single-parent families. The loss of a husband's income faced by divorced single mothers is often compensated for by moving in with extended family to save on housing and food costs, or moving near extended family in order to save on child-care. This kind of assistance may foster some degree of tension, resentment, and lack of privacy, but it is essential to the economic survival of these single-parent households.

With married couples, there is often some asymmetry in the relationships with extended family members; usually, either the husband's family or the wife's family is more involved. Sometimes this is a function of geographical distance, but sometimes it just reflects the closeness of particular relationships. This unevenness can lead to some tension between spouses even though the support received is needed and appreciated.

Family relationships form the foundation of community for the majority of workers I met. In this type of community, most social time outside of work is spent with relatives, not just for special occasions like birthdays, anniversaries, and religious holidays, but also for regular relaxation and recreation. These workers acknowledge a tremendous fragility and lack of security in the world of work, and they hold firmly to the belief that family are the people whom you can fall back on, the ones you can count on when all else fails.

There are two key variations in this type of community. Several biotech employees live with extended family members, either in the same house, or by having an "in-law" apartment, or sharing half of a two-family house. Their financial and dependent care arrangements are closely linked to this living situation. Other biotech employees live near extended family, across the street, a short drive away, or in a nearby city or suburb. Whatever the physical distance, interaction is frequent—sometimes, phone calls from work once or more a day—and relationships are emotionally intense. A few workers have extended family living out of state whom they see as their most important support. Perhaps most significant, this type of community is strongly shaped by reciprocity, and all those involved view the relationships as permanent.

Jessica Bromfield is a biotech professional with a specialty in quality assurance who works at a small biotech company. She is married to a full-time professional who also works in the biotechnology industry. They have twin preschool children. On Jessica's map, the majority of people are extended family members. This is not to say that she does not have other relationships, but she sees her support system and her strongest connections as family-based (see Figure 2).

Jessica begins with a bounded circle of herself, her husband, and her two daughters. Then she draws four lines that radiate out to four other circles. The first circle she draws includes her mother and two of her siblings. In the second circle, she writes the names of her mother-in-law, and father-in law who provide childcare two to three days a week. In the third circle, she writes "cousins"—she says she has 30 first cousins, many of whom are married—and then writes the names of two female cousins. Asked why she named these two, she answers, "Only because I know they would always be there, if I needed them." These two women give her personal support, provide backup childcare, and help care for her mother. In the fourth circle, she names her closest female friend, Angie, whom she grew up with and has known since childhood— "almost family." Angie has children the same age as Jessica's. Although they don't see each other often, they talk on the phone every other night. Angie works full-time for a medical device company—some days at home—and advises Jessica on how to negotiate with her boss for more flexibility.

Jessica's map includes both family she is responsible for and those to whom she looks for help. She gets regular help with childcare from her in-laws and backup childcare from her own relatives, and is involved in oversee-

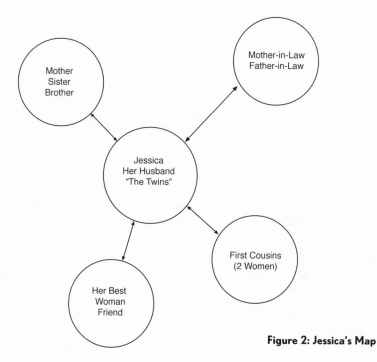

Figure 2: Jessica's Map

ing health care for the older generation, particularly her mother. She explains that because she lives farther away from her mother than her siblings do, she often turns to them to help their mother—another piece of the extended family care system. Everyone on her map, including her friend Angie, knows the others and has for a long time. The people she proposed for a family-community network interview were her in-laws. She and her husband not only rely on them for regular childcare but also live in the same town and spend significant time with them on weekends and some weeknights. In addition, her in-laws provide her a connection to community issues in her fast-growing suburb, participating in town meetings and a battle against out-side developers, something Jessica has not had time to do herself.

Jessica also makes time to visit her mother and her siblings, even though they live an hour away, and often goes to large extended family events on her side of the family. Although Jessica's map has a small number of circles and looks relatively simple compared to some others, the size of her network is large—between 80 and 90 people—and her network is highly durable, built on life-long relationships that she expects to continue, regardless of her job situation or the location of her employer. Jessica's extended family members form an asset in her work-family support system that has been tested and that she is confident will endure.

"A PLACE WHERE EVERYONE KNOWS YOUR NAME"

Neighbors and community of residence provide a strong sense of connection for about one-quarter of the workers I talked with. These workers often live in the same town where they grew up—and express "a feeling of being known." People from their childhood years and their high schools are still part of their lives. They describe a type of connection that is difficult to create in a single generation. Some biotech employees hope for this type of community in the suburbs where they have been living for five to fifteen years but lament the difficulty of achieving it. Some grew up with this type of community connection and express a sense of loss after moving away. The importance of extended family may be due in part to the difficulty of achieving a sense of community in some suburbs.

In the maps depicting this type of community, workers draw a mix of extended family, neighbors, and community institutions. Their narratives are filled with allusions to the insecurity of working in biotech, and their sense of a safety net revolves around people they live close to. They may see individuals on their map once a week or once a month, but frequency of contact does not seem to dilute the importance of these relationships. People on any one map may or may not know each other; it is common for some to be acquaintances while others remain strangers. There is reciprocity in these neighborhood relationships, but they may be short-lived and/or instrumental. For example, a strong relationship with a family childcare provider in the neighborhood may fade in intensity when the child goes to school, but the history of this relationship is part of what makes a worker feel tied to his or her neighborhood. Workers who rely on this type of community may be active in their local public school or parish, or have a spouse who is, which deepens neighborhood connections.

Frank Parsons is a research scientist with a master's degree who works at BioPrima. He is married and has four children. His wife, Natalie, worked as a family childcare provider for some time while their children were young and invests a great deal of time volunteering in their local public school and church. Frank lives in the blue-collar suburb in which he was raised. He and his wife bought a house on the street where his mother lived. They have been there for many years and express no intention of moving. Frank was involved in education issues in town, not in his children's school but as an elected member of the school council. He is not active in his church but supports his wife's and children's involvement and goes to services on important holidays and family occasions, like baptism or confirmation. He belongs to a men's recreational club in his neighborhood and often stops there on the way home to play pool and relieve stress. Many of Frank's high school friends live in the area, and although he does not consider them close friends, he enjoys running into them on the weekend at the local hardware store or around town.

Frank's map is dense and textured with many arrows connecting him and Natalie to their extended family and to community institutions in their neighborhood. Frank begins drawing his map with his wife: "Well, Natalie is first." He then adds himself and their four children. He makes a box for the neighborhood elementary school connected by lines to his children and to

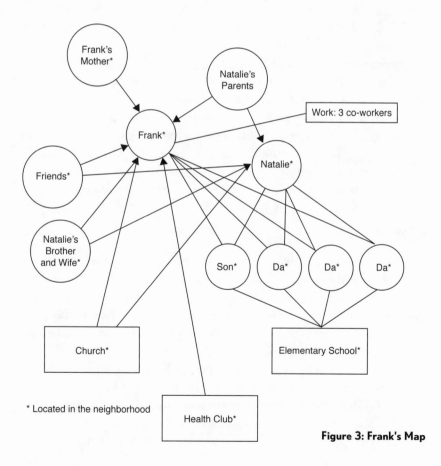

Figure 3: Frank's Map

him—he went there as a child—and to Natalie, an active volunteer there. He connects the church to both himself and Natalie. Natalie's brother, his wife, and their children, who live nearby and help a lot with the kids, are connected to him and Natalie. It is interesting that Frank draws no line connecting him and Natalie. His comments are replete with praise for Natalie—he admires all the volunteer work she does and is supportive of her new role as a college student. As a family in which Frank is the currently the only wage earner and Natalie is the stay-at-home mom, they have a very traditional marriage and very separate spheres of activity. Their neighborhood is their shared public domain.

The arrows on Frank's map go "every which way;" everything is interconnected, and most of the individuals (except Natalie's parents) and institutions are located in his community of residence. Only two lines join just two nodes on the map: one connects Frank to several named co-workers from BioPrima, and the other connects him to his men's club. As he is completing his drawing, Frank comments that he enjoys knowing a lot of people in his neighborhood and parish, and half-jokingly says, "It's nice to know that if you lose your job, other people will feed your kids!" His narrative is replete with stories of the contributions that he and Natalie make to people and institutions in their community *and* a strong sense that their family will be taken care of, if necessary, by people and institutions in their neighborhood. His map is filled with neighborhood-based assets and a set of highly reciprocal relationships. It is noteworthy that the men who, like Frank, take on volunteer positions are often those who have strong ties to their town and neighborhood.[12]

KEEPING THE FAITH

Religious affiliation is the path to community for almost one-third of the workers I met. They feel "known" by clergy and supported by fellow congregants with whom they share important values. Their membership in a religious institution is a strong element of their identity and the way they present themselves to others. They believe their religious institution will take care of them in a crisis, such as personal illness, the death of a loved one, or job loss. Workers express strong attachment to the teachings and rituals of their religious tradition, be it Judaism, Christianity, or Islam. The strength of their connection does not seem to depend on their level of involvement. Some attend religious services every week, teach Sunday school, or chair a committee, and some do less. They are united by an active search for meaning in their lives that transcends work, making money, and career advancement. They are seeking connections that will counterbalance the fragility of the biotechnology industry and the vagaries of a consumer culture. They are building connections they hope will last a lifetime—and that some believe will continue in a life beyond this one.

Despite busy weekend schedules, approximately half of those interviewed participate in a religious service or community activity. Some are financially supportive members of traditional churches, mosques, or synagogues, while others belong to looser groups with an informal, communal approach to religious holidays and observances. Most of these workers drew their religious institution on their map and reported regular contact once a week to once a month. Workers who belong to religious organizations know and socialize with other families who are members, creating social networks that are geographically and socially dense. In about half of the families who belong to a religious institution, both husband and wife are involved. Although the involvement of some husbands is minimal, these institutions appear on many of their maps. The single mothers, despite their busy schedules and lack of personal time, are all members of religious institutions, and fellow congregants are often described as friends.

Workers who experience a sense of community largely through their faith commitments often drew their religious institution prominently on their maps. Sometimes "God" is named and drawn inside a circle, or a clergyperson is included. Although there is a strong connection between the worker and their church, synagogue, or mosque, often there is little connection between members of that institution and other individuals on the map. A number of the workers who describe a sense of community through participation in a religious institution have extended family living out of state.

Rachel Warren works in a professional manufacturing-support position at BioTertia. She is a single mother who adopted a little girl from China. She often feels like an outsider in the white-collar suburban community in which she lives, but an insider in her church. She goes to services regularly on Sundays. She attends dinners organized by the church and goes on church retreats with her daughter. Hundreds of people attend these retreats, which include organized games for the children and communal dinners. Rachel describes these events in great detail, saying they are "just wonderful," and that when she returns to work she is better able to deal with the stress of her job and her long commute. Her church gives her a connection to clergy, other congregants, and God, allowing her a sense of perspective on her work.

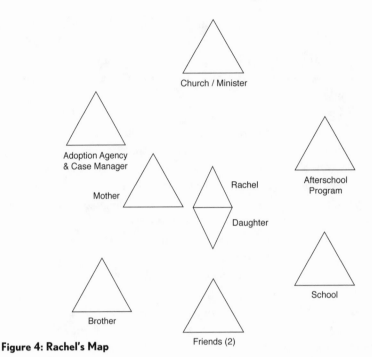

Figure 4: Rachel's Map

Rachel's map is a series of small triangles clustered on the upper half of the page with no connecting lines, perhaps indicating her sense of isolation as a never-married mother living in a suburban community of mainly married-couple families. As she draws, she talks about her worries that her daughter does not fit in culturally and her loneliness for extended family living out of state. On her map, she places herself in the center in a triangle, and her daughter in an adjoining triangle. She draws her church with the name of her minister directly above her. She explains, "That's what's leading my life. That's the head of my life. It gets me through the other things in my life until I can go next Sunday."

Rachel's church fills deeply personal and spiritual needs and provides a community life she cannot find elsewhere. She named her minister and the director of the adoption agency she worked with for family-community network interviews. She arranged for me to talk with her female minister, "who is absolutely a phenomenal speaker." Rachel describes her minister's sermons as giving her a sense of direction about how to live her life and "get through the day-by-day," especially the work week. Her minister helped Rachel move and paint her house. Rachel feels that her minister is an inspiring person, and that the church will be there for her and her daughter in both material and spiritual ways in the years to come.

Her key assets are her church, including both her minister and other congregants, and her adoption agency, which has connected her to other parents who have adopted children from Asian countries, and her daughter's school and after-school program. Although fellow congregants and other adoptive parents are a part of her narrative, they do not appear on her map, and there does not seem to be any overlap between the people or institutions she draws on her map. Work is notable by its absence. This is not to say that her network is not strong, but rather that its structure and size differ significantly from those of other networks. Her strongest ties are to her faith and her church; though not visible, they sustain her in her busy weeks as a single working mother—she marks her weeks as running from Sunday to Sunday, and church services are her "time to refuel."

TGIM—"THANK GOD IT'S MONDAY"

Professional or work-based friendships form the basis of community for a small number of workers. The nature of these ties is often instrumental, related to networking for new jobs or sharing information about scientific breakthroughs at other companies. But the language that is used to describe these relationships is that of friendship, not professional contact, even though these people rarely see one another socially outside of work. I was surprised that only 10 percent of those I talked to expressed a sense of connection and community from work-related friendships, given the fact that many biotech employees invest significant years in professional education.

This may in part reflect the fact that contact with friends—even strictly personal friends—is strikingly low over all in terms of duration, frequency, and regularity of contact. However, a number of workers say that, despite infrequent visits, their friends are their major source of emotional support, and they appear on the maps of two-thirds of those interviewed. Some friends are separate from daily life and yet are referred to as "my closest friend." Perhaps the distance of these individuals from daily routines makes the friendships particularly valuable. One woman described her relationship with her closest woman friend, whom she rarely sees, as "the one person I can really let down my hair with." Perhaps her friend's lack of connection with her work and family enables a degree of honesty she cannot afford in other relationships.

Community based on work and professional identity is found mainly among the postdoctoral research scientists interviewed, who derive a sense of identity from their professional training and collegial relationships. There are two variants of this type of narrative. One variant revolves around professional friends from college, graduate school, and/or postdoctoral positions. These friends often do not live locally, and in-person visits and interactions occur rarely. The other variant involves co-workers, either in the current workplace or a recent former place of employment. Whether or not one sees these friends outside of work, the salient theme is that some co-workers or professional friends are the people who really know you and understand you. This is the case with Fatimah Razad, a senior research scientist at BioPrima. As she draws her map, she says her closest relationships are to people at BioPrima, and that other relationships are superficial. She is a first-generation immigrant from the Middle East who completed a B.S. degree in her home country and did her doctoral work in the United States. Most of her close ties are with people she met in graduate school and in her workplace. She states, "Everyone here says, 'TGIF—thank God it's Friday,' but not me. I am sad. I say thank goodness it's Monday."

The frequency of contact between members of these communities varies greatly, from daily at work to once a year at a professional conference. The extent of reciprocity is narrow—the narrowest in the four narratives of community—and focuses almost exclusively on the work domain. It may involve help finding a new job or knowledge about a source of grant funding. There is no direct support for family care, although there may be supportive discussions around family, career issues, and job transitions. These workers have minimal involvement with their communities of residence or community groups, except indirectly through the volunteer work of their wives if they are men. They usually belong to professional associations in which their involvement varies. Several drew extended family living out of state on their maps, but they say the frequency of contact is once or twice a year for short-term visits.

George Stratton is a research scientist and senior manager at BioPrima. He is married and the father of two school-age children. When his children were younger, his wife worked in a full-time professional position. She is now a stay-at-home mom but does a little work from home. George completed college, graduate school, and postdocs outside Massachusetts. George begins his map with a circle that includes his immediate family, listing people by name: Elizabeth, his wife, at the top, then himself, then his son, then his

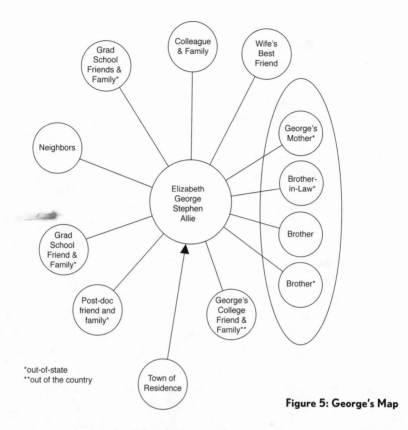

Figure 5: George's Map

daughter. Next he draws a large circle with four smaller circles inside it for his mother, his two brothers, and Elizabeth's brother, three of the four live out of state. Then he draws six circles arrayed around the circle containing himself and his wife and children. Five out of six of these are professional friends he describes as "close family friends" and "very important families." The fact that some of these families live abroad, some in the distant parts of the United States, and some in Massachusetts is not reflected in George's map. He indicates that he has not seen some of these colleagues for several years, but this is not reflected in his map either. He simply comments, "They are all very close." He talks about them as "friends" whom he met in college, in graduate school, or when he was doing his post-doc. He emphasizes their shared professional interests.

There is no indication on George's map of his children's school, the school committee that Elizabeth serves on, the other parents they know through the school, or the many children's programs and sports teams in their community that his wife and children are involved in. One wonders what a map drawn by Elizabeth might look like. It is not that George has no relationship to his community, but it is mediated through the relationships and volunteer work of his wife. After a pause, George draws a circle at the bottom of the page, at a great distance from himself and Elizabeth, and places the name of their town, Northridge, in the center. Then he draws an arrow toward the circle with his family, and comments, "The Northridge loop is moving in," explaining that he and Elizabeth are getting friendlier with some parents of their children's friends. He notes with a degree of irony how strange it is that the people they see frequently are the ones they are not close to. The relationships with people in the other six circles are the most important—"they are 15- to 20-year friendships"—despite their geographic distance. Even though George and Elizabeth moved to Northridge nine years ago, they have just started to build social ties to people in their suburban community.

As an afterthought, George adds a friend of Elizabeth's whom they see frequently and vacation with, and who helps with the kids. He indicates that it is a terrible omission to have left her out and recommends that I interview her. She is a friend of Elizabeth's from her old job, a professional colleague, the most important type of relationship. In George's view, it is this kind of relationship that forms the path to friendship and to community.

LOOKING AT COMMUNITY THROUGH A SPATIAL LENS

The narratives of community described above are based on social maps drawn by workers. Each map can be redrawn to create a spatial representation of the proximity between the individuals and institutions drawn. Differences in the ways that workers create community and work-family support systems produce different kinds of spatial maps. The maps of those who build community based on neighborhood ties and faith commitments show that the key people and institutions in their family-community support networks are geographically separate from the workplace, clustered near (if not in) each worker's community of residence. Despite the importance of extended family living out of state, the daily work-family support system is concentrated close to home. For example, if one were to redraw Julie Taylor's map as a spatial map, it would look like the diagram in Figure 6.

Most of Julie's key day-to-day supports cluster in and around the suburban town where she lives, including the childcare center, her church, her

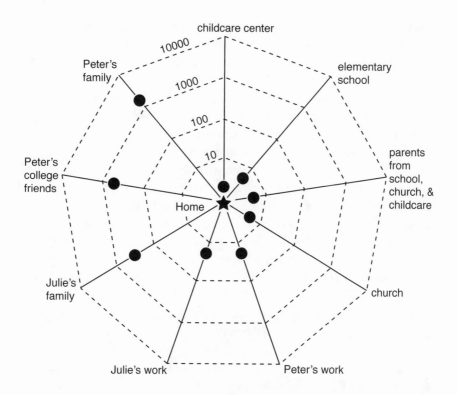

Figure 6: A Spatial Representation of Julie's Map

neighbors, and other parents. The distance between work and home (for Julie and other workers with long commutes) appears to be a factor in the construction of strong neighborhood networks.[13] Perhaps workers feel that they need many levels of backup in case they cannot get home quickly.

On Julie's map, there is one exception to the clustering of work-family support in her community of residence—her extended family. Although her parents live over 200 miles from her home and Julie visits them only a few times a year, her ties to her family of origin are strong; she says their emotional support and occasional financial assistance are essential to her family's well-being. Physical proximity to home is important in the construction of a durable, sustainable work-family support system, but elements of support can also be provided at some physical distance.

Workers whose sense of community derives from strong neighborhood and faith-based ties have spatial maps that are dense, with key work-family supports clustered in their communities of residence. The spatial maps for workers who build a sense of community around work and professional relationships vary in their configuration from moderately dispersed to very dispersed. If work-related networks are related to one's current job, they tend to be moderately dispersed and some people within the network know one another. If the networks originated in graduate school or membership in a professional association, they are significantly dispersed, and friends are unlikely to know other people in the network. None of the individuals George Stratton names as being close friends or close relatives lives in his community of residence. They are scattered across eastern Massachusetts and across several regions of the United States, and one lives overseas. In general, personal friendships are usually part of a geographically dispersed network.

The spatial maps of those workers who rely primarily on extended family do not fit one spatial pattern. Some have key family members living out of state, while others have extended family living close by. When those with extended family in Massachusetts move from cities or blue-collar suburbs to white-collar suburbs, they tend to maintain close geographical proximity to extended family members, even when the relocation increases their commute to work. This reflects their reliance on family members for help with childcare, an interest in making weekend and holiday visiting easier, and their desire to be available to care for aging parents.

LOOKING AT COMMUNITY THROUGH A LIFE COURSE LENS

The importance of a life cycle model for understanding the nature of the work-family linkage has been well formulated by Phyllis Moen, former director of Cornell's Employment and Family Careers Institute.[15] She writes that there are four life stages: the *anticipatory stage*, when couples are in their twenties and anticipating careers and development of their families; the *launching stage*, when couples have preschool children and are trying to build careers; the *establishment stage*, when couples have established careers and school-age children; and the *shifting gears stage*, when couples are thinking about a new career or retirement and no longer have children at home. Moen has shown how husbands and wives vary their paid work hours and career strategies at each stage to accommodate work-family needs.

This perspective suggests a number of questions about the family-community networks of biotech workers. Does the size or composition of these networks change as families move from one stage to another? What do the maps reflect about the life stages of the children, parents, or grandparents? Are certain community-building strategies more strongly correlated with families at a certain stage? Some of these questions can be addressed only by studying these same families over time, but some can be explored now.[16] The workers and family members I met fit into three of Moen's four stages (there are no families in the anticipatory stage). One-third of the families are in the launching stage, well over half are in the establishment stage, and about 10 percent are in, or moving toward, the shifting gears stage. Their relationships to community vary, and their stage of life, particularly the age of their children, does appear to shape their connections and efforts to build community.

The community connections for families in the launching stage revolve around their dependent care arrangements, including their ties to childcare providers and/or family members who provide childcare. Extended family members are also important for providing financial assistance and other resources, especially for buying houses and paying off educational loans. Friends, either from work or outside of work, do not figure prominently on their maps or in their narratives. The size of family-community networks is small, except in cases where extended families are large.

The community connections for families in the establishment stage revolve around their children's school and faith-based institutions. The maps of workers at this stage show other community-based groups, such as YMCA and YWCA, sports teams, Brownie and Cub Scout troops, and adoption agencies. Extended family connections are important for these families as well, but the maps show an increase in non-familial community-based connections, compared to the maps of those in the launching stage. Friends figure more prominently, and where friends are drawn, they are often the parents of children's friends as well as adults' friends from work or other activities. The networks of families at this stage are larger than those of families at the launching stage and tend to be geographically dense.

A few families in this book are on the cusp between the establishment stage and the shifting gears stage. Their maps show a dense network of familial and community-based connections. The school connections that are found in some form on the maps of families in the establishment stage disappear as children go to college, move away from home, marry, and start families. Connections to faith-based institutions remain for some families but disappear for others. This suggests that the religious education of the children, rather than the faith orientation of the parents, shapes the importance of religious affiliations for some families. Friends seem to play a larger role, and elder care providers and services emerge in their community networks. It would be interesting to explore the interface between life stage and community building strategy with a larger, more diverse group of working families.

FAMILY ASSETS: DIVERSE COMMUNITIES, COMMON CONNECTIONS

We hear many stories about the "time famine" that is depriving working families of dinners together, leisure, and even sleep. But a "deficit model" that focuses on what working families are lacking does not capture how the families I met actually live. These families bring multiple assets to the task of coping with work-family conflicts in their daily lives. They find assets in extended family relationships, in their neighbors, in secular and religious institutions outside the family, and at work. Most of these relationships involve complex reciprocity. Interviews with extended family members and community-based professionals reveal how pivotal these relationships are to all involved.

As I tried to understand what families do, rather than what they don't do, four narratives of community, which reflect different strategies for integrating work and family, emerged. These are not formal categories, and they are not static or neatly bounded; rather, they represent options that families may move in and out of at different points in the life cycle, or a way of reorganizing sources of support to reflect changes in the health, marriage, or job status of key family members. Some families may fit into more than one category or have a very unique way of connecting people and resources. It is important to highlight the creativity that families show under considerable constraints and to recognize the agency of families—powerfully conveyed in their maps—devising strategies for building work-family support systems.

Looking at the workers I spoke with as a group, several things stand out. First, the most prevalent narrative of community is the one that focuses on extended family. Interestingly, this group includes some families with relatives living nearby and a few with relatives outside Massachusetts. The strength of the extended family bond crosses state lines, and in one case national borders. The narratives that focus on neighborhood and religious affiliation are equally represented in the group. These are forms of community—especially the one centered on neighborhood ties—that many people think are out of date, but the evidence I found supports the idea that the ties formed where workers live and worship provide many of the supports that contemporary working families need. The community narrative that focuses on work relationships is by far the least frequent, despite the fact that this group of new-economy knowledge workers is highly educated and includes many professional workers. Perhaps the fragility of their industry makes biotech workers hesitant to rely on friends they meet at work. This provides an interesting counterpoint to the important research conducted by the sociologist Arlie Hochschild, who writes that, for the families she studied, work rather than home is becoming the "haven from the heartless world."[17]

The lives of the biotech workers I met are not entirely driven by the pressures of job and career. They seek, and often find, communities outside of work that sustain them. The connections they make with others—as shown in the chapters that follow—create durable work-family support systems and the foundations for community involvement and volunteerism. This involvement outside the nuclear family holds promise for three important changes: it can foster greater gender equality inside the family; it can strengthen our understanding of work-family issues as matters of social responsibility; and it can create the basis for a stronger civil society.

CHAPTER SIX

CHILDCARE AND OTHER BUILDING BLOCKS OF CIVIL SOCIETY

Sitting in my car outside the Apple Tree Child Care Center, I watch the comings and goings of parents and children. Some parents seem to be pulling their children inside, while other children seem to be pulling their parents. It looks like a dance in which the partners are not sure about who is leading. As parents leave, most are already rushing to work; some look back, but most do not. The center's director, Phoebe Walsh, told me that this early-morning separation sets the tone for the day. When I called to arrange a time for our interview, Phoebe warned me not to arrive too early, saying,

> I like to be at the door and greet my kids by name. It makes them feel known and welcome. It makes their parents feel more relaxed too—you know, about the "goodbye rituals" that every working parent dreads? Anything I can think of to make the transition easier, I'll try. I often wear a funny piece of jewelry— something to catch their eye, distract them. One time I even used face paint.

Phoebe has worked at the Apple Tree Child Care Center for 16 years. As she gives me a tour of the center, she comments on each new addition to the facility with pride. She points to the new water table in the toddler room, filled with bobbing rubber boats and animals, surrounded by splashing two-year-olds. Phoebe's brightly colored long skirt echoes the tones in the children's paintings and drawings on display throughout the building. She stops and squats next to three-year-old boy Jason and asks about his new sister, who arrived a couple of days earlier. He ignores her question and yanks her long braid. Jason pulls her over to see his latest Lego construction, signaling that this is a more important development than a new sibling.

Phoebe lived through the change in ownership at the center when it was acquired by a large national chain. She recalls how scared she was when the change was announced to staff: "I felt like I'd been sold." She believes the formation of the Parents Committee at the time was essential to the smooth transition. She still marvels at the fact that "we didn't lose a single family. We even have some of their kids coming back now as teenagers to help in the classrooms." Her long-term involvement with the center has created an environment in which teachers stay—"80 percent of my teachers have been here ten years or more," a very high retention rate in the early childhood field.[1] She attributes this not only to their attachment to the children they work with but also to the involvement of parents like Julie Taylor.[2] Julie has suggested that I interview Phoebe as a key person in her work-family support system.

Phoebe hands me the latest issue of the center's newsletter, *Under the Apple Tree*, which describes many different aspects of parental involvement. The committee that Julie started as the "Parents Group" is now the "Parent/Teacher Exchange," and the newsletter announces that Susie Stern, "mother of Matthew in the Big Bird Room," will be the new president, and that Dana Colby, "teacher in the Muppet room," has just been chosen to represent the teachers that work with the three- and four-year-olds. The newsletter is filled with information about the efforts of the center to attain accreditation from a national professional association of early childhood educators.[3] It states, "The first round of Parent Questionnaires were very helpful, thank you for your input. We are striving for improvements in the areas that we did not score well on." Phoebe explains that all parents had the option of doing in-class observations as well as commenting on their own child's experiences. The self-assessment of internal stakeholders around which the accreditation process is designed seems to be having its intended outcome, quality improvement. There are also newsletter items thanking the family who donated a new couch for the teachers' room and asking if anyone has access to a truck to take the old couch to the dump.

However, being involved in the center is not easy for many parents because of the pressure of their jobs. Phoebe says, "The parents here are so supportive. I just wish more of them could get time off during the day to participate in their child's field trips or regular activities. I know many of them want to." She adds, "It's nice for their child, and it's nice for them, because they get to know the other parents." She tells the story of a parent who works in a big downtown law firm and was called when her child developed a fever, but felt she could not leave work for several hours. Phoebe says sadly, "It's frustrating sometimes, [long pause] but I understand." She mentions the discussion/support groups they have on parenting issues, but says they have had to cancel some of them owing to lack of participation: "Many are just too tired to come out at night."

Phoebe insists that all these families need the type of support and connections a center like this can provide, and she believes that employers should allow parents time for regular involvement. Phoebe has observed that when families participate in the center over time, especially those that may have more than one child attending, they start to form social ties with some of the other families involved.

This happened for Julie Taylor, who helped to set up the first Parents Committee at the Apple Tree Center. The parents who met through these meetings decided to start having family picnics and cookouts outside the center, sometimes inviting the teachers too. Nowadays, Julie finds that many families whom she met through her children's childcare center are either the parents of children at her older daughter's elementary school, or parents of children at the Sunday school in her church. She likes the fact that most of them live in her suburban town, and some are neighbors. These connections with other parents provide her with logistical help. More important, they give her a feeling that there are other parents trying to build a supportive environment for families in her town—a feeling of belonging to a community.

DO MIDDLE-CLASS FAMILIES FACE A CARE CRISIS?

The need for out-of-home care has risen dramatically over the past 30 years, but there has not been an adequate response to this shift by either private sector firms or the government. Private sector companies have made some attempt to provide resources for childcare and elder care, but research has shown that these benefits go disproportionately to salaried workers in well-paying jobs.[4] Government has made some attempt to provide resources for child and elder care, and these programs—with the exception of income for the elderly through Social Security—are targeted to those with low-wage jobs or living in poverty. This is not to say that the targeted programs are adequate—in fact, they are often inadequate.[5] The point is that, in addition to the problems faced by low-income Americans, there is virtually no public childcare support for moderate-income workers, nor for elder care services, like home health aides. This leaves middle-class families largely to fend for themselves in finding and paying for care.

With almost three-quarters of women with children now in the workforce, that inadequate level of public and private sector support is setting up a family care crisis that affects most families, regardless of income.[6] For some Americans—especially those who are poor, work in low-wage jobs, or are people of color—the crisis is not new, and work and family care challenges have always gone hand in hand. Their strategies for meeting this challenge have revolved around their kin, and has been well documented.[7] It is frequently argued that these families use relatives as caregivers because they cannot afford to pay for childcare and because they work off-hours shifts.

Strikingly, many of the middle-class families I met have also turned to their kin for help with family care. Although their work schedules approximate a traditional 9-to-5 work day, and many have some financial resources to pay for non-family care, they strongly prefer to use relatives whenever they can, especially for the care of young children.[8] Some families use non-relative care for all their childcare needs, but more often than not they combine this with relative care. This preference means that extended family members play a much greater role in providing childcare than is usually considered the norm for moderate-income and professional workers, and again suggests that extended family may be playing a larger role in the lives of middle-class families than is generally assumed. In any case, the families I met have developed a cross-generational, extended family care system to fill the gap left by inadequate policies in the private and public sectors. As wonderful as this may be for individual families, it is actually obscuring the crisis from public view and may be decreasing public pressure for expanding and better coordinating existing childcare programs.

MOTHER CARE OR OTHER CARE?

Biotech workers with young children ask themselves the same nagging question as other working parents: "Will childcare help or hurt my child?" Although they may not have read scholarly studies about the quality of childcare, many are familiar with the basic findings as reported in women's magazines and other mass media. The vast majority of center-based childcare— 80 percent—is of poor or mediocre quality.[9] Similar problems exist in family childcare homes, many of which are unregulated. In these settings, 13 percent of regulated homes and 50 percent of unregulated homes are of substandard quality.[10] In addition, there is a class-based ambivalence about non-parental care because many middle-class Americans equate childcare with Head Start and see it as a social service for low-income families who need this "extra help" because they lack good parenting skills.[11] Finally, many working parents adhere to traditional gender roles and believe that women are better able to care for children than men. In a recent poll of voters in Massachusetts, 49 percent expressed a preference for mothers to stay at home and care for children under three years of age, despite the fact that almost 80 percent of mothers with children under three are in the workforce in this state.[12]

Many working parents do not know what high-quality childcare looks like, nor that—if they can find it—it can be very beneficial for their child's social, emotional, and cognitive development. This finding has now been well documented in a recent explosion of research on early brain development.[13] Taken together, these studies emphasize the importance of the educational component of childcare and the link between the quality of childcare and the extent of school readiness. They make a compelling argument for increasing the accessibility and affordability of quality childcare for all preschool children, not only for the positive outcomes it predicts for school performance but also because it lays a foundation for sustainable life-long learning and healthy social relationships.

Parents in biotech who have young children are caught in a bind familiar to many other working families. They need care for their young children in order to work, but they often feel that they have no care option with which they are truly comfortable. The supply of quality childcare in Massachusetts is actually somewhat better than in the country as a whole, yet this does not seem to have affected parental attitudes about who should be caring for young children. In Massachusetts, between 20 and 35 percent of center-based care has received accreditation from the National Association for the Education of Young Children (NAEYC), as compared with 10 percent accreditation for this type of care nationally.[14] Accreditation of family childcare homes is much less common and therefore low, but the extent of licensed home care is again higher than in most parts of the country. In terms of availability, 70 percent of children under five live in a family where their parents are employed, yet there are not enough childcare slots available. This is a particular problem for infant and toddler care; 65 percent of these programs have waiting lists.[15] Problems of accessibility and quality remain issues for working parents in Massachusetts, and biotech workers, like everyone else, struggle to find good childcare.

THE SEARCH FOR CHILDCARE

The group of families I met use three types of arrangements to care for their preschool children, sometimes in combination, and often they end up with a different arrangement than what they started looking for. A small number of families rely exclusively on the wife of the male biotech employee to care for their children (there are no "stay-at-home" dads). This is not linked to occupation and income level, as the fathers of these children work in a variety of scientific, managerial, and production jobs. One-third of the families rely solely on fee-for-service childcare by non-family members; this includes center-based core and family day care homes.

The majority of families with young children—almost 60 percent—combine childcare provided by a parent or a relative with a limited amount of fee-for-service care. The extent of parental care is worth noting, as there is a popular misconception that working parents have little direct regular involvement in the care of their children. Although none of the male biotech workers is involved in the daytime care of children, a few women workers are directly involved through a part-time or alternative work schedule.

Constructing these mixed systems of care is a constant challenge, and it is mothers who retain the primary responsibility for choosing childcare providers. The search for childcare is an unrecognized component of family caregiving that workers must fit into their busy schedules with no provision for time off to visit and interview prospective providers. Most parents I spoke to do not know that there are community-based agencies that can help them learn to identify quality care.[16] Monitoring a childcare arrangement and making changes when necessary also take a good deal of time. Many parents feel that "stable childcare" is an oxymoron; they are not surprised when things fall apart, and they have to start the search all over again, another reason many families involve relatives.

A number of mothers told me that they did not start their childcare search with the idea of using relative care. The majority started out looking for center-based care, feeling that it would be safer than a family childcare home, only to be disappointed and uncomfortable with what they observed. Laurie Pratt, a manufacturing supervisor at BioTertia, had her first child in her mid-thirties. She took a three-month maternity leave and then placed her son in a center that is part of a childcare chain with a good reputation. Her experience was quite negative:

Well, first of all, he was exposed to a lot of sickness. The first week he was there he caught a cold that lasted almost two weeks. . . . And also we didn't feel like they were watching the babies as carefully as they should. Frequently, my husband would drop the baby off and there would be nobody there to greet him. He'd have to call somebody from the surrounding area to say, "Look, my baby is here, somebody has got to stay with him now," which didn't make him feel very secure or comfortable about our child's safety. . . . There was a lot of rotation of people through the infant care center . . . sometimes as many as four to six people a day.

They kept their son in this center for only six weeks. Eventually, they found a licensed family childcare provider in their neighborhood with 20 years' experience caring for young children. This provider takes only two infants at a time. Laurie comments, "We were looking for the smallest caregiver-to-child ratio that we could find . . . you can't get much better than two to one!" Initially, Laurie wanted to have her son as near to work as possible, hoping she could continue breastfeeding and see him during the day, but her work schedule did not actually allow for this, and once she found a good provider in her neighborhood, she ended up feeling that proximity to home was preferable.

Laurie and her husband have also made other changes in their childcare arrangements. Laurie has changed her work to a four-and-a-half-day, Sunday-through-Thursday schedule so that she can care for her son half of Thursday and all day Friday. On Sunday, her husband is home with their son. On Friday, her mother drives from central Massachusetts to their home in a Boston suburb to care for her grandson. This allows Laurie to do errands and helps build a close relationship between her son and his grandmother. Laurie's ultimate childcare solution includes a non-relative provider, a grandparent and two parents.

Colleen McCarthy's story provides another account of these problems and an alternative solution. Colleen, research associate at BioPrima, is married, in her early thirties, and the mother of two boys aged two and three. When her first son was born, her plan was to put him in family childcare and, in fact, she had arranged this five months before he was born. At the last minute, the family childcare provider could not take him, so Colleen found another family childcare provider, a friend of the family, but this arrangement lasted for only eight months because the woman moved away.

At that point, Colleen started looking for center-based care, hoping it would be more stable, but the childcare centers she visited made her very uneasy. At one place, the infants were kept in a dark room. Even though it was a licensed center and a place other employees from her company used, it seemed as though the staff wanted the infants to nap all the time. Then she looked at another place and saw that the playground was not suitable for children's use.

These experiences led Colleen and her husband away from both family and center-based care to a new plan. First, Colleen dramatically reduced her work hours to a half-time schedule. Negotiating a 20-hour work week was not easy, and Colleen had promised her supervisor it would only be temporary until the boys enter public school. Second, her sister Margaret rearranged her own work schedule so that she could be available to do some regular childcare. Colleen now works two ten-hour days, one of which is a weekend day when her husband can take care of the boys. On Wednesday, when both Colleen and her husband are at work, Margaret does childcare for the entire day. She says, "I'm kind of old-fashioned. I think daycare is good for people who don't have a support system from their family. But I think that the family should do everything they can to help with the kids so that they don't have to go to daycare." Colleen's children are now cared for by a parent or relative every day of the week; her search for childcare has ended and her worries have greatly diminished.

THE AFFORDABILITY ISSUE

Although none of the families interviewed relied on a relative for all their childcare needs, many relatives provide a significant amount of care for children of all ages. One reason is a matter of childrearing philosophy; particularly in the case of children from infancy to three years of age. There is a strong feeling that young children's development will be best advanced by the involvement of family members. Another important reason is financial; paying for childcare is expensive, sometimes prohibitively so.[17] Parents want to help adult children save money and attain a middle-class lifestyle. There is a cross-generational sharing and shifting of family care "costs" through the provision of unpaid care work.[18] Older relatives donate their time and labor to care for children so the younger generation can get financially established.

Then the younger generation donates their time and labor to care for elderly family members when their health is failing.

Maria Cabral, a production worker at BioTertia, uses fee-for-service care for her older son and relies on her mother and mother-in-law to care for her six-month-old son on an alternating basis. She does this largely for financial reasons and partly because "it's nice to keep the babies in the family." She inquired about having her infant son attend the same center as his older brother and was told it would cost fifty dollars a day. "That's my whole pay-check!" she said. She values the experience her three-year-old son is getting in a center—it "helps him get ready for school"—but having two children in childcare simultaneously is simply unaffordable for her family.

Relatives also provide care during after-school hours. Maureen Stendall, a regulatory affairs specialist at BioTertia, planned for the involvement of her mother in her daughter's care as a permanent arrangement and a sound financial investment. When her daughter was born, she and her husband bought a house that included a small apartment with a separate entrance. This enabled her mother, Theresa, to move to the Boston area from the Midwest and help with the care of Kristin, her granddaughter. When Kristin was little, Theresa cared for her part-time—"Nana days"—cutting down on childcare expenditure and the amount of time Kristin spent in a nearby child-care center. Now that Kristin is in grade school, Theresa brings her grand-daughter to the bus each morning, meets the bus after school, and takes care of her after school every day, saving Maureen the expense of after-school pro-gram tuition.

The tight finances of women workers who are single parents pose addi-tional childcare challenges. For example, Barbara Feldman calls on her mother as well as her sister, who lives nearby. After Barbara separated from her ex-husband, she moved back to her parents home with her two young children. She could not afford the childcare she needed to keep her job. She explains the variety of ways she relies on her mother:[19]

> My mother gets [the children] off to school. She's home with my son in the morning because his preschool doesn't start until 11:30. . . . Then when my daughter has soccer after school, my mother picks her up and gives her a ride to practice. And when the kids get sick, usually my mother can cover for them. . . . So many things happen in the middle of the day while I am working.

RELATIVES AND BACKUP CARE

Many workers who rely on fee-for-service childcare during the work day use relatives for backup and emergency care. Mike Sinclair, an associate scientist at BioPrima, explains that he and his wife, Lisa, rely heavily on Lisa's sister, Elise. Elise lives ten minutes away from their house and has a lot of flexibility because she works part-time out of her home, helping do the books for her husband's construction business. Mike says that he and his wife try to stay home with their kids themselves when the children are sick, but when that is not possible, Elise often takes over. She also picks them up from preschool and extended daycare when Mike and Lisa have to stay late at work, She says she's just doing what a sister should do: "We were brought up that way. . . . Being there for family is the most important thing."

Some grandparents provide backup and emergency childcare even when living outside the United States. Lily Huang, a biotech research associate at BioSegunda, is a first-generation immigrant, and her parents still live in the Asian country where she was born. When Lily had her first child, her mother came and stayed with her for several months to help with the new baby. When her second child was born, both her parents came before the baby was due, to become familiar with the area where their daughter and son-in-law had recently bought a house, and stayed for almost six months. Lily explains that they were busier the second time because she needed help with her three-year-old son as well as her new daughter. Sometimes her parents would help with the new baby, giving her a bath or a bottle, or they would pick up their grandson at his childcare center. Most evenings, they would cook dinner so Lily could play with her son and attend to the baby. Lily says wistfully, "So I have the luxury right now," recognizing that when her parents leave she will not have this kind of dinner-hour help. She does have some childcare help from her husband's parents, who live nearby, but they are older than her own parents and both have health problems. Lily recognizes that they may not be able to continue to help with childcare as they have in the past, and that she may be asked to get more involved in her in-law's care. Thus, the care equation—from childcare help to elder care help—is constantly shifting within this family.

The workers who have relatives helping with childcare often refer to themselves as "lucky," but these relatives insist they are not doing anything special and, like Colleen's sister Margeret, articulate well-worked-out philosophies about the role of extended family. They claim they are doing "what family should do" and "what they were brought up to do," honoring extended family obligations.

THE QUALITY OF CARE RELATIONSHIPS

THE PARENT-PROVIDER RELATIONSHIP: ALMOST LIKE FAMILY

Most parents whose children are being cared for by non-relatives portray the quality of this relationship as overwhelmingly positive and describe favored providers in familial terms. They reserve negative comments for providers or centers they chose not to use or are no longer using. The strength of their negative comments reveals the underlying anxiety these parents (like Laurie) feel about leaving young children with non-family members, and the familial language for "good providers" helps to mitigate these negative feelings.

Parents and childcare providers collaborate on building a relationship based on familial feelings from the early stages of the care arrangement. Christine Donnelly, a single mother, explains how she chose her son's family childcare provider. When Christine was interviewing her future provider, a small child in this woman's care "ran up to her and said spontaneously, 'I love you Francie.' And I thought, you can't pay a two-year-old to say that . . . my son will go here." Francie, on her part, refers to the children in her care as "my children" and tells Christine she treats them "just as I would my own." On some level—not always explicitly stated—parents are hoping that their provider will love their child and their child will love the provider, and the relationship will feel like the child is being cared for by a relative. Family childcare providers emphasize the "homey" quality of the space they have, and sometimes the presence of their own family, especially their children.

The contrast between Laurie Pratt's description of the teachers at the center she left and the way she describes her current provider is striking. She praises Marguerita, emphasizing their closeness:

> We give her the report in the morning, how his night was, and then she gives us a report at the end of the day. And I'll typically bring the baby's supplies to her, you know, the food and all that. And I'll have long conversations with her about how things are going and, just in general, what his trends have been. And we talk on the phone as well, you know, when needed . . . the communication is very close.

These sentiments are echoed by Marguerita. She describes how she interviews "her parents" before accepting a child into her home. She explains that she chose Laurie and her husband because she could see what good parents they were, how much they loved their son, and how well they interacted. She also tries to make the relationship familial; she taught Laurie's son to call her "Tia," which means "aunt" in Spanish. She takes pride in the fact that both the parents and the child call her by that name.

NEGOTIATING CLOSENESS AND DIFFERENCES

When relatives are the care providers, workers describe these relationships with a great deal more nuance and acknowledgement of conflict than they do their relationships with paid providers. Workers express a great deal of appreciation for help from relatives, but some say frankly that although it is "free," it may come with an emotional price. Maureen Stendall, whose mother lives in her house, experiences her mother as very critical of her own mothering skills. She describes their arrangement as "a double-edged sword." On the one hand, her mother cooks dinner most nights, does laundry, and provides after-school care each day, all of which helps Maureen's budget, work schedule, and responsibilities. On the other hand:

> If Kristin's class is going on a field trip, like berry-picking, then [my mother] is the one who remembers to send in the five dollars. I have a hard time remembering stuff like this. So it's good that she remembers, but it makes me feel bad that I'm not on top of all these details.

Maureen therefore never knows whether to keep certain concerns about Kristin to herself. For example, a family power struggle of sorts emerged about the direction of Kristin's education. When first interviewed, Maureen and her husband, Clifford, were debating public versus parochial school for Kristin. Maureen was leaning toward public school, while Theresa was advocating parochial school, and Clifford chose the diplomatic path of remaining neutral. During a follow-up interview one year later, Maureen reports that Kristin will be attending the parochial school affiliated with their church. She explained that she too had gone to parochial school as a young girl, so the choice carried on a family tradition. But if her mother had not been living with them and, providing such critically needed family care, Maureen admits she would probably have sent Kristin to public school.

Generational differences between parents and their relative caregivers also arise around lifestyle choices and consumer behavior. Estelle, Fran Steinberg's mother, was explicit on this issue. Estelle does not question the fact that her daughter is working and is proud of Fran's professional accomplishments at BioPrima, but she sees a stark contrast between the life she led as a mother of young children and that of her daughter and son-in-law:

> The way of life was different then. Women stayed home and were satisfied with what men made. . . . You made it manageable. You didn't think about things that you wanted. Young people today like more things. They think they need things to be happy . . . luxury things and nice cars . . . videos and electronic games. These things are so expensive and they aren't necessary. They need to say, "This is what we are going to spend. Period." You can't do this all your life—work, work.

Estelle also thinks parents put too much emphasis on buying things for their children. She says, "Parents are eager to please their children . . . so they buy them fancy toys. One toy is enough. They are looking for ways to make up for their lack of time with their child." Underlying these comments about consuming too much there appears to be a deeper critique of the limited time that children have with their parents when both are working.

FINDING A NEW PURPOSE IN RETIREMENT

Criticism is only one side of the story, however. In several families, retired parents have literally organized their time and routines around the care needs of their grandchildren and community issues as they arise. They find that this level of involvement brings fulfillment they often did not derive from their paid work.[20] Joseph and Kathleen Bromfield, whose daughter-in-law, Jessica, and son, Ron, both have stressful professional jobs in biotech, typify this feeling. They both worked while their own children were growing up, Joseph for three different companies in various blue-collar jobs, and Kathleen part-time as a waitress, keeping "mother's hours" so she could be home after school. Their jobs paid the bills but were not particularly gratifying in other ways. Now retired, they take care of their twin granddaughters with pride. Kathleen explains:

> Two days a week was a regular thing . . . and then if they needed us, say Jessica had an important meeting or something, we would take them the extra day.

You know we were very flexible. It wasn't a rigid schedule. I mean basically it
was, but if she traveled, we switched everything around . . . we were flexible
whenever they needed us.

In fact, they take pride in being more flexible than Jessica's employer,
BioTertia. Joseph says:

Well, I think they [the employer] should be more flexible for these mothers
that want to work. If they want to work, that's their choice. Some of them
have to work; they have no choice. So they should make it a little easier for
them. What would they rather do, have them go on welfare or something?

During a visit to Joseph and Kathleen's home, we sit in the kitchen
because the living room is overflowing with age-appropriate toys, books, and
mini-play structures. Their other daughter is visiting, as she often does, with
her four-year-old and new baby. The whole house is childproofed, with elec-
trical outlets covered and breakables out of reach; it looks like a licensed family childcare home. Joseph and Kathleen modestly downplay the value of
what they are providing and emphasize the rewards they derive from caring
for their grandchildren. Kathleen explains:

Our whole life has changed now with grandchildren, by choice. You know, if I
don't see—if we don't see them for a day, my gosh, I miss them. . . . And it's
just part of our life, that's the way it is now, and we're doing this by choice. . . .
We love it.

Joseph adds, "We absolutely love it when they come over. I don't know what
our life would be without them." When asked how they would feel if their
son's and daughter-in-law's jobs took them out of state, Kathleen jumps in,
"I'd be broken-hearted. We'd both be broken-hearted." Joseph jokes, "We'd be
saving up money for plane tickets!" Kathleen quickly strikes a more serious
note, saying, "Exactly. I couldn't imagine [life] without them, you know,
they're such a plus in our life."

THE BENEFITS OF RELATIVE CARE

Overall, biotech workers who have relatives living nearby have far more
choices regarding childcare than those who do not. Combining the families

who use parental care and those who use relative care, a substantial majority of these families organize their childcare around a close family member. Relationships between parents and the family members they rely on for care may cause strains, such as divergent ideas about discipline, education, and consumer spending. On balance, workers believe that relative care provides greater continuity and safety than fee-for-service childcare for young children. The more they can "keep the babies in the family," as one mother put it, the more relaxed they feel—and this is particularly true for mothers—about their own inability to be involved in their children's care. The period of using fee-for-service childcare is also the period when many young families buy their own home. Relative care provides financial relief and allows young families to save for their first mortgage and attain that all-important part of the middle-class American dream, homeownership. Relative care also provides the realization of another American dream, a retirement involved in the care and development of the next generation.

FAMILY CARE AND COMMUNITY CONNECTIONS

Most of the workers with preschool children in childcare full-time or part-time use providers in the suburbs or cities where they live.[21] They emphasize the proximity of the center, family childcare provider, or after-school program to their home in describing why they chose a particular arrangement or program. This underscores parents' desire to create a familial feeling in their relationships with non-relative childcare providers and specifies an important connection to their community of residence.

Childcare arrangements near home also create links between families who share a common provider. Parents see each other at drop-off and pick-up times and begin to form casual acquaintances. These may deepen over time, depending on several factors. Parents may become involved with other parents on volunteer committees and governing committees of a childcare center. A parent who is concerned about a particular teacher or policy may call other parents to discuss it. Families who participate in a center over time may start to form social ties, just as Julie Taylor's involvement with the Parents Group at the Apple Tree Center led to friendships with other families.

For parents who use family childcare, connections with other parents may be less formal but equally important. For example, the family childcare provider Laurie Pratt uses in her neighborhood takes one other child. Laurie and her husband have become quite friendly with the other parents. They are very aware of the other child's developmental issues and think about them as they continue to monitor the suitability of their provider for their own son. They often keep their son at home if he is sick so as not to infect the other child. Laurie sometimes speaks on the phone during weeknights with the mother of the other child if a problem comes up between the children or with their provider. Laurie and her husband occasionally arrange weekend outings, to a zoo or local farm, with this other family.

Moving parent-to-parent contact from acquaintance to friendship is largely "women's work." It is the mothers who nurture and promote this shift in the relationship. Fathers' involvement in childcare is usually confined to drop-off and pick-up, and sometimes discussions with childcare providers and teachers about their child's day, including illness and medication issues, but mothers' involvement often goes beyond the day-to-day necessities. Their initiative determines the extent to which friendships with other parents develop and a parent-to-parent support network is established and sustained.

Parental involvement in childcare exists on two levels: formal volunteering to help with the activities and funding of childcare centers, and building family-to-family ties between parents whose children use the same childcare provider. Too often this second type of involvement is not recognized or valued in the way that serving on a fundraising committee or parent board is valued, but these informal relationships provide practical support and information about child development and childrearing, and they may—as in Julie Taylor's case—be the foundation for deeper ties between families as the children get older and move into public school. The fact that many children go to childcare in their community of residence, and then go to school there, shows how the spatial relationship among home, childcare, and school may help to create an infrastructure of support that working families can rely on.

NECESSITY IS THE MOTHER OF CONNECTION: CARE FOR SCHOOL-AGE CHILDREN

The lack of after-school programs for children ages five to fourteen is a national problem. Over two-thirds of school-age children—about 28 million children—have either both of their parents or their only parent in the workforce.[22] Approximately 80 percent of these parents work full-time, making after-school care a necessity for most school-age children.[23] The U.S. General Accounting Office has estimated that only 25 percent of the demand for after-school care can be met by existing programs.[24] Estimates of the number of children who are home alone, sometimes called "latchkey children," vary from five to fifteen million.[25] Studies by the National Institute for Out of School Time (NIOST) at Wellesley College has estimated that approximately eight million children in elementary and middle school spend time after school without any adult supervision or organized activities.[26] This is the case despite overwhelming and consistent research findings that children who do attend after-school programs benefit greatly from their participation. These children have better school attendance, work habits, academic performance, and peer relationships than children who do not attend these programs.[27]

One of the most important initiatives, and the only government program, to address this problem is a U.S. Department of Education program called 21st Century Community Learning Centers, which awards grants to public schools and community programs for after-school care that includes academic enrichment and targets children in low-performing schools. It began in fiscal year 1995, and by 1998 had $40 million in funding.[28] In 2002, funding for Community Learning Centers had grown to almost $1 billion. This started as a federal program but was turned into a grants program to the states through the Leave No Child Behind Act of 2001, and its funding levels are in jeopardy. The Bush administration has proposed a cut of almost 40 percent for the 21st Century Learning Centers in FY '04, a cut that would hurt many working families. It would adversely affect the number of subsidized after-school slots available to low-income children as well as the viability of programs that also serve children from moderate-income families.[29] The day when we see a universal approach to funding for after-school programs that could benefit children from all income levels seems further away than ever.

In Massachusetts, the situation mirrors that in the rest of the country. More than half a million children have parents who want more after-school programs, but they cite the following obstacles: there are not enough programs, existing programs are too costly, and the quality of programs is low.[30] This is the situation facing biotech workers with school-age children. Most of these families report using some type of program in or near the community where they live to provide academic enrichment, art, music, dance instruction, or recreational opportunities. Participating in such programs is advantageous for the children in providing a range of extracurricular activities not available through most public schools, but transporting children to these activities often proves a significant challenge. It is obviously easier for the "stay-at-home moms" than for parents who are working full-time. The latter either pay for transportation between school and after-school, or find a relative who is free at that time of day, or ask another parent for help. Of the

351 cities and towns in Massachusetts, after-school programs in the public school are available in only about 25 percent of communities, and only one-tenth of the families I met with school-age children have access to school-based programs.[31]

The extent and diversity of children's activities varies with parent availability. For example, George Stratton, a biotech research scientist at BioPrima, and his wife, Elizabeth, made a decision for her to leave her job partly to accommodate the after-school needs of their children. Elizabeth devotes her afternoons to driving their children from place to place. Both children take lessons in piano, swimming, and tennis. Depending on the season, their older son plays soccer or baseball and needs rides to practices as well as games. Two afternoons a week, the children take classes at a local art school, and Allie also takes ballet and gymnastics lessons. Elizabeth is relieved that Stephen chose soccer over hockey because hockey requires a huge commitment of time and money—$1,500 a season, and four to five practices a week. George says he did not realize how much Elizabeth had organized for the children in the after-school hours, and how complicated the schedule was, until she left town unexpectedly to take care of her mother. He had no idea where each lesson was, or how long it lasted, or how his wife managed to coordinate both children's activities so that neither child was late or left waiting.

In families that do not have a "stay-at-home" mom, the after-school hours often present a logistical nightmare. School-age children either attend an after-school program in or near their school, or rely on babysitters and extended family members to take them to after-school activities. When full-time workers do get involved in these activities, however, there are opportunities for connections with other families in their community. Julie Taylor, for example, tries to participate in some of her daughter's Brownie troop events, even though they meet every other Friday afternoon right after school, a difficult time for her to leave work. She told the troop leader, "Anything that's on an evening or a weekend, call me." She proudly reports that she took Sarah's troop on a nature walk one recent Saturday. Julie values not only the time with her daughter but also the contact with other working mothers involved in running the Brownie troop.

COMMUNITY-BASED PROGRAMS FOR FAMILIES

After-school programs are not the only community-based organizations that tie working parents to their communities. For example, Barbara Feldman, a single parent, uses her local Y as a place to do special things with her kids and to meet other parents. She regularly takes her two children to swimming lessons, and sometime takes them to a puppet show or "game night." She particularly likes the Y's "family nights" with pizza and salad for dinner, and an opportunity to do creative small-group activities with other parents and children, from pumpkin carving at Halloween to making gingerbread houses in December.

Adoption agencies are another type of community-based family program that serves both social and recreational functions. These agencies play a continuing role in the lives of adoptive families.[32] For example, Rachel Warren, a biotech manager at BioTertia and single parent of an adopted daughter from China, frequently attends support groups for adoptive parents, where she meets others who are facing similar issues of integrating a child from another culture into a predominantly white, middle-class American suburb. Rachel also goes to social events with her daughter and the parents and children of other adoptive families. These gatherings feature Chinese cuisine and are often held at important holiday times such as the Chinese New Year. Rachel hopes these events will help her daughter make friends with other Chinese children. Agency events also help Rachel to feel she is not alone in meeting the challenges of cross-cultural adoption by developing relationships with other adoptive parents. Mike Sinclair, a biotech technician, told a similar story about the adoption agency that helped him and his wife, Lisa, adopt their son from a Latin American country. In fact, Lisa feels so strongly about the value of this agency to their family that she now serves as a member of its advisory board and volunteers to speak with prospective adoptive parents whenever asked.

Again, there is a pattern of informal and formal participation in community programs, both of which build ties between working families and they communities where they live. Barbara Feldman's use of her local Y is an example of informal community involvement. The volunteer work of parents in after-school programs, Brownie troops, and Cub Scout troops exemplifies formal community involvement. The unmet needs of working families, especially those with school-age children, often compel them to seek connections to other families and involvement in local community programs.

ELDER CARE: AN EMERGING FAMILY CARE ISSUE

The aging of the population in the United States is one of the major demographic shifts shaping family life in the 21st century. It is estimated that more than 14 million American workers today are caring for an elderly relative.[33] The Family and Medical Leave Act (FMLA) provides leave for workers with a parent who is "seriously ill," but it does not provide leave for less serious medical conditions or other routine needs of the elderly, such as doctor's appointments. There are many community services that now offer care for the elderly, but employees are not always aware of the services that exist, and employers do not always have resource and referral agencies to compile and provide this information to those who need it.

Most of the workers I met are in their mid twenties to late forties, and consequently their parents are mainly in their fifties and sixties, with a few in their seventies and eighties. Although many of the workers profiled here have parents and in-laws who are still in good health, others have parents who are experiencing the social or physical challenges of old age. These families are already dealing with elder care issues that demand their time, financial resources, and emotional stamina. Regardless of where their parents live, some employees need to leave work to take a parent to doctor's appointments, or they need a short-term leave to provide care in a distant city. There is also the need to arrange time for regular visiting and household help. Hank Bartholet, a production worker at BioSegunda, visits his elderly mother every Saturday morning. He goes over to her house and she makes him an omelet, a tradition that started when his father was still alive. After breakfast, he helps his mother with household chores, repairs things that are broken, and in summer helps her plant and weed her vegetable garden. She is nearing eighty and does not drive, so Hank also helps with weekly grocery shopping and other errands.

Some workers have elderly parents with significant health problems. For example, Fran Steinberg, a senior biotech manager, uses a home-based health care agency to provide her mother with a companion during the day. Finding the right agency and person, getting the companion oriented to the particular health issues and social needs of her mother, and maintaining a relationship with the companion entails a significant amount of work. Fran shares some of this with her sister, and the fact that both sisters live in the same city as their mother makes things easier. However, Fran's responsibilities for her mother's care are becoming a daily occurrence, and are difficult to fit in with her full-time job, a long commute, and the needs of her school-age daughter. Much like finding quality childcare and building a close relationship with a childcare provider, arranging and maintaining good elder care are not activities that biotech workers are given time off to accomplish. Again, these tasks are largely "women's work," falling more to daughters and daughters-in-law than to sons or sons-in-law.[34]

The medical crisis of an elderly relative can also complicate childcare arrangements. This happened in George Stratton's family. When his mother-in-law had a stroke, his wife, Elizabeth, needed to go to Arizona to care for her mother. Elizabeth is one of the stay-at-home moms who handles virtually all the childcare and housework, so her absence for a few weeks required significant reorganization of arrangements for their two school-age children. To deal with this family care crisis, George asked his mother, who is in good health, to come from North Carolina to take over care of the children while Elizabeth was away. George said he could not have maintained his work commitments without her and was grateful for the way she pitched in, saying, "She's a real help with the kids." George is not anticipating any health issues with his own mother, but he is ready to reciprocate when the need arises. His mother, in fact, has elder care issues of her own, as she is still caring for her own mother, who is ninety. So while Elizabeth and George are typical of the "sandwich generation"—caring for Elizabeth's mother and their own children at the same time—George's mother has added another layer to the family care "sandwich," needed for both her mother's regular care and the occasional care of her grandchildren.

Three important points emerge from the elder care experiences of biotech workers. To state the obvious, physical proximity makes involvement much easier. Almost three-quarters of these families have one or both spouses' parents living in Massachusetts, and almost all visit their parents regularly and are able to assist when needed. Second, and perhaps unexpected, elderly family members who live far away sometimes provide childcare themselves, especially at special times like a birth or adoption, or for backup and emergency childcare on a limited basis. Extended family ties are strong, and care relationships are not determined by state boundaries. Third, biotech employees facing care issues for elderly relatives frequently use community-based services and programs for elder care, creating important connections for themselves and their relatives, as clients and sometimes as volunteers.

AN EXTENDED FAMILY APPROACH TO COMMUNITY INVOLVEMENT

Elderly family members are often consigned to the role of a passive recipient of health care or other forms of assistance with daily living, but in the families I spoke with, elderly relatives are not only childcare providers but also volunteers in community-based programs. For example, Theresa, the mother of Maureen Stendall, volunteers regularly in their local church, an effort she makes for both religious and social reasons. Through the church, she joined the local Catholic Women's Club and became an active member, arranging monthly meetings or serving as correspondent secretary. Theresa also frequents the senior center in her suburban town, where she meets other women her age and plays in a bridge club that meets every Tuesday. She has developed friendships with some of her bridge partners that extend beyond card games. Several of the women meet regularly for a dinner out on Friday nights, and she has even traveled around New England and to Europe with some of the women she met through the senior center. These friendship ties and volunteer work are important to Maureen for several reasons. They give Theresa a sense of independence and her own social life, making her less dependent on Maureen and her husband, and they provide a connection for the whole family to their local church and other parishioners in their suburban town.

Theresa has also been important in helping her daughter and son-in-law get to know their neighbors. Theresa tells the following story of an event that occurred when she was taking her granddaughter to the bus that takes her to kindergarten,

> I saw a little girl waiting for the bus one day, with her babysitter or caretaker. And I said to [my granddaughter], "There's a little girl that looks about your age." So I walked over and talked to the woman and this little girl was already in [second grade]. She's just a year older than [my granddaughter]. So I said, "Maybe Katy would like to play some day." So now they've been playing together.

Theresa explained that Katy and her family live on the next block, and that the two sets of parents became friends once the two girls started playing regularly after school. Maureen invited Katy's parents to a dinner party, and they reciprocated with an invitation to a Fourth of July cook-out. Theresa says proudly, "So Maureen said, 'Gee if it weren't for you, I wouldn't be meeting these people' . . . I have the time. Maureen would never be around to see that little girl waiting for the bus."

Joseph and Kathleen, who provide regular care for their preschool grandchildren, are also community volunteers, engaged in a controversy about land preservation in their suburban town. When their children were growing up, the town still had a good deal of open space and house lots were large. Since 1980, that situation has been changing as developers have come in with plans to build new housing with no consideration of the pressures that would put on schools and other resources. By attending the local town meeting, Kathleen and Joseph got involved in opposing some plans that would have dramatically increased population density and decreased open space in their community. Kathleen explains:

> They wanted to put in a 72-unit apartment and we cut them down to six houses . . . on my grandmother's old land, it is. But we went [to meetings] for months and months. You have to be involved if you want to help save what's left. There's not much left on open land. It was beautiful here. You know?

Their stake in the issue was partly personal and partly civic. Their involvement in the controversy surrounding outside developers was done on behalf of their children and grandchildren, and on behalf of preserving open space. While their son, Jeff, came to a few town meetings, their daughter-in-law Jessica could not attend any due to her work schedule, so the involvement of the older couple in a critical community issue became important for both generations.

FAMILY CARE AND CIVIL SOCIETY

Working families in biotech face the same family care challenges that working families face across America. They have a hard time finding quality out-of-home childcare that they are comfortable with and can afford. For those with school-age children, the paucity of good after-school programs and the lack of transportation is a constant dilemma. Those with elderly relatives struggle with their need to be at work and their desire to be at a parent's home or hospital bedside. They face the difficulty of finding reliable elder care services and paying for them. But within this fragmented and inadequate family care system, many are finding ways of coping. They rely on both extended family members, neighbors, friends, and an array of community-based services and programs.[35] No one family can meet all its family care needs alone; they are impelled to reach out to others, forging community connections vital to family well-being.

Although these connections are not usually thought of as of community involvement, I believe that the formation of informal social ties—parent-to-parent and parent-to-provider—and formal volunteer work in childcare and after-school programs are, in fact, creating the elements needed to form a strong social fabric.[36] Civic-minded families are not simply found at the polls on Election Day; they are doing the daily work that helps children grow up and elders grow old with dignity. No society can be called "civil" unless its members invest time and resources in the care needed by each generation.

Childcare is rarely looked at as a civil society issue, but I believe the development and sustainability of strong community-based childcare programs is one of the most important building blocks of a healthy civil society in a country where most families work. As consumers, clients, and/or volunteers in programs for preschool children, parents learn basic lessons of community involvement that may lay the basis for their participation in school, neighborhood, or civic activities when their children are older. When working parents have children in childcare, they meet and develop relationships with other families with young children. Parents share a wide variety of ideas and contacts—teenage babysitters, discount clothing stores, good pediatricians and dentists, and new recreational opportunities for weekend family outings.

Some parents, like Julie Taylor, become volunteers on the parent committees of childcare centers and help sustain these important community institutions. They organize pot-lucks, family fairs, and fundraisers. They become voices for parent input on governance, teacher salaries, and curriculum. Serving on a parent committee is visible volunteer work, while building parent-provider and parent-parent relationships is largely invisible "volunteer" work. In making both kinds of work visible, it is possible to see the different kinds of activities required to create high-quality care environments for young children, and a support system for their working parents.

A similar process occurs around the challenges of after-school care. The mismatch between parental work hours and children's school hours, along with the lack of after-school programs, makes out-of-school time particularly difficult. What is often obscured is the extent to which parents help each other, and extended family members help parents. This assistance may take the simple form of a carpool or the complex form of starting and running an after-school program. From Girl Scouts and Boy Scouts to soccer teams and Little League, these community activities rely heavily on the involvement and creativity of parents. As children enter school, parents are brought together not only through their participation in and leadership of after-school programs but also through children's friendships. Like ties between

parents who use the same childcare provider, many parents of school-age children say that their "friends" during this stage of family life seem to be the parents of their children's friends. These relationships are often instrumental—"If I take your child to practice, will you bring mine home?" But bonds may deepen as their children's spheres of activity form interlocking circles of contact and connection between families.

The needs and demands of elder care provide two avenues for community connection. One is through the use of community-based services—adult day programs, senior centers, senior transportation programs, Meals on Wheels—that link working families to a specific set of community services. Second, and largely unrecognized, is the volunteer work of elders that create community connections for them and their working adult children. Through memberships in neighborhood book clubs and bridge clubs, volunteer work in religious institutions and schools, and participation in local town meetings, elders are providing time and expertise to community-based groups. This generational division of labor, in which one generation works for pay and the other generation volunteers, has positive outcomes for all involved.

Whether consciously planned or simply a product of new work-family realities, in each family care arena, from preschool care to elder care, working parents and their extended family members become agents for community connection. When the responsibility for family care moves out of individual households and into the community sphere, caregiving work can be a vehicle for transforming the relationship between families and the multiple "communities" on which they rely.

CHAPTER SEVEN

The PTA Is Not the Problem

As Congress reconvenes each fall and the school year begins anew, "improving our schools" has become a mantra for both political parties. One side advocates vouchers and local control; the other promotes reducing class size and investing in early education; and both emphasize that children should be ready to learn when they enter first grade. Whatever the differences, one thing that politicians and voters agree on is that our public education system is sorely in need of reform. But absent from most of these conversations is the important role parents play at the community level. This chapter highlights parents' actual and potential roles in the lives of their school-age children, suggesting that new forms of parental involvement are needed and, in fact, are developing.

IS THE 21ST CENTURY THE AGE OF PARENTAL ANXIETY?

While Congress debates new education bills, working parents worry about their school-age children. What is not being taught in the classroom that should be? Are their children physically safe while at school? Are their children safe after school? If they are home alone, are they doing their homework or getting into trouble? These questions are on the minds of parents I spoke with, and surveys show they are on the minds of parents all across the country.[1] Studies documenting the rise in juvenile crime between the hours of 2:00 p.m. and 6:00 p.m. are not reassuring.[2] Negative comparisons between the math and science skills of American children and children in other industrialized countries are further cause for concern.[3] Parents know in their gut that there is a link between what goes on academically in school and what goes on in the after-school hours, a link documented in research by educators and child development specialists.[4]

Most of the parents I spoke with want to help fix their children's schools,[5] and want to find either a good after-school program or volunteer to help run one. They feel that if they could help out in the schools by volunteering in the classroom, chaperoning field trips, or being part of curricular and staffing decisions, they could improve the quality of their own child's education. Many workers told me they wished they could leave work early to take their children to after-school activities or start homework help before dinner.

The story of Pamela Bodajian is about one parent who was able to bridge the gap between what she wanted to do and what she was actually doing. In the mid-1990s, Pamela was a biotech manager on the fast track at BioSegunda. Just at the time that her son was born, she was asked to travel more, take on new projects, and supervise a key department. When her son was little, she tried to "do it all." With a supportive husband, extended family members willing to help, and a good childcare arrangement, it seemed possible that Pamela's star would continue to rise in her company without short-changing her family. However, when her son began kindergarten, things began to unravel. Part of it was scheduling problems. He was too young for an after-school program, yet his school day ended well before his parents' work day. Pamela organized an elaborate system, with five different adults involved, for his mid-afternoon pick-up. She wanted to volunteer in her son's classroom but could not get time off. The distance between her son's school and her workplace created an additional obstacle to volunteering. Pamela's frustration peaked at the end of the kindergarten year. She made a decision to quit her job, believing that was the only way she could have more time with her son and be more involved in his school.

When Pamela told her supervisor she planned to resign, she found out there were other options. Thanks to a responsive vice president in her company, a working mother herself, Pamela negotiated a reduced schedule. With newfound time, she not only volunteered in her son's first grade classroom but also co-chaired an important planning committee for the local school board. The following year, with this committee experience under her belt, she decided to run for a school board seat. Her campaign was a major undertaking, involving her extended family, neighbors, and friends. When the votes were counted, Pamela won. Pamela and her department head then devised a job-sharing arrangement in which Pamela shares the full range of responsibilities in her old portfolio with another employee. She has more time for family and community, and the company has adequate staffing. Despite some ups and downs, Pamela and her employer achieved a "win-win" solution with clearly perceived benefits for work, family, and community.

Pamela's situation is not unique, but it is not common either. Most working parents have not been able to craft such a neat or meaningful resolution. Many have experienced the kinds of conflicts Pamela experienced when her son began public school but have not found a satisfactory way out. However, I found that many parents are involved in their children's education in ways that are not always visible. Though often unable to do as much as they would like, they do find time for activities that express a piece of the potential solution to increased parent involvement with their children, their schools, and their communities.

A HISTORY LESSON

In the past, one key way parents could get involved in their child's education was to join the PTA. In his book *Bowling Alone*, Robert Putnam argues that, in order to understand how involved parents are in their children's school, we must look at changes in community involvement in our society at large. He notes that for the first two-thirds of the 20th century, Americans were increasingly involved in community institutions, including the national Parent-Teacher Association (PTA), but in the last third of the century, "Active involvement in face to face organizations has plummeted whether we consider organizational records, survey reports, time diaries or consumer expenditures."[6] Around 1960, PTA membership peaked, representing approximately 50 percent of families with school-age children,[7] but by 1980, only 20 percent of families with school-age children were paying PTA dues.[8] This decline is often attributed simply to the rise in maternal employment from 1970 to the present—women left the PTA when they went to work. This explanation ignores other possible reasons, however, and it blames working mothers rather than deeper sources of the problem, such as workplace policies that make unpaid volunteer work difficult.

Although I do not dispute the overall downward trend in PTA membership, I do want to raise an implicit question: how much should we focus to the PTA itself as a barometer of parental involvement in education since the 1960s? I believe that there has been too much emphasis on the PTA per se, and not enough on other kinds of school involvement that are more feasible for—and often more compelling to—working parents. I also think that the

history of the PTA, and the fact that it has not been responsive to the changing nature of work and family for much of the past three decades, is central
to understanding how working parents today view this organization.

The PTA was founded in 1897 as the National Congress of Mothers
(NCM). Its founder, Alice McClellan Birney, was a strong proponent of
"maternalist thinking," a set of concepts about private and public life popular
at the turn of the century.[9] This ideology reinforced the idea that it was
women's job to care for the home and for children, and that they should enter
public life only as an extension of their role as mothers. Maternalist thinking
legitimized women's involvement in selected public institutions in which
children were involved, such as schools. Although the NCM changed its
name to the National Congress of Parents and Teachers in 1924, its organizational goals and structure were shaped early on by women who were not
members of the workforce, and who in fact pitied, if not censured, women
who had to work for wages outside the home. The only time the PTA explicitly supported women working, and the necessity of childcare for working
mothers, was during World War II.[10] Although PTA publications and rhetoric did begin to reflect current realities of women's increased employment by
the late 1980s, its earlier history has shaped its contemporary image damp-
ening the involvement of many of today's working parents.

While parents have always been concerned with what their children are
doing in school, today parents are also concerned with what their children are
doing when they are *not* in school whether they are eight or eighteen. Although
after-school programs have expanded since 1980, there is still a huge unmet
need for after-school care.[11] Parents have worked to get schools to give space and
set up after-school programs. They have served on boards of after-school programs in their communities, and gotten involved in committee work and
fundraising for extended day programs. Parents lead Cub Scout packs and
Brownie troops and coach Little League and youth soccer teams that sometimes
complement, and often substitute for, after-school childcare programs. Focusing
exclusively on the PTA obscures many forms of parental involvement.[12]

Parents are also involved in trying to preserve cultural programs such as
art, music, and theater classes, which have often been subject to state and federal education funding cuts, and to introduce new issues into the curriculum
that increase respect for diversity and other cultures. Many working parents
try to volunteer during the day. They chaperone field trips or read to a class
in order to increase time with their own child and make a contribution to the
school.[13] Many working parents, reluctant to give up precious family time, shy

away from becoming formal members of groups that require dues and attendance at evening meetings, but that does not mean they are not involved.

I think the question "How can we revive the PTA?" should be changed to "What have we really lost with declining PTA membership?" And we should add, "What can been gained by new forms of parental involvement, especially in after-school volunteerism?" The following stories from the lives of biotech parents with school-age children document the variety, creativity, and impact of parental involvement in a number of urban and suburban schools and communities. They suggest that another type of organization than the PTA may be needed to facilitate parental engagement.

NEW QUESTIONS, NEW ANSWERS

When I started talking to parents about school involvement, I fell into the trap of asking about the PTA, equating the PTA with parent involvement. Not surprisingly, I found very few parents are involved in the PTA, and their reasons are not surprising either: lack of time, busy schedules, and the desire to spend time with family. Almost two-thirds of parents in one recent study said that "lack of time constrained them the most."[14] Many time issues actually reflect workplace constraints: the nature of full-time work, resistance to part-time work arrangements, and the lack of flexible scheduling and leave policies that would facilitate volunteerism. Several parents said that half the meetings of their PTA are during the day, so those are out, and they feel conflicted about going to the other half, in the evening, because they will miss time with their children. Barbara Feldman, a single mother, manages to go to some PTA meetings because she lives with her parents and has childcare in the evening if she needs it, but the other single mothers, who lack extended-family backup, say that finding evening childcare is difficult. Even if childcare were available at the meetings, these single parents express great ambivalence about disrupting their children's evening routine by taking them out to be cared for by a stranger so they can attend a PTA meeting.

A number of parents who are not active in their local PTA express resentment about two particular aspects of the organization. First, they do not like that fact that most PTAs see fundraising as their primary business. They do not think that bake sales, raffles, and silent auctions are a good use of their time. The parents I spoke with who have modest incomes are particularly resentful about this type of activity.[15] They feel that they work full-time and pay their taxes, and they question why the schools still need more money out of their pockets. Issues of income inequality and the difficulty that some working parents have making ends meet negatively affects PTA involvement. Second, some working mothers say, with thinly veiled hostility, that the PTA meetings are like a social club for the stay-at-home mothers. The divide between mothers who work and those who don't is exacerbated by the fact that many school volunteer opportunities still exist only during the work day.

While my questions about the PTA did not seem to lead anywhere— and perpetuated a picture of parental noninvolvement—my questions about the daily work-family routine and the family care challenges of having school-age children produced quite a different picture.

HOMEWORK HELP

Assistance with homework is something that all the parents I met do as part of the evening routine during the work week. In families where mothers and fathers are both working full-time, they spend roughly equivalent time with their children, although there are some gender-related subject differences: fathers help more with science and math, while mothers help more with language arts and writing.[16] In families with a stay-at-home mom, mothers provide most of the homework assistance. Many mothers and fathers read to their younger children as part of the bedtime routine or have their elementary school children read to them.

Parental involvement with homework sounds like an activity of unqualified positive value for both child and parent, but some workers have a different perspective. They report that the school's expectations regarding the level of parental help can be burdensome for tired working parents, and homework time can promote conflict and tension. Beth Finley, a senior scientist at BioSegunda, started encountering these kinds of problems when her daughter was only in first grade. At the end of that year, a large science project was assigned that required a lot of parental help: Beth explains,

> She did ladybugs . . . so we made a model of a ladybug, and she and I pretty much did that part of it together. . . . Then she made a big poster board where she'd written a little story about ladybugs, and my husband helped her get some pictures of different ladybugs off the Internet so she could put them up there. . . . So it worked out well, but it was work.

Beth feels that the school expects a lot of parents, whereas she and her husband "want [our daughter] to do the work herself." There is some resentment on Beth's part about her daughter's homework—"When she gets home from school she wants to play?"—and some fears about what will be expected as her daughter grows older.

Another area of parental involvement is attendance at regular parent-teacher conferences. All the parents interviewed, mothers and fathers, make it a priority to fit these sessions into their schedules and find it feasible since they are routinely held in the evenings. Schools that are more sensitive to the complexities of scheduling in families where both parents work may also provide conferences in early-morning "before-work" hours. Schools that provide afternoon hours to accommodate the work-family pressures of teachers are viewed as being insensitive to the needs of working parents. Only mothers, not fathers, said they make calls to teachers between parent-teacher conferences if a problem arises. Most mothers report that this happens a couple of times a year, and issues can usually by resolved over the phone. This is another invisible aspect of parental involvement.

VOLUNTEERING AT SCHOOL

Volunteering during school hours is a challenging area for school involvement in families where both parents work. Fran Steinberg, a senior manager at BioPrima, and her husband both try to volunteer a couple of times a year at their son's public school. Fran has chaperoned some field trips and wishes she could do more, but says it's impossible because of her job demands and her commute, at least an hour each way. She expresses a certain amount of resentment toward the stay-at-home moms who volunteer regularly in the library or bring in food for the morning "snack cart." Fran says wistfully, "I would love to do that." When asked if she could negotiate with her supervisor for that kind of time, she responds, "Going in a few times a year is one thing, but regular volunteering? It doesn't fit with my job description!"

Rachel Warren, a single mother of an adopted child, Liza, has been able to do a little volunteering in her daughter's public-school kindergarten class, but only by using sick days, since she lives an hour and a half from her job at BioTertia. For example, during National Adoption Month, she arranged with her daughter's teacher to come in and read a story to the whole class about a bird who gets adopted by a bear. She also volunteered to chaperon a field trip to the aquarium in Boston. In addition, Rachel donates about $100 a month to the teacher for art materials and school supplies. She feels that this benefits both the class as a whole and her own child.

Rachel feels that her efforts have paid off for her daughter's school experience. During the first half of the year, Liza was so timid she did not speak at all, and Rachel talked to the teacher about this. The teacher noticed that Liza was an excellent reader and asked her to read aloud at "circle time." This strategy has worked, and now Liza is much more talkative in class. The teacher has also sent Liza home with books that are above her grade level so that she won't be bored and will continue to improve her reading skills; Liza rose to the occasion and read them all. Rachel feels that by volunteering whenever she can, she is building good communication with Liza's teacher. Rachel expressed ambivalence about getting involved in the PTA, because, as a single mother, she would need evening childcare and have to leave her daughter.

Even attending occasional events at school can be difficult to manage for full-time working parents. Beth, the biotech scientist who sometimes feels burdened by her daughter's homework, recalls that when her son was in kindergarten, she would try to go to "little plays or singing things," but when they had his "graduation" she had to take a whole vacation day off work because it was in the middle of the day. For her daughter, she says, "At least I feel like I've tried to be there for certain in-school little performances or whatever they have, and you know if they need something, snacks . . . but as far as organizing things, and being responsible for something for the whole class, you know, I haven't been able to do any of that."

Attending school events often seems to be measured—especially by mothers—against some higher standard of participation that is simply not possible given the constraints of their present jobs.[17] Beth does not go to PTA meetings, and adds wistfully, "If I for some reason didn't work full-time, I would get more involved." However, when asked about whether she would consider a part-time job, Beth says the real reason she wants a part-time job is to be home with her children several afternoons a week and ease her worry about the lack of an after-school program in their town. On the question of whether other parents in her firm would like to be more involved with their child's school, Beth answers, "More of the women might. I just would like to not feel so pressured about the school, and the kids, and the job."

WHERE'S THE WELCOME MAT?

In discussions with both working parents and stay-at-home moms, several issues surfaced that dampened their impulse to get involved. The first concerns the uneven quality of teaching staff and the lack of input parents are allowed in selecting teachers for elementary school children each year. Fran Steinberg, the mother of a second-grader, expresses some of her frustrations. Her daughter's current teacher is "perfectly nice, but does not challenge [Rebecca]." Her daughter reads at a fourth- or fifth-grade level and needs harder books and harder math than she is getting. Her kindergarten teacher was great, but there were problems with her first-grade teacher. Fran complained about her seating assignment, but the teacher did not intervene. Now she feels there are problems with Rebecca's second-grade teacher, and Fran does not know where to turn. She says the principal is not great, and "You have to be careful what you say. You can't ask for specific teachers." When she tried to talk to the principal about the next year's assignment, she was told in a patronizing tone, "They [the children] *do* get through this." Fran felt she was being told, "Be patient. It's just a stage." When I ask whether this might be an issue to raise at the PTA, Fran responds, "It's *not* an agenda item in the PTG [Parent/Teacher Group]."

Another parental concern, touched on earlier, is the volume of homework in elementary school, and the extent to which assignments cannot be completed without the help of parents. Several parents say that teachers' expectations about the quality of graphic presentation for reports and poster boards are very high and often require the purchase of materials they do not have at home. They complain about the additional expense, the unexpected trips to office supply stores after work hours, and the fact that unless they themselves spend a considerable amount of time on these projects their child will not get a good grade. They are irritated about the use of photocopied worksheets instead of assignments that will stimulate creativity, and are skeptical about homework that emphasizes memorization. Some parents worry about raising homework issues with teachers for fear of appearing "anti-academic," but they—especially those who lack college degrees—often feel that teachers cannot be challenged about these issues because they are trained professionals who are somehow protected from questions about their area of expertise.

Several parents raised concerns about their school's sensitivity and responsiveness to differences in children's learning styles and special needs. Scott Porter, a senior manager at BioTertia, and his wife used public schools in their community for both their children, who are now in college. Scott's wife, Jackie, a stay-at-home mom, devoted many hours over many years to classroom-based volunteer work. Although the school was well suited to their daughter both academically and socially, it did not work well for their son, who had problems academically. According to Scott, the school kept saying he was "lazy" and needed to work harder. Finally, Scott and Jackie went outside the school to have their son tested, and he was diagnosed with attention deficit disorder (ADD). Scott credits the outside professional with making the correct diagnosis of his son's condition and figuring out what needed to be done. Scott is very critical of the school and its failure to pick up the fact that his son has a learning disability. He says they figured out a plan, based on outside testing, then went to the school and said, "This is what we want." Scott reports that his son's grades immediately turned around. Although Scott is currently serving on a science subcommittee of his town's school committee, he was not involved in education issues during the period when his son was having difficulties.

Class and/or racial bias on the part of school staff can also adversely affect parental involvement in education. Malika Shaheed is a college-educated single parent of Afro-Caribbean descent. She works as a mid-level technician at BioTertia. She attends all the "breakfast shares" in her sons' homerooms, and all parent-teacher conferences, despite working full-time in biotech and holding a second part-time job. She says, "I never miss them [parent conferences]. That's one of the things I cleared with my boss to let her know." Despite this type of involvement, Malika found the attitudes of many teachers and administrators at her sons' school very patronizing:

> My first year at the school was a hard year for me, because they automatically degraded me. They thought I had no education, I knew nothing about parenting. And they would brush me off and any concerns that I had. So it was a big struggle for me to get them to understand and listen to me and let them know that I was educated . . . and even now there is still some prejudice. Because sometimes the boys will go to school and they'll be a little tired and the teacher will think that I'm doing something that I'm not supposed to be doing. But I'm very straight up. My children go to bed at 8:30, they're very disciplined. I'm always involved . . . just because I don't have a husband does not make me less of a parent.

Malika often takes her sons to plays on the weekends because their father is a theater artist, yet she finds that the teachers in their school always act surprised when they find out that her sons have been exposed to this kind of cultural experience. She mentions another problem that she feels has not been dealt with at all: the lack of black teachers and male role models. She says there has been little progress on this issue at her sons' school, although it has been brought to the attention of the principal by several parents of color.

Finally, parents report that high schools organize few opportunities for them to come to the school. Across the grades, there is the standard annual "Back to School Night." However, one-on-one parent-teacher conferences are done only through eighth grade, not in high school. In grade school, it is fairly common for parents to be invited to an event where children's artwork or writing is displayed, but this kind of event is rarely organized in high schools. Of course, adolescents may prefer that their parents not make a public appearance at their school and may feel infantilized by being asked to do a joint activity with their parents. Nonetheless, parents of high school students express a keen interest in what is going on both academically and socially in their children's lives, yet feel they have few avenues to get information or meet with other parents.

Jane Forrester, a senior manager at BioSegunda, has noticed a change in her relationship to her children's school between elementary and high school. She has two children, a son in high school and a daughter in middle school. She recalls being more involved in her children's elementary school and was a founding member of their after-school program. However, starting five years ago, her involvement began to decline. She attributes this in part to a change in her marital status (she and her husband separated at that time), and in part to increasing responsibilities at work, but she also attributes it to a "hands-off" attitude the high school has toward parents. She has recently joined a group of parents with children in her son's high school, called "Parent Boosters," which was started by other parents who were also feeling uninformed and disconnected from school. The group provides some parent-to-parent support on issues affecting teenagers outside of school—support parents feel they cannot get from the school itself.

Sometimes parents feel put off by what is said by teachers and school administrators; sometimes they are put off by what is *not* said, and an overall lack of outreach to parents. In these examples, the impediments to parental involvement in school do not always lie with a lack of time or interest on the part of parents, they sometimes lie with the school, its policies, and its staff's attitudes.

PARENT POWER: WHAT DOES IT TAKE?

Only a handful of biotech parents are regularly involved in their child's school as in-school volunteers or in a leadership role. These kinds of roles are mainly held either by stay-at-home moms—some of whom have flexible, home-based, part-time work—or part-time biotech workers. Full-time paid employment and significant volunteerism in the schools are incompatible; less than one-tenth of the parents I met with full-time jobs are involved with their child's school. Nevertheless, women workers, both full-time and part-time, consistently express a greater sense of responsibility for monitoring what is happening in their child's school, and more worry more about the quality of schools, than do their male counterparts.

THE OLD MODEL OF PARENT INVOLVEMENT

An interesting example of the way the "old model" of parental involvement in education works is evident in the family of George and Elizabeth Stratton. George is a senior biotech scientist and manager who is not involved with his children's public school at all. He does not have time, he says, given the level and scope of his professional responsibilities. He is explicit about the fact that the decision that he and Elizabeth made about her leaving a full-time professional position is making her school volunteer activities possible. He explains that Elizabeth is on the Parent/School Advisory Committee, goes to regular meetings, and has gotten to know the principal and teachers quite well. She also volunteers in the classroom, this year focusing on her youngest child's kindergarten. George believes Elizabeth's involvement is valuable to the school and to their family, and his overall view of his children's school is positive and uncritical.

In my conversation with Elizabeth, an "insider's" view of the school emerges. She discusses her concern that there have been three principals in three years, for example. The first principal had problems delegating and resigned. The second principal was "wonderful" but was arrested for allegedly using drugs and was immediately fired by the school superintendent. Elizabeth thinks action was taken too quickly and without hearing the principal's side of the story. The third principal is "all right"—she thinks well on her feet, but is not as warm or personable as the second principal. Elizabeth is reserving judgment.

On the Parent/School Advisory Committee, Elizabeth helped carry out an extensive needs assessment, but little has been done to respond to the problems reported. The language arts curriculum is very weak and needs attention. The math program is good, but the science curriculum needs to be overhauled, and Elizabeth is concerned because "there is very little science coming home [in terms of homework]." She would like to work on the sci-

ence curriculum but is also worried about the fact that music and art classes
were cut last year owing to budget shortfalls. She has thought about running
for the town's school committee (similar to a school board), but the fact that
the meetings are at 3:30 in the afternoon, when her kids need her for after-
school activities, makes this impossible. Even stay-at-home moms have
scheduling problems that limit the extent of their school involvement.

The difference between George's and Elizabeth's perspectives on the
quality of education in their children's school is striking. It is unclear whether
George is uninformed, or whether he is not identifying problems because he
feels assured that Elizabeth will help fix whatever problems exist. Regardless,
this suggests that among families where both parents work, and neither parent is involved in the school, knowledge about what is really going on with
staffing and financial and curricular issues is likely to be very limited. George
and Elizabeth's decision that Elizabeth would put her career on hold was
based in part on a commitment to parental involvement in their local school.
George says that when he was growing up, "church was the center of the
community," but he thinks that is no longer true. He says, "Nowadays schools
are more important than churches." He describes himself as "kind of on the
edge" of his community with little time to get involved in local issues. He is
very preoccupied with work and because "Everything is up in the air at
BioPrima."[18] His community ties exist by proxy, embodied in the sustained
involvement of his wife in their local school and in a variety of community-
based after-school programs.

This division of labor between spouses, with a male breadwinner and
female community activist, is characteristic of the families where women
remain out of, or marginal to, the paid labor force. George talks with pride
about how "Elizabeth is a really important part of the school," and how he
has encouraged her to run for the school committee. Elizabeth's work in the
school is meaningful to their family and an important contribution to their
town, but this situation is based on an all-or-nothing model of community
involvement. Elizabeth is responsible for all of the school volunteering,
George only attends an annual "Back to School" night. Elizabeth does all the
volunteer work described, as well as frequent parent-teacher conferences,
reporting the conversations to George when he comes home from work.
They discuss issues and problems as they arise with each child, but it is
Elizabeth's job to have follow-up conversations with the children's teachers.

The only exception I found to this pattern among the stay-at-home
moms is Ellen, the wife of Jim Dugdale. Ellen and Jim have worked out an

interesting division of labor: he is a full-time research scientist with high-level project management responsibilities at BioSegunda, and Ellen stays home to take care of the kids. For a number of years, Ellen was a full-time mother and active volunteer in the LaLeche League,[19] but nowadays she works part-time out of the home. She writes self-help books on dieting and exercise, sometimes traveling to speak about her work. In their current arrangement, Ellen is responsible for their children after school, five days a week: picking them up from school, working on homework, making dinner. So they agreed it would be only fair for Jim to attend the PTA meetings of the school all three children attend once a month. It is interesting, though, that Ellen is the parent who develops and maintains ties with other parents in the school, and this mirrors the more traditional gendered division of labor found in other families. Now that she has to travel for work, she occasionally needs other parents to bring her kids home from school in the afternoon or invite her children over for after-school play dates. She reciprocates when she is not traveling.

NEW MODELS OF PARENTAL INVOLVEMENT

It is hard to avoid the conclusion that parents have to essentially leave the workforce in order to assume a significant degree of involvement in their children's schools. However, there are three promising new developments in parental involvement among the workers I spoke with that suggest otherwise. One is the involvement of women with part-time or alternative work schedules; another is the involvement of a small number of men in town-wide school committees; and the third—discussed in detail below—is the involvement of women and men in after-school activities. Although the numbers are relatively small, they may be a harbinger of changes to come, stretching our imagination to think about what would make greater involvement possible.

The women working in biotech who are most involved in their children's school work part-time, like Colleen McCarthy, who works 20 hours a week. She initially went from a full-time to a part-time schedule in order to care for her two preschool sons. Though planning to return to full-time when her children entered school, she found that she needed and wanted to continue these hours, both to take care of her boys after school and to volunteer in their school. Colleen is able to volunteer in the school library and computer lab and serves as a lunchroom monitor. She explains that her children are just starting to form important friendships centered in their town, and her involvement helps cement those relationships. As she puts it, "I need to know the children, parents, teachers, coaches, and priest that my children will be associating with."

Only one full-time worker I spoke with has been able to become a regular school volunteer, thanks to an alternative work schedule at her company that makes her "weekend" fall during the work week. Helen Rafferty is a middle manager at BioTertia. In the past, her long hours and extensive responsibilities meant that she came to her children's school only for back-to-school night and parent-teacher conferences. A number of the mothers in her community stay at home and are often at school. Helen typifies the pressure and guilt that haunts many mothers who work full-time. She was devastated when her ten-year-old daughter asked, "How come *all* the other mothers come to my classroom? Why can't you come in for something?" She would answer weakly, "I'm sorry, I have to work." When her company restructured hours of operation and asked her to work full-time from Wednesday through Sunday, her first thought was one of horror—how would she cope on the weekends? Her next thought was, "Now I can volunteer at the school!"

So Helen went from being a parent who never volunteered to being a regular school volunteer. She goes in Monday mornings from 9:30 to 11:30 to help with writing skills, and Tuesday mornings to work in the school library. As soon as she finishes at school, she runs to do the grocery shopping and chores she used to do on the weekend so she can be home with her children after school. When asked if she had any time for herself before going back to work on Wednesday morning, Helen laughs, saying that she still has to fit in the accounting for her husband's small business on Mondays and Tuesdays. She seems physically exhausted and admits she may be "a bit overextended," but at least, she says, she doesn't need to feel as guilty as she did before when she was unable to volunteer in her children's school.

Although it is mainly women who have significant volunteer roles in their children's schools, there are two male biotech workers I met involved in education issues. It is interesting that both men became involved in education issues when their children were older, and only on the town level, not in their own child's school. One of these men served on a short-term committee to review and revise the high school science curriculum, and the other served on the local school board. It is not happenstance that both men also have stay-at-home wives who have been regular school volunteers for years. It seems that the long-term visibility of their wives as dedicated volunteers

and members of the PTA laid the basis for their husbands to take on more
public, town-wide volunteer positions.

NO MORE MILK AND COOKIES: WORKING PARENTS AS AFTER-SCHOOL ACTIVISTS

Nowadays, most mothers are not home in the afternoon, waiting for their
children with milk and cookies—an image from the 1950s that hangs over
working mothers today like a wagging finger. Parents today still have several
hours of work and a commute ahead of them when their children are "free"
and finished with the school day. After-school care is critical for working parents with children ages five to thirteen, and a constant worry for the parents
of teenagers, who often don't want to be supervised but may need structured
activity nonetheless. Some working parents look for after-school program
slots they can purchase and use on a fee-for-service basis that does not require
any involvement on their part. Many parents, working and not working, want
to be involved with their children in the after-school hours, whether they are
in formal programs or enrolled in a set of unrelated lessons, recreational activities, and sports teams. The story of Jane Forrester illustrates the choices of
many other biotech parents—to focus on after-school activities.

Jane Forrester, a senior manager at BioSegunda, has never been a PTA
member. She and her husband, from whom she is now separated, both work
full-time and have no extended family in Massachusetts to help with daily care.
When their two children were little, they relied on full-day childcare, and the
hours of coverage worked well. When their older child, Chris, started public
school, with classes ending at 2:00 p.m., Jane learned there was no extended day
program in the school, nowhere for Chris to go. First, she panicked. Then she
started talking to other parents from her old childcare center. The parents
decided to start their own after-school program. They petitioned the principal
of their elementary school for space, hired three teachers for 15 kids, and created a Parent Advisory Committee to oversee the program. The first couple of
years were rough: negotiating with the school administration, hiring teachers,
buying food and supplies. Their sliding-scale fee structure meant constant fundraising. The program has now grown and stabilized. Both of Jane's children are
now teenagers and outgrew the program around sixth grade, but Jane remains
proud to be a founding member of her school's extended day program.

Problems with after-school care are partly an issue of supply and
demand—too few programs, too many kids.[20] Another problem is the location of the programs that are available. Most working parents do not have

after-school care in their child's public school, and when they don't, they worry about how they are going to get the child from school to the after-school program.[21] Only 10 percent of the families I met with school-age children had an after-school program available in their child's school, a fact that has prompted three different types of response. One-fifth of families decided to have the mother stay home, or leave the paid labor force, in order to have an adult available to take children to team practices, lessons, and so on. In another third of these families, a member of their extended family—usually a grandparent—provides transportation. Over half of the parents have created, run, or in some way supported their child's after-school program. These parents usually are not involved in their child's school beyond annual parent-teacher conferences and back-to-school night. Instead, they are devoting time and energy to sustaining community-based after-school programs, an alternative type of parental school involvement with many positive results for their children and their communities, as the following story illustrates.

THE WORK OF "HOMETOWN HEROES"

Mike Hallowell is a production technician at BioSegunda. When I first met Mike, his son Joey was twelve. From the time Joey was six years old, Mike devoted himself to running three different kinds of after-school programs. Joey's enthusiastic engagement with sports prompted Mike to coach both football and softball every fall and spring. In addition, because of the lack of a school-based after-school program, Mike encouraged Joey to join the Cub Scouts and soon found himself among the active father-organizers of Cub Scout events such as field trips, dinners, and weekend camping trips.

In Little League, Mike started out as a coach. He eventually became a member of the Parent Board of Directors that ran the League, and for three years served as its vice president. As a board member, he had "on-duty night" once or twice a month and a number of other jobs: getting umpires or being an umpire if one did not show up, cleaning up the field after the game, making sure there were people to run the snack bar. It even involved dealing with disputed calls, especially when a parent behaved badly. As vice president of the League, Mike also had to recruit other parents to become and stay involved.

One of the parents Mike recruited and worked closely with is Dennis Roper, a full-time professional in the financial services industry, whose son is the same age as Joey. Dennis and Mike have become friends through their work for the Little League and enjoy the comaraderie that developed among the fathers involved with the League. Dennis says Mike's leadership of the League is important not only for Joey and his own son, Tom, but also for the quality of life in their neighborhood:

> I think [the boys] love playing the game. I think they love competing with one another. I think they all walk away from it with some sense of accomplishment. Our League has been consistently successful over the years as far as making it into tournaments and winning. . . . So I think they take pride in the fact that they're from our neighborhood. They take pride in the fact that our fields look nice, and people want to come and play in our fields. They take pride in the fact that, you know, their brothers and sisters, and sometimes cousins and fathers and mothers, have played in this league. So, you know, I think all these things have a beneficial effect on our neighborhood.

Dennis says the pride is shared not just by the kids but by the parents as well. He recounts how one of the girls' softball teams was so good that they got invited to play in tournaments in Delaware and New York, but their families did not have the money to send them on these two trips. So ten or fifteen parents involved in the boys' Little League got together and raised money to send the girls to these two tournaments. He comments, "It was really neat, you know? It was a great team effort and accomplishment . . . I think we generally recognize that what we are doing for our own kids, we're doing for the kids next to them."

Another area of Mike's after-school activity was his five-year involvement as a coach in a fall football league. This league was started by a good friend of Mike's and, over five years, about 500 children participated. One of the things Mike liked about this league, which made him feel it was not just another sports team, is that when kids sign up, they have to agree to do a service project. Mike liked the idea of Joey learning football and doing something to help the community as well. One year, each team adopted the house of an elderly person in the neighborhood and kept the yard raked and clean all fall. Another year, they cleaned up a local park. The last year that Mike was coaching, the kids on his team did a clothes drive for a local homeless shelter. This football league has 18 teams, so each fall they complete 18 community service projects.

Finally, Mike served as a "den leader" of Joey's Cub Scout pack, coordinating all the different levels of Cub Scouting up to the two-year program for fifth and sixth grades, "Webelos" (which stands for "We Be Loyal Scouts"). He eventually became a member of the "pack committee," analogous to the

board of directors of the Little League and responsible for the overall administration of all the different levels of scouting. While den meetings are held
in the homes of each boy, the Pack Committee convenes and organizes pack
meetings of all the dens several times a year, and also coordinates community
service projects. Mike arranged for pack meetings to be held in the neighborhood Catholic Church and initiated many service projects that Joey and
Tom participated in. Dennis, who also served as a den leader, stresses the
importance of Mike's work in Cub Scouts:

> The best thing about Cub Scouts is that it is not dependent on any kind of
> physical capacity at all . . . you're learning about . . . other things, about
> respecting one another, real, you know, basic stuff about how to be a good per-
> son. . . . Each program still focuses on that part of it—"What are you doing for
> the community? Not just for yourself."

Summing up his feelings about Mike's contribution, Dennis says:

> I think Mike is a very unassuming guy . . . you know, I think of him as a classi-
> cal hometown hero . . . [he's one of the] people that you never hear about, that
> really do yeoman's work, because these things make a better life for their kids
> and the kids around them.

Mike Hallowell did much with and for his son from ages six to twelve,
but the amount of time he is now able to devote to his son and community
volunteer work has been greatly reduced. Part of the explanation is Joey's
age—he has outgrown Cub Scouts and parent-coached athletics. Another
part is Mike's recent promotion in the production area at BioSegunda which
means he works much longer hours, and the relocation of his company which
has increased his commute time so he doesn't get home till late. He would
like to get involved with issues at his son's high school but feels he does not
have time.

The impetus for parental involvement in after-school programs is a failure of private and public policies to come to grips with the disconnect
between work hours and school hours. The good news is that some parents,
both mothers and fathers, are filling the void. They are building programs
that are good for kids, neighborhoods, and community cohesion. The bad
news is that the structures of the workplace and full-time jobs still make it
difficult for many parents to be involved, and stay involved, with their chil-

dren's lives after school. It should not have to be one or the other. As a society in which most parents work, we need public policies to expand the availability of after-school programs, and workplace policies to make parental involvement possible—both in school and after school.

SCHOOL INVOLVEMENT AND CIVIL SOCIETY

When I asked workers to draw me maps of their work-family support systems, "school" as an institution appeared on the maps of only one-fifth of the families. When I asked workers to name the three most important people in their family-community support network, not one person mentioned a teacher, principal, or other school-based professional. However, a number of people gave me the name of another parent of a child at their children's school, or another parent who helps them during after-school hours. These ties are based on sharing information, exchanging goods and services, or working together on a community project. These parents discuss and debate controversial school issues, coordinate their work schedules, and create carpools for after-school activities, sports events, and practices, and a few serve together on the parent boards of after-school programs.

THE PARENT CONNECTION

If working parents get the time and flexibility to work together more on behalf of their children, then perhaps they can strengthen the community institutions vital to children's well-being. The efforts of Pamela Bodajian, who works on school and town-wide education issues, and the efforts of Mike Hallowell, who has run three neighborhood after-school programs, together may hold the key to a new approach for strengthening parent involvement. There seems to be a basis for trust and mutuality of interest between parents that does not often exist between school teachers and administrators on the one hand, and families on the other. Perhaps if schools focused more consciously on facilitating parent-to-parent connections—parent support groups and parent networks—both schools and school-age children would benefit.

In an era when the majority of parents are in the workforce, the quality of life for school-age children is crying out for attention and resources. My experience with families working in the biotech industry suggests that we need to decisively sharpen our focus on this age group and support their parents to be involved in their lives in any way they can. Among the workers I met with school-age children, roughly 90 percent do have some level of involvement with their child's education, usually helping with homework and attending annual parent-teacher conferences and occasional special events (plays, concerts, science fairs). Most parents say that if they had a real choice, they would volunteer in their child's classroom because this would give them additional time with their child, and benefit the school. However, only 9 percent volunteer regularly, and only 18 percent sporadically. The hard truth is that unless there is one parent at home or working part-time, regular volunteer work in the schools is the exception, not the rule.

Does this mean that the quality of civil society in our communities is declining? I would answer "No." If one looks beyond PTA membership, which in this group of parents hovers around 15 percent, one finds a family-to-family support system for school-age children. Membership in these networks, which includes over 80 percent of the families I met, links working parents and stay-at-home parents in a variety of ways. They help children build strong peer relationships, participate in sports teams, and attend after-school activities. They provide support to one another, not only with car-pools, but also with advice on work, child-rearing, elder care, and careers. A few parents attend PTA meetings, but many more are volunteering in after-school programs. This is a community-based effort in which parents are stepping in to bridge the gap between the need of employers to keep parents at work, and the needs of school-age children to have parents at home.

However, there is not the level of parental involvement in education issues that is needed, or is desired by parents themselves. With most parents working, we need multiple avenues for connection between all the adults in school-age children's lives. This includes parents and other family members, teachers and principals, coaches, clergy, and after-school childcare providers in both school and community programs. The idea of one organization that will meet the needs of all parents and all schools is outmoded. Differences in ethnicity, culture, and family structure affect parents' ability to get involved. New approaches to promoting parent involvement are needed: sensitivity to the needs of single parents; outreach to fathers; and knowledge and respect for the languages and cultures of all families.

LEARNING NEW SUBJECTS

Along with overemphasis on declining PTA membership, there has been underemphasis on what it is about paid work in the lives of both men and

women, especially full-time jobs, that makes it so difficult for working parents to be involved with schools. There has been too little discussion about
how the drastic shortage in after-school programs is creating an additional
impediment to parents' involvement in schools. Many parents feel they have
to put their energy into after-school programs instead. While there are no
simple answers, there are several ideas that can be used to jump-start the
search for solutions.

First, we need an expanded definition of parental involvement in education to acknowledge and value the unpaid work of parents who have built an
informal support system to meet the daily needs of their school-age children.
Many parents depend on one another, and this is a good thing not a bad
thing. These informal ties should be strengthened and may provide the basis
for more formal kinds of volunteerism and a movement to expand after-
school programs.

Second, we need to rethink how schools are organized in a society where
most parents work. If the goal is ultimately to get more families involved in
their local school system, it may require some changes in the way schools
relate to families. Schools need to understand how parents' jobs and schedules constrain their lives and plan school functions accordingly. Schools need
to be more cognizant of the diversity of families and the differences between
the pressures on married couples and on single-parent families, and how to
make all families feel welcome.

We also need to learn subjects not often taught in school—work redesign
and community planning. The experiences of the parents in this book
strongly suggest that the inflexibility of paid work hours, the disconnect
between school hours and work hours, and the physical distance between the
workplace and the schoolhouse all need to change. It may not be possible—
or even desirable—for work hours and school hours to be identical. It may
not be possible to move all workplaces and schools close together. But if more
employers can redesign work and increase flexible work arrangements to
facilitate parental involvement in education, then we will be creating conditions for change. If more community planning efforts can address parental
involvement education along with environmental, transportation, and housing issues, then we will be further creating such conditions. If employers,
educational institutions, and government can work together to expand community after-school programs, then increased parental involvement in
schools will grow.

CHAPTER EIGHT

NOT BY BREAD ALONE

It is Saturday morning, and I am driving out to Westville to attend shabbat services at Temple Shalom. I feel honored that Fran Steinberg, one of the biotech managers I have came to know through the work for this book, has invited me to her adult bat mitzvah ceremony. As I enter the synagogue, I do not expect to know anyone there, but before I find my way to an empty seat I have already seen several familiar faces—people to whom Fran had introduced me as members of her family-community support system. There is Fran's mother, Estelle, sitting up front with her granddaughter, Rebecca, beaming as friends come up to congratulate her. There is Nelda Jorgenson, the family childcare provider who took care of Rebecca when she was little. And there is Gerald Cohen, a senior vice president at BioPrima, where Fran works. He and his wife have driven over an hour to be present.

I have some sense of what this day means to Fran, as she has shared with me some things about her childhood and the recent loss of her father. As the ceremony begins, I watch Fran reciting the prayers, the rising on her toes for the Kadosh, the section of the service where people reach symbolically for what is holy. When the Torah is taken out of the ark, Fran and the other women in the adult bat mitzvah class move to the *bima*. They stand by the open Torah scroll holding a *yod*: each reads a few lines of the week's Torah portion, first in Hebrew, then in English.[1] Then each bat mitzvah has a chance to speak. Fran talks about prayers that her father had taught her as a child, and how, after many years of not praying, she has returned to one of his favorites. She now begins each morning by reciting it. She reads the prayer, a blessing of appreciation for the beauty of each day.

Fran's religious involvement is a story of return. She was raised in a Reform Jewish synagogue but did not participate as a teenager or young adult. When she married a non-Jew, Fran and her husband had decided to raise their daughter as a Jew and send her to religious school. They became members of the synagogue to which Fran's parents belonged, but their own participation in the temple remained limited. Fran felt that she wanted to continue some of her family's Jewish traditions, but she was not sure how this would fit into her life as a busy working mother with a full-time professional job and a long commute. That was true for many years, until the recent death of her father. She was devastated by his loss, and her personal struggle to accept his death prompted her to learn more about Judaism and get more involved in her synagogue, eventually joining the adult bat mitzvah class. Fran prepared for this special "coming of age" ceremony for months, studying with the rabbi and improving her Hebrew. She feels her father would be proud.

Fran finds her involvement with Judaism increasing, not just for the sake of her daughter's education, but also for her own. Her busy work life made it difficult for her to mourn the loss of her father as she wished, but her synagogue has given her time and a place to express her grief. She is quick to say that her co-workers were very supportive when her father was sick and she had to take time off work, but she needed time outside of work to grieve. Fran's reengagement with Judaism has also made her closer to her mother, an observant Jew. Her bat mitzvah brought honor to her parents and was admired by her parents' friends in the synagogue. Fran's participation in the adult education program has strengthened her ties to other temple members of her own generation, too. She is especially close to the women in her class, most of whom are working mothers. She says they share stories about their jobs and try to resist being super-moms. Fran's ties to both family and peers reinforce her ties to her community, the city where she was born and raised and now raises her own child.

FAITH AND COMMUNITY IN THE 21ST CENTURY

The religious journeys of working parents like Fran Steinberg are taking place against a backdrop of renewed public debate about religion and public life. The creation of the White House Office of Faith-based and Community Initiatives by the Bush administration in 2001 reignited controversy that started long ago. In the 1770s, the nation's founders pondered whether it was desirable for government and religious institutions to form an explicit partnership. Their denial was codified in articles of the U.S. Constitution. Elected officials today are asking similar questions and coming up with diverse answers. Recent legislative proposals to use federal dollars for the anti-poverty work of religious institutions have been opposed by many Democrats on the ground that this violates the principle of the separation of church and state, but it was the Democratic administration of President Clinton that took the first step in encouraging this use of federal funds. The Personal Responsibility and Work Opportunity Act (PRWOA) of 1996 includes a provision called "Charitable Choice," which allows any faith-based institution that complies with federal nondiscrimination laws to receive federal funds for the delivery of services to people transitioning from welfare to work.[2]

Despite some serious limitations, the 1996 welfare reform law is significant in recognizing that community-based religious organizations may be effective partners with government in reducing poverty and promoting personal responsibility and economic self-sufficiency. There are some compelling examples of church-based activism in inner-city communities that support this view. For example, the Ten-Point Coalition in Boston, initiated by Reverend Eugene Rivers, is based on a partnership between clergy and Boston police officers. These two unlikely allies have successfully taken on gang violence, teenage drug use, and out-of-wedlock pregnancy, issues that have plagued many poor inner-city neighborhoods across the country.[3] Despite such inspiring models, however, some social commentators say that religious institutions cannot fully eradicate poverty or address other social welfare issues because they are not in a position to alter the fundamental structures of inequality that underlie our economic system. Others fear that some religious groups might use government funds to impose their religious beliefs on nonbelievers who are in need,[4] or that this modest funding could be used to absolve the government of any further responsibility to ameliorate the social welfare of the poor. However, those wanting to advance a "new perspective" on church-state relations, such as Mary Jo Bane and Brent Coffin write, "that partnerships will involve inescapable perils; but those perils should not be allowed to overshadow the promises that religious organizations hold for renewing our obligations to one another."[5]

While new laws and White House initiatives have focused on the role of religious organizations in poor communities little attention has been given to the role of faith institutions in middle-class communities. Children there may not be considered "at risk"; however, violence, drugs and teen pregnancy are also found in suburbs and in upscale urban enclaves, along with less visible problems. It is widely agreed that the lack of decent employment opportunities for parents holding low-wage jobs negatively affects poor youth; it is less commonly acknowledged that the long work hours and demanding jobs of middle-class parents create a somewhat different, but nonetheless disturbing, set of problems for their children.

This chapter explores the role that religious institutions are playing, and could play, in the lives of one group of middle-class working families. These families may be materially comfortable, but they are physically exhausted—and, some of them would say, spiritually exhausted—by the struggle to cope with their jobs and family responsibilities. Depending on their income level and care options, they often spend a sizable portion of their paychecks to pay others to do what they might prefer to do themselves, leaving them troubled about the quality of their relationships with others and the value of their time-consuming jobs. Many are looking for ways to re-create a sense of connection to others and to find new pursuits with a purpose that transcends their daily lives.

SEARCHING BEYOND THE SECULAR

Many of the workers I spoke with expressed feelings of spiritual yearning and have turned to religious institutions in their communities to provide for an alternative framework for their lives, as well as for opportunities to provide service to others, possibly as a counterbalance to the self-promotion often required by professional careers. They look to religious institutions for help finding inner peace and fraternity with their neighbors, as an antidote to unending work, consumerism, and competition. Of course, religious institutions are not exempt from problems, but these shortcomings can actually spur increased involvement by lay people to ensure that their religious denominations are true to their core ideals, beliefs, and commitments.[6]

More than half of the families I met are involved in religious institutions, and almost all of the workers in this group drew their church, synagogue, or mosque on their maps of family-community support networks. Another quarter of the families expressed their intention to join a religious institution soon; these are mainly families with children who are not yet old enough to attend religious classes. Finally, one-quarter of the families are not involved at all in religious institutions and do not indicate interest in them. These findings are fairly close to data from national surveys of Americans' participation in religious institutions.[7] What the survey data do not reveal, however, is why some people participate and others do not, and how the nature and meaning of participation changes over the years while families are working and caring for children and elders.

There is a wide spectrum of involvement in religious institutions among the families I met. For some workers, participation is confined to attendance at special holiday and ritual events. Christians attend midnight mass before Christmas day and Easter services. Jews attend the High Holiday services observing Rosh Hashanah and Yom Kippur, the Jewish New Year and Day of Atonement. Muslims observe a holiday at the end of the fast for Ramadan, and a holiday commemorating the sacrifice of Abraham. Other workers attend services regularly, once a week or a couple of times a month. Most workers with school-age children arrange for them to take religious education classes, especially during the elementary-school years. A few workers not only attend services but also volunteer on committees, teach in religious education programs, and get involved in administration. The religious institutions attended are located in an employee's community of residence or in a nearby town. About 20 percent of the biotech employees who are religiously involved mentioned that their move from a blue-collar suburb to a white-collar suburb was accompanied by a decline in their participation, but these families usually maintain a relationship with their old religious institution, attending family events and other special occasions, while searching for a new affiliation.

RESHAPING FAMILY RELIGIOUS TRADITIONS

Religious involvement is shaped primarily by the religious tradition in which people were raised. Some work to preserve these traditions, some break away from them completely, and others break away and return. The following two stories are about workers who have continued to participate in the religious tradition in which they were raised, although they have reinvented the tradition, bringing to bear their adult perspective and their needs as working parents.

For Mike Sinclair, a scientist at BioPrima, and his wife, Lisa, their current ties to the Roman Catholic Church were shaped by their childhood experiences. They grew up in the same blue-collar suburb, and ties to their local parish were very important to their parents and grandparents. They went to catechism classes and attended mass when they were young. In the early years of their marriage, they lived in the town where they grew up and were involved in the parish in which Lisa was raised. Mike says that this particular church is still important to them; it is where their children were baptized. Since they moved to a white-collar suburb almost an hour from where they grew up, that church is too far away to attend regularly, and their involvement is limited to attending ceremonies for extended family members.

The distance that has arisen between Mike and the Catholic Church is not only geographic. He is disappointed with the parochial school affiliated with their old church. Mike and Lisa tried sending their daughter there, but found the teachers were "very strict" and used an outmoded approach to teaching. This was one of the factors motivating them to move. The part of the Catholic Church that Mike finds the most meaningful is the tradition of being a godparent. He and Lisa chose siblings as godparents for each of their children, and Mike is the godfather for both of his brother's children. Mike says that their children's godparents are the key people in their family-community support system. He and Lisa have chosen to continue some aspects of their Catholic upbringing while forgoing others, preferring those that reinforce extended family bonds. They have a more critical attitude toward church teachings and church-affiliated schools than did their parents and grandparents. Their daughter now attends public school, but they insist that she receive a basic Catholic religious education. Their decision to hold her first communion in the church they used to attend attests to their continuing attachment to the religious tradition in which they were raised.

For Barbara Feldman, a single parent who works at BioTertia, her participation in Judaism has shifted over the years. After her divorce, she could not make ends meet and moved back in with her parents. She started attending their synagogue—the one she grew up in—but she found it was not for her:

> I used to go to the one my parents were going to, but they're not very family-friendly. It's mostly older people, and they don't have activities for children. Of course, I just thought, you know, I spend enough time with my parents. I just kind of wanted a little bit of separation. Plus, it's better for the kids, 'cause there's more that they can be involved in.

Barbara joined a Conservative temple that has "a lot of younger families" and children's services, a congregation in which the members are more involved than the people in her parents' synagogue. Her new temple does not have its own religious school, but it subsidizes tuition at the school of a nearby synagogue. Barbara's daughter attends classes there on Sunday mornings, and her son will start when he is old enough. She hopes that her children will both become bar and bat mitzvot, but she is already anticipating that her ex-husband will not participate in or pay for it. Barbara's parents are very much in favor of the bar and bat mitzvah process and will help with expenses so their grandchildren can reach this milestone in Jewish life—but Barbara feels it will cost her both financially and emotionally.

Barbara is frank that her motivation for joining a new temple is partly social: "I wanted to expand my social life." She is pleased to meet other working parents who have children the same age as her own and who are also struggling with combining paid work, time with children, and religious involvement. In choosing a new synagogue, Barbara is making a choice that links her past and her future. She has found a place to ensure her children's religious education in the Jewish tradition, while also joining a social community that will lessen her isolation as a single working parent and facilitate her religious observance.

There is no simple path to follow in choosing to continue the faith tradition of one's parents. Mike and Barbara both left the particular institutions in which they were raised, but they did not leave the faith tradition. Their reasons for being involved differ: Barbara, as a single parent, values the support and connection with other parents; Mike values the role of godparent, which strengthens his ties to extended family. Each, however, continues some level of religious involvement in order to pass on faith traditions and values to their children that were important during their own childhoods.

CREATING NEW TRADITIONS

Several biotech employees I spoke with see their involvement in religious institutions as part of a personal spiritual journey that diverges significantly from the family tradition in which they were raised. The following story illustrates the challenges and the rewards of pursuing a new religious path, and how involvement in a religious institution can significantly enhance work-family support.

Beth Finley is a research scientist at BioSegunda and the mother of two school-age children. Her commitment to a spiritual life is central to the way she chooses to live. She is a member of a Christian denomination that has no buildings for worship and blends traditional and alternative approaches to religious observance. She attends services twice a week, on Wednesday evening and Sunday morning, usually at the homes of other members. Sometimes her children accompany her on Wednesday evening, and sometimes she goes alone. The church provides Bible classes for the children on Wednesday nights, as well as an adult service. Beth also belongs to an a cappella choir that rehearses on Tuesday nights. It is a little tricky when her son has T-ball practice at 6:00 and she has to be at choir practice at 7:30, but they manage. They have dinner early, and then Beth or her husband takes her son to practice.

Beth was not raised in the church that she currently belongs to; in fact, her father was a Methodist minister. She did not leave the Methodist church until a year after she married Charles, a Catholic. There was some tension between them about whether she would convert to Catholicism, but they have worked out a fairly complex faith compromise. Their daughter attends catechism classes at a local Catholic church twice a month, and goes with Beth to her church services on Wednesday evenings. On Sundays, both children go every other week with their father to Catholic services, and alternate weeks with their mother. Beth had hoped they could attend both services as a family of four, so she proposed to her husband that they go to mass on Saturday evening and spend Sunday morning at her church. Charles did not agree, but he does go with her to some church events and spends social time with friends from her church.

Although her decision to change her religious affiliation has brought some tension into her marriage and complicated their schedules, Beth feels it is well worth it:

> I really believe that it's made a huge difference in terms of how I can live the life that I live. And people look at me like how can you do all these things? Work full-time, have kids, have a family, you know, be part of this church, which is very consuming. But I really feel like if you're spiritually at peace, and you've been able to fulfill that part of your life and rely on the friendships that I have, and the relationship with God that I have, you know, everything is better.

When I asked how her being part of her church helps her to manage her job and her family, she elaborated, "The stress of my life doesn't consume me as I have seen it consume other women."

Beth is one of a small number of women in her church who work full-time; most of the women work part-time, and that has helped Beth to manage the difficulties that come with a full-time career. She often calls on her friends from church to watch her children after school. "People do that all the time, we babysit each other's kids, or help other people do errands and things like that." She and her family also socialize with other families from the church at pot-luck dinners, apple-picking trips, or religious holidays. The structure of the church, organized in small groups of people who live in neighboring towns, enhances the possibility of this type of social connection for busy working families. These "neighborhood groups"—usually spanning several suburban towns—are also the basis for informal Bible study groups. The social and the religious are strongly linked in the church's culture, and both personal and institutional relationships are characterized by a great deal of reciprocity. On Beth's map, she drew one circle for her immediate family and four others for extended family, church, neighborhood, and "other community neighbors/friends." All the circles are connected by double lines with arrows pointing in either direction. At the top of the page she wrote "God"—not in a circle—connected to her family by double lines with reciprocal arrows.

One of the part-time working mothers in her church with whom Beth is particularly close, and on whom she relies on for work-family and spiritual support, is Margaret. Margaret and Beth met through their church six years ago, but they did not become close until Margaret's family moved to the same suburban town where Beth lives, and they became part of the same church "neighborhood group." They organize Bible study, a women's prayer group, and a women's breakfast series. Margaret explains the importance of these meetings:

> That's [these meetings] how I got to know Beth a little bit more. I really do appreciate Beth's friendship a lot. And I think our common denominator is God. It's really God and how we trust what we say—I trust her love for God. So then you have that common bond.

Through the women's group meetings, Beth and Margaret try to apply their understanding of the Bible to current issues in their marriages, parenting dilemmas, and work-family conflicts.

Margaret, who holds important lay leadership positions in their church, is no stranger to the problems of balancing work, family, and faith-based commitments. She worked full-time for a nonprofit organization until two years ago. Owing to the needs of her three children, two school-age and one preschool, she recently quit her job and now works for her former employer as an independent contractor, taking on small projects at home. Although she has lost her benefits, this arrangement gives her the flexibility to invest time in her children and her church. When asked what kinds of issues they discuss, Margaret says the biggest problems in dual-earner marriages are "Pride and selfishness and finances . . . who earns the most, and who has the control of the finances, and who has the power to decide." The two women seek help from each other—and from the Bible—to be more flexible and less competitive with their spouses.

Their church is organized around ministries that serve different age cohorts and work around different issues. They have ministries for infants, preschoolers, preteens, teens, and single parents. One of the most popular ministries, to which Beth and Margaret both belong, is the "parenting ministry." There they seek support and advice from other parents about how to help their preteen and teenage children resist drugs, alcohol, and premarital sex without losing their popularity with peers. They learn how to convey their values to their children. Margaret explains:

> There's no way to put your kids in a bubble and protect them. . . . It has to be their conviction, rather than their parent's conviction, or the teacher's conviction. . . . God's view of family is that he didn't mean for parents to be authoritarians, or just tell their kids what to do, but rather to train them . . . consistent, gentle pressure. . . . The scripture says, "Be quick to listen, slow to speak."

When Beth comes home from a Wednesday evening Bible study or her women's prayer group, she says she feels strengthened and renewed to face the challenges of being a full-time professional, a wife, and a mother: "Gaining peace of mind—even if for only a few hours a week—is priceless." The neighborhood organization that her church uses facilitates connections between families on a religious and material level; weekly prayer meetings and services are easy to attend; and backup childcare and carpooling are easy to organize. It is unlikely that either religious observance or family-to-family support networks would be as durable if the denomination was organized in a more geographically dispersed pattern.

CAN WORKING MOMS BE LAY LEADERS TOO?

Some biotech workers have created a faith community outside any institutional setting. This is the case for Helen Rafferty, a biotech manager, who was raised in a Jewish family. Helen married Albert, who is not Jewish. Although he agreed to raise the children as Jews, he did not want to make the financial commitment necessary to join a synagogue, so Helen looked for an alternative to provide religious education for her children. Her family childcare provider told her about a parent-led group that she herself belonged to. Helen joined this group, the Jewish Family Havurah,[8] composed of about 15 Jewish families who come together to celebrate the Jewish holidays, usually three or four times a year. Many of the families involved include interfaith couples. The Havurah provides a level of participation in Judaism that Albert feels comfortable with, and it gives the children some knowledge of Jewish ritual and identity. Helen is active in organizing activities of the Havurah, serving on various committees and organizing a Passover seder.

Helen views her involvement with the Havurah as central to her sense of community. She suggested that I talk to her friend Sarah, who also belongs to the Havurah, as a key person in her family-community network. They met because their daughters are friends in public school. One weekend they took their daughters to an amusement park and began chatting about the Havurah. Sarah's daughter had expressed an interest in going to Hebrew school, but most temples hold classes two afternoons a week, and Sarah could not get time off from her full-time job to do the necessary driving. Helen explained that in the Havurah, religious education classes are held once a week on Sundays, a better schedule for working parents. Sarah joined the Havurah, and now the two women see each other at events and share driving their daughters to religious education classes.

The connections and conversations between Helen and Sarah are not always, or even largely, about Judaism and religious issues. They tend to be about the difficulties both women are having trying to fulfill work and family commitments. Sarah says, with a laugh, "That topic is the primary subject of our relationship!" They do a certain amount of shared childcare beyond carpooling so that each couple can have some weekend time alone. If a schedule conflict comes up during the week, Sarah is the first person whom Helen calls, and vice versa. Sarah thinks that Helen takes on far too many tasks, feels too much guilt, and does not take time for herself: "I think it creates an enormous amount of stress for her. There's physical stress, in her body, you can see the tension and anxiety." She thinks Helen does not get enough support at her workplace in regard to family needs. When Helen's daughter was very sick for a week Helen was allowed to take the time off to care for her, but did not feel comfortable about taking it, worried that the firm would question her commitment and say she was setting a bad example for the employees she supervises.

Asked whether the Havurah addresses any of these time pressures and other work-family issues, Helen is ambivalent. In a religious community with no clergy or physical facility, there is enormous pressure on the lay members. So while the families in the Havurah are saving the money that would otherwise go to large annual synagogue dues, their alterntive commitment takes a large chunk of their time. Membership in the Havurah requires being a "monitor" at Hebrew school several Sundays a year, serving on two committees a year, and attending four services a year; Helen also serves on the board. Helen hints indirectly that her husband's lack of involvement is a problem. The Havurah designated Sunday as "Family Day," but Helen's husband usually does not come, so Family Day is Helen's day to be with the kids. On the positive side, the Havurah gives Helen a sense of community that she does not get at work; she feels that it is important for her children, and this gives her a positive feeling about herself as a mother.

Helen now has a four-day work week, from Wednesday to Saturday, which has made it easier for her to fulfill her commitments to the havurah. On Sunday she does grocery shopping and takes her children to religious school. On Monday and Tuesday, she does committee work for the Havurah (and volunteers in the local school). But with her long commute, her work days run 13 hours, from 6 a.m. to 7 p.m.—"Those are very hard days." Helen says that if her job were closer to home, she would bite the bullet, join a synagogue, and send her kids to Hebrew school, so she would not have to worry about helping to sustain a lay-led religious organization. These are the complex trade-offs for working parents.

GENDER AND RELIGIOUS INVOLVEMENT

Among the families portrayed in this book, the women carry most of the responsibility for religious involvement.[9] This is particularly evident when husband and wife are not of the same faith, or when husbands are involved only nominally. This gender-based division of labor is similar to the pattern already described for childcare settings and school activities.

The special responsibility women take for religious practice and education is evident whether one talks to male or female biotech workers. When I asked George Stratton, a senior biotech scientist and manager, whether his family had any religious affiliation, he answered, "No, we are not religious." However, his wife, Elizabeth, spoke with conviction about how important it is for their children to have some kind of religious education. The children have begun to ask her questions about God and heaven, and she feels the "need for some kind of framework" to help her answer them. She has been actively "shopping around for something that is not too religious" because for many years she has not attended the Episcopal church in which she was raised, and George, who was raised Baptist, does not espouse any religious beliefs at present. This has left Elizabeth in a quandary: on the one hand, she and George have no obvious religious home; on the other, she feels strongly that her children need the kind of instruction and guidance that a church-based education can provide. Like a number of other mothers, Elizabeth is taking on their children's religious education as her own—rather than a shared—responsibility.

Another mother with young children seeking a religious home is Colleen McCarthy, a biotech bench scientist at BioPrima. Colleen was raised Catholic and attended a parochial high school in the blue-collar city where she grew up. Colleen married someone of her own faith, and she and her husband agree that they will raise the children in the Catholic Church. Her challenge is twofold. First, she and her husband have just moved into a new suburban community. There are two Catholic churches nearby, and Colleen is debating which one they should join; the choice seems to be hers to research and make. One parish is dominated by wealthy families; the other parish is one town over but seems more economically diverse. Colleen is concerned about whether she will be able to be as involved in their church as she would like because of her current work schedule. In order to maximize her time at home with her two preschool children, Colleen is working two ten-hour days a week, Wednesday and Sunday. Although this schedule gives her time with her children, it means that she is not available to teach CCD classes on Sundays, as she did before the children were born.[10] Once again, the trade-offs between flexibility of schedule and community involvement are complex. But whatever her schedule, it is Colleen, not her husband, who is responsible for choosing a church and shaping the specifics of her children's religious education. Even in marriages where couples are from the same faith tradition, decisions about religious affiliation and ongoing faith-based involvement are usually women's work.

CAN FAITH-BASED INSTITUTIONS ERASE INEQUALITY?

Of the nearly 300,000 religious organizations in the United States, over 90 percent report some activity serving the needs of the poor.[11] Usually this is done by volunteers from the congregation, and most activities focus on filling immediate needs such as for food, shelter, or clothing.[12] Although the percentage of faith-based institutions involved in social service is large, the percentage of people involved in this type of volunteer work is fairly small; most congregations mobilize around 30 volunteers a year.[13] These figures create an important context for understanding the social service work of biotech employees and their families.

For many workers I met, religious institutions are not only a place for family support, community connection, and personal spiritual fulfillment; they are also a place to give back, to attend to some of society's ills, to increase social justice. Beth Finley explains that her church does a lot of work to raise money for the needy in the area where she lives. For example, her church runs a food pantry in Framingham, in which she works three hours on many Saturday mornings. Once a year, Beth takes up a collection for the food pantry in her biotech company. When her children get older, she hopes to involve them in this work "because I'd like to expose them to people who are worse off." This volunteer work is central to Beth's definition of herself as a Christian, and to her sense of what she is trying to teach her children about being a good Christian and a caring community member.

Not all the congregations of these workers are located in affluent suburbs serving moderate-income or affluent middle-class families. Some are in poor inner-city neighborhoods, such as the mosque of Malika Shaheed. Malika, an Afro-Caribbean single mother who works full-time at BioTertia, is a practicing Muslim. She finds it difficult to attend weekly services because they fall on Friday and conflict directly with her work hours. Her three sons attended a Muslim school when they were small and lived in another city. Now that they attend a secular public school, their religious education is difficult to maintain. She prays with them at home every night, and when her three boys have a half-day of school on a Friday, then she takes the day off of work and brings them to their mosque in Boston.

Even though her participation in religious services is sporadic, Malika is involved in community service projects through her mosque. As a member of the Sisters Group, she counsels young women in inner-city Boston about "how to be a young lady, how to function, how to carry yourself." The Sisters

Group offers workshops on everything from job networking to combating domestic abuse. Malika says that the young women who come are not just Muslims, and that the Sisters Group is not trying to proselytize. She feels that her religious tradition has much to offer young African-American women from poor inner-city neighborhoods who are trying to grow up to be self-respecting and economically self-sufficient. The Sisters Group provides a mentoring project, like the Big Sister Program but with a distinctive faith perspective. As a middle-class professional woman, Malika considers her work with less affluent African Americans an important part of her faith, as well as of what she is trying to teach her sons about Islam.

Some biotech employees voiced a desire to do more service work related to poverty, hunger, and homelessness, but it is impressive how many of them already find time for this. Participation in religious activities in general seems to take a higher priority than, for example, school involvement. Most of the women described in this chapter hold full-time jobs; two of them have commutes of over an hour each way; two others are single parents. Despite these impediments, they are all involved in religious communities, and not as nominal members; they are doing committee work and volunteer work among the poor. Each woman, in her own way, says that religious involvement helps bring some perspective to her busy life, a sense of order into the chaos of commuting, working, and caregiving.[14] Through service to the poor, they believe they are making a difference in a world filled with pain and inequality.

THE CLERGY PERSPECTIVE

A number of workers arranged for me to interview their priest, minister, rabbi, or imam, describing these professional clergy as key people in their family-community support networks. These individuals provide both material and spiritual support and understand the challenge of managing work and family. Speaking with the clergy, I learned that they face their own set of challenges produced by the current system of long work hours and inadequate family care.

VOLUNTEERS FOR THE ANNUAL CHURCH SUPPER?

Father Paul is the pastor of a small church in a working-class town near Boston. The church is going through a crisis: its membership and financial resources are diminishing. He does not want to be the one to "preside over the death" of the church, which has been an important community institution for many years. Father Paul is looking to Natalie Parsons and her family to help him revive the church. Natalie is a stay-at-home mom, and her husband, Frank, is a full-time scientist at BioPrima. Father Paul says Frank and Natalie have one of the few "intact," healthy families in the congregation, and he is hoping their example and leadership will help to bring in new members.

From this pastor's perspective, churches like his—located in blue-collar suburbs—are experiencing significant attrition as more and more residents move to white-collar suburbs. The pastor sees it as his job to create and maintain an active membership base in this difficult environment. He knows he cannot do it alone and is grateful to have a skilled volunteer like Natalie to help him. She is chair of the Administrative Council and runs the church's steering committee, serves as co-president of the Women's Group, and teaches at the Sunday school. Natalie's consistent presence on church committees helps her church to be an anchor institution in a community undergoing rapid social change and some deterioration. Her volunteer work makes it possible for the church to continue to provide a spiritual home for her family, her friends, and her neighbors.

Several other clergy I spoke to sounded a similar call for volunteer help, although their institutions were not facing quite the same difficulties as Father Paul's. Joshua Lowenthal, the rabbi at Fran Steinberg's Reform synagogue, told me that with increasing numbers of women at work, he is facing a dire lack of volunteer labor. The ranks of the temple's Sisterhood are depleted. He asks with urgency, "Who will do the *onegs* [social receptions after the service]?" He recognizes that women's roles have changed, families have changed, and Jewish institutions must be responsive. Not only does the temple need to provide childcare for meetings and rethink scheduling of adult education classes, but it must also design its programs to attract the dual-earner couples who increasingly constitute its membership.

Father Flanagan is a Catholic priest in a large suburban parish attended by Maureen Stendall and her mother Theresa. He explains that, in the past, it was not uncommon for one parish to have three or four priests to share the work, "but now with the shortage of priests, we're relying more and more on the people of the parish to start taking over." He sees this as a positive development, in the sense that lay church members should be taking a greater role in the affairs of the parish; however, with so many parents working, people have little time. Father Flanagan says the same people volunteer for everything, and there's a need to get new people involved. He participates in an ecumenical clergy group in his town and reports that the need for more volunteers to support religious institutions is an "across-the-board issue."

Imam Abdul Hasan, who serves as the only cleric in a small inner-city mosque, has also found difficulties with getting enough volunteers, but he manages to maintain six active volunteer committees. He himself holds a full-time position outside the mosque to support his family, so he must rely on congregants like Malika Shaheed to do some of the work. The active committees include the Ways and Mean Committee, which handles fundraising; the Hospitality Committee, which greets visitors at weekly Friday services and other public events; the Maintenance Committee, which cares for the physical upkeep of the mosque; and the Security Committee, which ensures the building is properly locked and guarded when not in use. There is also a Health Committee, who visit the sick at home or in the hospital and prepare the bodies of the dead for burial. Finally, the Sister's Group, to which Malika belongs, brings women together to discuss "problems of the secular world" and perform community service on behalf of the poor. This group is setting up a food pantry in the mosque that will be available both to members and to the poor in their neighborhood, regardless of faith. They participate in the annual Walk for Hunger and volunteer at a local women's shelter for victims of domestic violence.

Speaking of the importance of this volunteer work to the mission of Islam and to their mosque, the imam says, "I always tell the believers that there's a concept that we don't have in Islam: that's unemployment. You're not unemployed because there's so much to do." He does acknowledge that the current structures of paid work leave some congregants with little time to work for Islam:

> The need is to take care of yourself and your family; they keep us busy doing that, and there's no time for anything else. So really I see society as a great deal at fault. You know, really, a man providing for his family should work about five hours a day and get something that's comfortable for that person. Five hours a day. And then go home to his family.

All these clergy, representing three different faith traditions, have their own experiences with the changing nature of work and family care and the visible impact of this change on the pool of volunteers. But there is an invisible component of contemporary family life that has also been affected—a component clergy must address on a spiritual level.

FINDING MEANING BEYOND PAID WORK

When professional clergy talked about the biotech employees they know and serve, I heard repeatedly about the extent to which work is dominating people's lives. Several clergy portrayed the families they know as constantly rushing—rushing to work, rushing home from work, rushing to drop children off, rushing to pick children up. Amid this rushing, they see parents attempting—sometimes successfully, sometimes not—to make a place for community and religious commitments. There is a perception among these clergy that this endless rushing may be linked to a kind of spiritual impoverishment on the part of many working parents. They see a genuine spiritual search on the part of a few for a different pace, a different path.

Reverend Simmons, the minister of a church in a middle-income, white-collar suburb attended by Rachel Warren, comments about the difficulties that working parents have with time:

> Time is the biggest thing that people in this congregation are struggling with. "How much time do I have and how am I going to spend it?" And that is something we talk about a lot as a religious community, you know. Trying to decide what your priorities are. We actually have people in this community who have . . . made intentional decisions about how much time they are going to spend with careers.

Reverend Simmons gives several examples of families who scaled down—sold an expensive house, or had one parent change to a part-time job or leave work completely—so that they would have more time to be with children and to participate more fully in the church. She is sensitive to the particular constraints of single working parents. But for all working parents, married or single, Reverend Simmons feels that the church can play a positive role in making work-lifestyle decisions:

> And I've been with a lot of these folks as they've been making those decisions. You know, "How can we cut back?" . . . And I think the church has been important. The community has been important for some of that, in that these are not people who are going in, you know, to have season tickets to the symphony. . . . Instead they are electing to have their entertainment costs be minimal . . . to remain out here and go to a three-dollar cinema, and have their social life kind of revolve around their community here.

But for those families who have not scaled back, for the working parents who are still rushing around, clergy are struggling to define what role religious institutions can play to address the pressures that so many working parents feel. Reverend Simmons explains what her church is trying to do, both on the programmatic and spiritual level:

> We try to arrange our program to be family-friendly, so that we can provide things where families can come together to do things. A lot of intergenerational types of activities . . . the church is the one place for the whole family to come together. We try to be more careful with what we ask people to do. . . . So that you take time, even in committee meetings, to check in with each other . . . talk about some deep things with each other.

She has encouraged the director of religious education in the church to think not just about what the children need to learn, but also about what adults need to learn to deepen their spiritual quest:

> We also focus on, What are you learning? How is your spiritual life being enriched and deepened? What is this bringing to your life, by taking on this responsibility? So we talk a lot about shared ministry. And what we would really like everybody to have is a sense that they are part of the ministry of the whole church.

Reverend Simmons feels that, in many churches, there is too much emphasis on what she calls a "vertical relationship." Whether it is between the clergy and the layperson, or between God and the individual, it is top down. In her church, on the other hand:

> Our focus is not on the vertical relationship, but on the horizontal relationship. So after [services], in our church, people hang around and they'll talk over coffee. And they want to develop relationships with each other, and it's really the development of religious community, you know, the focus on the community.

Reverend Simmons's observations about the lives of busy working families are also voiced by Janice Thompson, the religious education director of Julie Taylor's church. Janice discussed the difficulty of getting working parents involved in teaching in the Sunday school. She noted that when parents are involved in thinking through the curriculum and team-teaching with other parents, this type of volunteer work becomes meaningful for their own spiritual growth. She says, "What began as a chore may become a growth opportunity." Janice worries about why it is usually the mothers, and not the fathers, who do this kind of work:

> Why do the moms feel more responsible for religious education, even when they are working full-time or part-time? Why is it the moms who are still buying the gift for the teacher, sewing the Halloween costumes, and baking for their child's school project?

Whatever the answer, Janice says her church is trying to support these mothers and provide "a wholeness for families." She says the church can address this by focusing on values, and this is what families are looking to faith-based institutions to provide. "They want a wholeness, a wholeness their children have not found in our culture, a culture where there is too much mobility and not enough community." Janice says:

> It is hard to stave off a culture of entitlement and consumerism. Kids are handed everything they want, so it's important for the church to show them how to serve and help others. . . . Sometimes parents can't see that the choices that they make are disabling the values they say they care about.

Janice believes that part of the role of her church is to help parents forge a closer alignment between their choices and their values:

> I want to give parents in our church a chance to get off the treadmill, to walk their own spiritual path. This will bring them and their children to a better place. Everyone is on the fast track. There's so much pressure from jobs, schools, the media. People need tools to break away from all that. Sometimes a death or a vacation will jolt them, but then they lose it. Many have good values, but the values are rhetoric, they are not lived. The church can help them live as they want to live.

Not all the I met clergy are dealing with congregations where parishioners are struggling against a culture of affluent consumerism and trying to get off the fast track. At Imam Hasan's congregation in a low-income inner-city neighborhood, parishioners are looking for expanded economic opportunities. His mosque has recently purchased an abandoned building and has

plans to rehabilitate each floor and build apartments that will provide affordable housing for the community. They are going to use the first floor for a
store that sells staples and household supplies at a significant discount. The
imam explains the rationale for this project:

> Take charge of our own lives, and be able to, at some point in time, you know,
> be entrepreneurs, and won't have to worry about the things that you worry
> about when you're not an entrepreneur, you know when you are dependent.
> But it's time for us as African Americans to become entrepreneurs and be able
> to do for ourselves. We should be able to work for ourselves and begin to build
> schools for ourselves, and to employ members of the community in a meaning-
> ful way . . . as any other community in America has done.

Linking a religious institution to an economic development strategy and a
community empowerment objective gives this mosque a distinct sense of
purpose and a social action agenda on behalf of those who see themselves as
disenfranchised. Some may find meaning through, not beyond, paid work.

In order to move away from being disenfranchised, the mosque must
struggle with mainstream American institutions. For example, Imam Hasan
joined with religious leaders of other mosques in the Boston area to negotiate with the Boston Public Schools for two religious holidays for Muslim students. They have written letters to employers of their members, asking that
they be allowed to leave work early on Friday to attend midday services. Each
initiative has demanded action on the part of the imam and mosque members to confront the Christian majority culture and seek their rights as a religious minority in a pluralistic secular democracy. It is significant that the
imam does not see the position of Muslims as that of victim:

> The problem is not so much on the secular world, and it's not so much on the
> employer. The problem is on us as Muslims, of coming together in a commu-
> nity context and having those things that every other community has, and
> coming together and coming up with the necessary institutions.

In this way, the desire for a decent "material life" is not separate from following the way of a Muslim believer. Imam Hasan says, "For the person of faith,
certainly we're trying to get what we're supposed to get here, in this life. . . .
God tells us that certainly you'll get it in the next life, but you're obligated to
get something in this life." In his sermons the imam exhorts his congregants

to pursue the "material life," not just for themselves, but so they will have something to leave to their children and to the Muslim community.

RELIGIOUS INVOLVEMENT IN A WORKAHOLIC WORLD

In all of three faith traditions—Christian, Jewish, and Muslim—involvement in a religious institution gives new meaning and new focus to paid work. In some faiths, diminishing the importance of paid work in one's life, living more simply, and serving the poor enhances the meaning of life. In others, the call to build the community, increase each family's material resources, and escape poverty enhances the purpose of paid work and life's meaning. Though the needs of the families I met are diverse, many are looking to religious institutions to help them raise their children in a way that is consonant with their highest values. How successful this will be, whether it is a goal shared by husbands and wives, and to what extent children will participate, are all questions that must be evaluated over time as families move through the life course. For the present, their clergy are aware of the pressures that paid work puts on families, regardless of income level, and they are trying to give families support to manage their complex lives.

FAITH IN EACH OTHER: BUILDING RELIGIOUS INVOLVEMENT AND COMMUNITY

The choice of whether to be involved in a religious institution starts inside the family of origin, and this in turn shapes the choices that people make once they become adults. In the generation that formed families right after World War II, most people married someone from their own family's faith tradition. Although their orientation might have been quite assimilationist, many were children of first-generation immigrants and did not question whether to join religious institutions. This is much less true today; some have kept their distance from organized religion, and 20 percent of the couples profiled here are in interfaith marriages. Whether it is Jews marrying non-Jews, Catholics marrying non-Catholics, or Christians from different denominations marrying each other, faith orientation can pose a challenge for marital relationships. In some cases, one partner is religiously involved and the other is agnostic or atheistic. More often than not, it is the wife who takes primary responsibility for decisions about the children's religious education, and who investigates different religious institutions, decides where the family will affiliate, and maintains the family's link to church, synagogue, or mosque. Ties between individual

families and religious institutions constitute an important part of the social
fabric of support for working families, and these threads are woven largely by
women, whether they are employed full-time, part-time, or not at all.

Religious involvement also affects extended family relationships in varied ways. For Estelle, Fran Steinberg's mother, her daughter's return to
Judaism strengthened their relationship. Estelle herself is deeply involved in
the Jewish community; she volunteers at a local Jewish Community Center
(JCC) and attends religious services regularly on Fridays and Saturdays. Fran
tends to go less regularly, and only on Saturdays. Despite their differing levels of religious observance, their faith and the activities of their synagogue are
important for both on two levels: they ensure that family religious traditions
will be carried on; and both mother and daughter rely on the work-family
support services offered through the temple.

When the faith choices of adult children diverge from family tradition,
the involvement or noninvolvement of the adult children may be a source of
tension in extended family relations. This is true, for example, in George and
Elizabeth Stratton's family. Although George is completely nonreligious, his
mother is very religious and is disturbed by the fact that her grandchildren do
not attend church. She mentions this frequently when they visit or talk on the
phone. This is one of the factors spurring Elizabeth's current search for a congregational affiliation. It is complicating the search, because Elizabeth needs
to find something that will assuage her mother-in-law's concerns while not
alienating her husband, who would be perfectly happy with no formal religious affiliation at all.

The impact of religious involvement on peer friendships and family-to-
family bonds seems to be positive overall. Common membership in faith-
based institutions creates ties between working parents that helps mitigate
work-family conflict and provides concrete assistance through carpooling,
backup childcare, help with routine errands, and so on. Friendships between
women with the same religious affiliation make a particularly significant difference in helping them maintain full-time careers and manage responsibilities at home. With Helen Rafferty and Sarah, their Jewish identity seems
secondary to their professional identities; in the case of Beth Finley and
Margaret, their religious identity and spiritual commitment are primary in
their lives and choices. In both friendships, the opportunity to talk to another
woman from the same religious community is meaningful; it relieves stress
and provides emotional support for dealing with marital tensions, parenting
challenges, and work-family issues.

Finally, on the community level, religious involvement is also having a positive, but perhaps more limited, impact. On one level, it builds bridges of connection and support among working families, providing a safety net for childcare crises and other family support problems. This is particularly important for working families who do not have extended family nearby. On another level, it builds bridges between families from different income groups. The efforts of middle-class families to work through religious institutions on behalf of the poor creates a sense of caring and social responsibility. The lessons that middle-class children learn from this type of community service are important in reinforcing what they learn in religious school—such as being one's brother's keeper, or treating others as you would have others treat you.

But questions of tokenism and paternalism cannot be ignored in evaluating the impact of volunteer service work. The persistence of poverty and the depth of class divisions in American society cannot be overcome solely by activity that occurs for a few hours per week or per month. It is not useless, but it is limited. Religious institutions are uniquely positioned to address the persistence of inequality in our society, but not necessarily by doing what they have always done. The ability of each church, synagogue, and mosque to engage children and adults in meaningful dialogue and practice regarding poverty and the wealth gap in our society remains a profound challenge across denominations. Community service projects based in different faith traditions are helping to mend holes in the fabric of civil society. But full repair—what is called *tikuun olam* in the Jewish tradition—is a far vaster project.

To begin that larger project, there is a need for families across the class divide to recognize that they all share "a certain kind of impoverishment," as one clergyperson expressed it. Some biotech employees look to religious institutions to provide a nonmaterialistic worldview for their children, to counter a materialistic culture with an anti-consumerist perspective. Others say they need their religious institution to speak loudly against a workaholic culture that devalues taking time for children and elders, because they know that their employers will not speak out. Many want their religious institutions to preach in word and deed about the need for key social institutions to invest in community-based supports, and to create policies that will support time for working families to care for their "community," however one defines that term.

WHAT CAN RELIGIOUS INSTITUTIONS DO FOR WORKING FAMILIES?

This chapter has documented how the ties between congregants, and the ties among congregants and clergy, are often critical components of a family's work-family support system. But working families need more. The clergy I spoke to are acutely aware of the toll that the current work-family system is taking on the children and families in their congregations. They must find a way to engage others—in their own denominations, and across denominations—to expose the inadequacy of the public response to work-family conflict. As community-based institutions, they are well-positioned to expand and mobilize community resources in childcare, after-school programs, elder care, and other areas. Too often, religious leaders are used as pawns in struggles among politicians over what constitutes "family values." Faith-based institutions and religious leaders are important stakeholders in creating a better work-family system. We need to hear their voices more consistently and to see their institutions offering the programs that working families need.

It is critical that faith-based institutions become allies of all families across the economic spectrum. If the Office of Faith-based Initiatives in the White House, or any other ecumenical effort, serves only the needs of poor families, its potential will be severely limited. We cannot pretend that poor families need faith and middle-class families do not, or that poor families have problems and middle-class families do not. When there are religious initiatives that speak a language that transcends racial, gender, and class divisions, and envision a society where community and caregiving are valued, then religious institutions will have found their place in destroying all forms of inequality and building a civil society. Many workers are looking to their clergy to provide a counterweight to the values and practices of the workplace and the market economy. Many are lending their own voices to that message with their participation and volunteerism in religious institutions where they live.

PART III

INVESTING IN COMMUNITY: EVERYBODY'S BUSINESS

CHAPTER NINE

THE TRIALS OF A FULL-TIME WORKING MOM

OR, HOW I BECAME A PART-TIME WORKER AND A PART-TIME COMMUNITY ACTIVIST

The story of Pamela Bodajian is one of the most promising and inspiring that I heard about new approaches to community involvement. It is important both in showing the obstacles working parents face, and in demonstrating that these obstacles can be removed. If one working mother can change the relationship between paid work, family care, and community volunteerism in her life, other working parents can too. This book asks, "How can we create healthy families and caring communities?" Pam's story reveals a part of the answer—it is being constructed daily by working families themselves, who recognize that the challenge of work and family requires neighborhood connections, community resources, and collective action.

A STORY FROM THE FRONT LINES OF PARENT ENPOWERMENT

Pamela Bodajian, a quality assurance manager, has worked as a full-time professional in the biotechnology industry for 15 years, five of these at BioSegunda. Though committed to her job and her career, Pam has always struggled with issues of professional advancement, especially when new opportunities came her way. Before she came to BioSegunda, she was working at a biotech company that moved its headquarters from Massachusetts to the West Coast. Pam had an opportunity to move to the new headquarters, but declined. She explains her decision:

> A huge part of it [was] community for me. I lived down the street from the house I grew up in. . . . My mother grew up in the next town over. My dad

grew up in that town. All of my siblings live nearby. I had a huge support network from my family when I went back to work when my son was an infant.
We moved—sold [our first] house at a horrible time in the market—just to
move back there to where my family lived, because it was one way I could go
back to work and not have to worry about putting an infant in daycare, which
was something that concerned me at the time . . . community was a huge piece
to me. Always has been.

When Pam's son, Jason, was a year and a half old, she found a childcare
center that she felt comfortable with, and her involvement with his early education began almost immediately. She volunteered as a parent reader at the
center and encouraged other parents to do the same. Her husband, Joseph,
who works full-time in a high-tech company, started coming in occasionally
"to do little science talks with the kids." They both talked regularly with the
two women who owned the center, offering their ideas for improvements:

> We always participated in their extracurricular things. They always did special
> holiday parties and events. We were always very, very involved with it and
> helped to shape some changes at the center. . . . There was no such thing [as a
> Parent Board], but we kind of created our own.

Having created close relationships with the owners and other parents
with children in the center, Pam and Joseph faced a difficult transition when
Jason started kindergarten in public school. To begin with, the hours were all
wrong: Jason's school started later and ended earlier than his parents' work.
The school bus picked him up at 8:35 a.m., and Pam could not wait that late
to leave for work. Luckily, her husband was able to negotiate flexible hours
with his company and could take Jason to the bus every morning. This made
it possible for Pam to leave the house before 8:00 and be at work no later than
8:30.

Difficulties in the early morning were just the tip of the iceberg. While
in kindergarten, Jason finished school at 11:30, but he was too young for the
after-school program. He did (by lottery) get into an "all-day" kindergarten
program, but it ran only until 3:00 p.m. A bus dropped him off at 3:30, with
no one home to pick him up. Joseph couldn't leave early because he had to
work late to make up for coming in late. Pam went to her employer and was
able to negotiate leaving work early two days a week. By the time she had
organized adequate coverage, there were five adults involved.

Summing up Jason's first year in public school, Pam calls it "total tur-moil," much harder than the years when he was in childcare:

> I call those the easy years, the years when you feel safe and secure. You drop
> your child off in the morning; you know he's fed, cared for, loved, playing with
> other children, safe most importantly, and you pick him up at the end of the
> day. And you're not worrying, did he get on the bus? Did he get on the bus to
> the after-school program? Did he have a problem with the nurse at school?
> Did he have a bad day and no one's talked to [him]? Those were the years
> when he had everything that I could have given him, even though I wasn't
> there. . . . And it was all in one place. Self-contained!

Pam trusted the owners of the center, the teachers, and the other parents.
Bestowing the ultimate compliment any childcare center can receive, Pam
comments, "If I had another child, I would entrust my child to these people."
For her, part of the experience of being a parent entering the public school
system was a loss of that trust. She no longer felt that the teachers were giving Jason everything that she could have. She was not certain of his safety,
especially when he started in an after-school program in first grade. His trip
from school to the after-school program was a time of daily anxiety.

Two different places, two sets of teachers, transportation without a parent—all these factors influence how parents of young children feel when considering whether to become involved in their child's elementary school.
Whatever the difficulties, though, Pam was not deterred from involvement.
During her son's kindergarten year, she started volunteering a little in his
classroom, but only infrequently:

> I was [involved]. But it was so stressful. I mean I was totally, totally stressed
> out that year. I wanted to be more involved with his class. . . . I really couldn't
> do that much. I would take vacation time every couple of months and go in
> and work with his class. . . . Because of my "special hours," I couldn't possibly
> participate in the things that I wanted to participate in.

In other words, because Pam had already negotiated with her supervisor to
leave early two afternoons a week to pick Jason up at the school bus, she did
not feel she could take time off to do what she really wanted to do—volunteer during the school day.

Pam's response was to do more at night: "I did all of the nighttime things that you could possibly do. I was a member of the PTO and on the School Council."[1] The School Council worked directly with the principal and was responsible for writing up school improvement plans for the following year. Just as the school year was coming to a close and her work with the Council was winding down, Pam heard about the formation of a new committee that interested her. It was to advise the town's school board on issues of space and building expansion. The town recognized that the population and thus the demand for full-day kindergarten were growing, and there was not sufficient classroom space for other grades. Pam knew that the resolution of these issues would affect her son's education for many years to come, especially in terms of class size and student/teacher ratios. She spoke to someone on the school board and indicated her interest. She was appointed to the Building Committee and by the second meeting had been elected as co-chair. When I asked how that happened, she modestly said, "I think I coughed or something, and they thought I volunteered!" In fact, she had just completed a year chairing a comparable committee for her biotech company, which was relocating its facilities, so she had a good deal of relevant experience.

While Jason was in first grade, Pam co-chaired the Building Committee. The other co-chair was from the school board, but the committee was supposed to be parent/community-driven. It turned out to be a huge undertaking. Pam put together a task force of about forty people and created a process in which everyone was heard. She wrote up all the input from engineers, current parents, former parents, and those living next to the school, and presented a plan to the school board, which unanimously approved it. Pam got high marks on her ability to listen, synthesize perspectives, and draft a plan acceptable to many members of her community.

Sometime during that year, Pam began to consider running for the school board. There were no women members or candidates, and Pam felt that the board should be more "demographically representative." She had learned a great deal from her experience on the Building Committee and had ideas about other issues. She explains what happened during her stint on the Building Committee:

> I worked very closely with the superintendent. And kind of from hanging around the school administration office a lot, you hear things, you see things, that just educate you about your educational system. Things that you just

wouldn't even think to question as a parent. Not bad things: just things that you don't know from reading the paper or volunteering at the school. Elections were coming up in April. I don't even know how I decided!

In fact, a number of consultations were involved in her decisions. First, Pam needed the support of her husband. Joseph thought she should run, but he had some conditions. Pam said,

> He made me promise that I would stop doing everything else: PTO, and read-ing programs, and everything else [she was also cultural coordinator, arranging plays and concerts and other cultural events for the school]. I would give up everything if I did this, and I agreed.

In addition, Pam consulted people from the Building Committee and the school board to see if they would support her, and got a positive response. Her parents had mixed feelings: "My parents were less than excited about it." Being longtime residents of the town, they had many friends there of differ-ing political persuasions. They did not want Pam to be in the middle of highly contested political issues, and they also were not sure that a woman—their daughter—should run for public office. Over time, they both got involved, even excited. Her father and her husband managed her sign loca-tions. Describing her father's role, she says, "When push came to shove, I couldn't get him away from the campaign—once I was affirmative with him and I decided that I was going to do this. You know, 'It bothers me that you're disappointed, but I am doing it.' And then he more than rose to the occa-sion!"

The campaign was demanding. Pam was working full-time and spend-ing every minute of non-work time researching the voting history of each precinct and going door to door asking for votes. She explains her approach:

> I had to do things that did not come instinctively to me at all. I had to ring doorbells and introduce myself. I grew up in the community with a Lithuanian name. There is a very big Lithuanian community in Stoneridge. And I am now married and have an Armenian name! So . . . I had to say my entire name every time I went to a door. My signs were like larger than life, because they had to say both names! No one would have recognized my married name. . . . Stoneridge is that kind of community; you'll always be what you were.

In the final days of the campaign, three other women threw their hats into the ring, making the race extremely tight. Pam tried to steer away from the controversial issue of standardized tests and to focus on broader themes of town growth and accountability in educational performance. She spent time campaigning in nursing homes and retirement communities, and she understood the feelings of the elderly, who had paid their taxes and did not want to face tax overrides while living on a fixed income. As a parent with a child in the school system, Pam also understood the needs of families like her own and their interest in improving the schools. She campaigned on quality education linked to fiscal responsibility. When all the votes were counted— much to her surprise—Pam won.

COMMUNITY INVOLVEMENT AND WORK REDESIGN

As Pam became more and more involved with school issues and school board politics, she was simultaneously rethinking and then reshaping her job. She began negotiations at BioSegunda by asking for more time with her son, and eventually gained the confidence to negotiate time for her community.

She first asked her direct supervisor if she could leave work early two days a week to pick up her son from the school bus at 3:30. She promised to maintain all her responsibilities if they would agree to give her a flexible schedule. She did not, in fact, reduce the number of hours she was working, rather, she worked four to five hours at home to complete her work. These negotiations were handled informally with her supervisor and did not require approval from the human resources department or the CEO. Although Pam was relieved that her supervisor was willing to allow such an arrangement, things did not always go smoothly. In order to be at the bus stop at 3:30, she needed to leave work by 3:00 at the latest, but sometimes pressures made that difficult. In the middle of a meeting, she would sometimes have to say:

> "I have to go. It's almost 3:00 and my kid's going to be standing at the corner." It was tough; it was tough. I rode home with my heart in my throat because many times I overstayed. . . . Many times I'd call my neighbor from the car phone. "It's 3:30, they're going to be getting off the bus in two minutes and I'm nowhere near home!" And she would keep him in her house and get him a snack.

Pam could not control traffic either. To meet all these contingencies, she had three levels of backup—her neighbor, her parents, and her sister, who teaches in the local high school. The flexible hours Pam arranged were helpful, but they did not entirely resolve her work-family conflicts.

The kindergarten year was one of tremendous stress and soul-searching for Pam. Then she started worrying about what she would do with Jason in the summer between kindergarten and first grade. She felt that she was not spending enough time with him. He was too young for full-day camp. The only summer program he was eligible for was a half-day program, and that would have entailed the same drop-off and pick-up problems. She and her husband agreed that, between her increasing school-related activities and her desire to spend more time with Jason, her full-time job was becoming impossible. They decided Pam would ask her supervisor for a one-year leave of absence:

> I had been building up to it the whole winter. . . . We had looked at our finances; we decided that I was going to take a year off. I was going to spend the entire summer with my son, and I was going to get involved in his school in first grade. I still hadn't really quite thought about the School Committee then. That was still further out on the horizon.

Pam did not breathe a word of this to anyone at work. She lived with that decision for several months before talking about it. She said, "I chickened out for the longest time. It was awful." Eventually she confided in a co-worker and found out that this co-worker had been contemplating something similar, for a different set of reasons. Pam gained courage about talking to her supervisor. When she finally went in, her supervisor responded, "Yeah, what's going on with you?" Pam said she had not been herself. Her supervisor, Jane Forrester, knew her very well and sensed this. When Pam spoke to Jane, she did not even make a specific proposal. She talked about how working full-time was too much for her. The whole year had been a struggle; she "always felt like [she] was in the wrong place at the wrong time"; her job was really important and her family was really important, and she wished she could do both but she couldn't. She did not mention a leave of absence or any other arrangement:

> I didn't propose anything. I honestly believed that they were going to say, "You know we already gave you flexibility to leave early while he was in kindergarten. You know Pam, come on, enough is enough," is what I expected them to say. My husband and I had it all resolved in our minds that I was taking time off, because it wasn't even going to be remotely possible that they were going to give me some other kind of hours.

Pam was taken aback when Jane asked, "How many hours do you want?" Pam asked if working part-time was really an option. Jane did not know the answer definitively, but from her own point of view, she was happy to consider it. Being a single mother with two school-age children, Jane was personally sensitive to the pressures facing working parents. Jane did say, "This is one that now has to go up the ladder," meaning that the human resources department and the president of the company would have to approve it. There were many issues, such as whether or not Pam would get benefits, whether she could keep her title, and whether she could still run her own division of the department. After the initial discussion, both Pam and Jane avoided the subject, which was without precedent in the company.

When the discussion resumed a few weeks later, Pam came back with a full-blown proposal. She wanted to work 20 hours a week—two full days and one half-day; she wanted to work certain days; she wanted to keep her title; she wanted to continue running her division; and she wanted all her benefits on a prorated basis. She would give out her e-mail address and home phone number, call in on the days she was out, and otherwise be accessible. She would come in on days that she wasn't supposed to be there if needed—no questions asked. The company accepted her entire proposal, except that she had to give up her life insurance and long-term disability insurance. One year into the plan, Pam says it is working very well. She has more time with Jason, more time to be active in her son's school, and time to be involved in the school system as a whole as an elected member of the school board.

Are there any negatives, I ask? Yes, and all on the work side of the equation. Pam says, "You have to kind of suck it up when promotions come by or opportunities for new projects." For the moment, this has not been a big problem; Pam is so committed to her current priorities at home and on the school board that she says it does not bother her. But this could change over time. There has also been some grumbling from her co-workers. People say they don't know her schedule, even though that was made public immediately and repeatedly, and she comes in for special meetings at the drop of a hat. Although her supervisor has been consistently supportive, other high-level managers have not been. Even Jane has received some complaints from her peers in the company, and the person she reports to, the CEO. Jane, however, is emphatic in saying that Pam's part-time schedule has not hindered the work in any way. Pam appreciates Jane's attitude:

Jane is so flexible. Like I said, she is very goal-oriented. If you get the job done, and you get it done well and to the best of your ability, it doesn't really matter so much to her when you are here, when you're not here. When she asks me to be here on a day that I'm not supposed to, I don't even have to question whether it's important. . . . I know it's important to her, and I do it. It's that simple.

Pam's relationship with her supervisor has been a key to her success in having more time for her family and her local school system while still meeting her work commitments. However, the continuing grumbling from co-workers and Jane's boss led to a third and final stage of restructuring Pam's work—a job share. Because of the volume of work in Pam's division and co-workers' discontent, Jane and Pam created a second part-time position to cope with the full-time load of Pam's responsibilities. After a year of Pam's "doing it all" on a half-time schedule, Jessica Bromfield was hired to work with Pam for 20 hours a week.[2] Although this is not a job share in the conventional sense (Pam is Jessica's supervisor, not her peer), they do share responsibility for the full range of tasks that were once entirely Pam's. Now there is always someone in the office to answer questions, attend meetings and delegate new projects. Pam and Jessica overlap one half-day a week to coordinate their work. One of the greatest benefits of this is that when Pam or Jessica is home, she can truly be at home—and not working—because her counterpart is in the office. From Jane's point of view, much has been gained for the company:

I feel it's working well. Sure there are times when I wish that I had full-time people, but one of them is here every day. I feel that I get more than I would if I just had one person. I have two bright people and two sets of ideas. Sometimes the scheduling is a little wild, but they work hard because they are so grateful to have the part-time option.

Although scheduling does present some challenges, the company is benefiting from this job share,[3] and Pam and Jessica are benefiting from the flexibility it provides for their lives inside and outside of work. By experimenting with the organization of work tasks and expanding flexible work practices, a "win-win" was achieved with significant benefits for Pam's community.

PARENT-TO-PARENT SUPPORT: FRIENDS AND ORGANIZERS

Not only did Pam need the support of her family and her workplace supervisor to become significantly involved in school issues, she also needed other parents. Her friend Abigail Gilcrest was part of the story of how she became an education leader in her community. Pam suggested that if I really wanted to understand her support system, I needed to talk to Abby.

On a Tuesday morning around 10:00 a.m., I arrive at Abby's home in the suburban outskirts of the city where Pam lives. Her kids are at school, and the house is quiet. Abby escorts me into her kitchen, a sunny room filled with plants, and very clean. The door of her refrigerator is covered with family photos and drawings by her children. While she makes a fresh pot of coffee, she explains that she is home that day because she works part-time. After years of trying to combine a full-time professional career in the healthcare industry and significant time with her children, she has cut back her work hours, just like Pam.

Pam and Abby met when their children were in preschool. Abby had recently moved to the town and was looking for a good childcare center for her oldest daughter. One center gave her Pam's name as a parent reference, and Pam highly recommended the center. When they met in person at a Mother's Day coffee, their connection was immediate. For the next three years, they were parents together in the same childcare center, and their children became friends too.

Pam's and Abby's relationship always combined friendship and community involvement. On the social side, the childcare center organized events for the families to get to know one another. They had holiday parties and outings, and the two couples got together on "PJ nights"— "You bring your child in their PJs [pajamas] and they watch a movie and have childcare providers there . . . you pay like ten dollars, and the parents get to go out." When Abby's second child was born, even though she had not known Pam a long time, she asked her to be the baby's godmother.

On the community side, Pam and Abby saw eye to eye on things that needed attention at Jason's and Chelsea's childcare center. Abby explains, "Pam would have been the ringleader—and I mean that in a nice way—by getting the parents together to meet with the two owners of the daycare about issues." Pam started a series of informational meetings for parents with the directors of the center as a forum for discussing issues such as mixed-age classrooms. Abby joined the newly formed parents' group and became involved in educational policy issues. Acknowledging the strength of the bonds formed at that time, Abby comments, "And I know the parents in that group, and the kids, are still all friends, which is really neat."

When Jason and Chelsea were ready for public school, they were assigned to the same kindergarten classroom. Both mothers tried to volunteer in the classroom, although Pam could not do it very often. Abby recalls that occasionally Pam would take a "sick day" from work and then go into the classroom to do a special project with the children around holiday time. Abby, who was working part-time at that point, was going to the classroom once a week to help with math and reading skills, and she kept Pam up to date.

Pam and Abby also attended PTO meetings together, always with mixed feelings. Abby sums up their mutual ambivalence:

> Some of the stuff is a waste of our time. I go with the view that everything we are doing should be geared toward the school. If the teachers need money for something, I don't even want to hear the details, they should get the money [from the school budget]. . . . Pam and I were at a couple of fundraisers that we were adamantly opposed to.

They were opposed to the PTO's raising money for a local charity when the school did not have enough money to make up for state budget cuts to the performing arts program. At a PTO meeting around that time, Abby and Pam heard the call for volunteers for a town-wide Building Committee. Abby recalls, "Pam told me at that meeting that she was interested, and I said to her, 'Well, good, you do it. I don't need to—I just need to know someone who is doing it so I can get my comments in!'" Abby supported Pam's work on the committee in two ways: acting as a sounding board—"just being there to listen"; and sharing with Pam the positive feedback she heard. Learning that people valued her work on the Building Committee was part of what led Pam to run for the school board. When Pam announced her decision to run, Abby's enthusiasm was instant. She and her husband quickly sent Pam the first donation to her campaign, along with a note saying, "We're totally supportive. We want to make this happen for you."

Abby joined Pam's campaign committee and became a key organizer. She chaired a huge fundraiser, including a bake sale. Pam was very grateful and later told her, "You got me the money I needed!" Abby also reviewed Pam's campaign materials, helped get ads, and held signs on election day. Now that the campaign is over and Pam is on the school board, Abby's role has changed, but it is still of mutual importance and benefit. Abby explains what she does now:

> I watch her [on cable]. I watch the School Committee meetings. And I call and keep her informed about the issues from my view. There is one school committee member who has got a child in special education, and he's really pushing the issue. But he has a very gruff way about him. . . . He was getting ignored a lot, but now he's got Pam kind of championing also. She's able to do it where she doesn't make people lose face, and that has worked well.

Abby sees herself as Pam's "special education advisor, without portfolio." Abby is well informed about special education because her second child, Sage, has a number of learning disabilities. To educate Pam on how special education works—and, often, does not work—Abby recently invited Pam to attend one of Sage's IEP (Individual Education Plan) meetings. Abby and her husband were touched that Pam took the time to come, and impressed with the way in which she contributed. Abby says:

> Pam came to the [IEP] meeting, and as only Pam can, she can't be quiet. . . . It was great . . . it's always nice to have someone else who isn't quite as emotionally involved. Because you never know what—not that the staff is mean or anything, but they tell you, "Well, your child can't do this and this and this." . . . So it's nice to have her to bounce stuff off of.

Pam and Abby share a deep friendship, providing personal support, exchanging town news or intimate worries in late-night phone calls. They get together one on one, with their spouses, and with their families. They share a special relationship around Sage, Abby's second daughter and Pam's godchild. There is a great deal of reciprocity in the relationship. They provide backup childcare for each other during the week if one has to stay late at work. They are partners in seeking solutions to work-family conflicts, in advocating for their children's educational needs, and in promoting quality education for all children in the city where they live.

IT TAKES A FAMILY, A NEIGHBORHOOD, AND A WORKPLACE TO CREATE A COMMUNITY CAREGIVER

Pam's ability to spend more time with her son *and* more time in her community did not happen by accident or simply because of the magnitude of her energy and commitment. Pam had the support of both her husband and her extended family to become an education activist and seek elective office. Joseph's support was evident in his willingness to share housework and childcare so Pam would have time to volunteer. Her parents and one of her sisters helped with the care of her son, and her parents became actively involved in her campaign for the school board. Their help with childcare gave her the time and flexibility to attend meetings, and their campaign work contributed to her becoming elected.

The willingness of Pam's employer to be flexible and innovative about her work arrangements was also critical to her increased community involvement. Pam had the full support—practical and emotional—of her immediate supervisor to change her hours and the way she fitted work into the rest of her life. She had the formal agreement of the human resources department and company president to adopt a part-time work schedule and ultimately a job share. The type of restructuring she negotiated with management met mixed responses from her co-workers, but the fact that she was allowed to reduce her hours and maintain her title and level of responsibility encouraged her to expand her commitments to both family and community.[4]

Pam also had the support of her friends and neighbors. Living in a small city where many people knew her made her feel comfortable asking for help. Her next-door neighbor provided backup childcare after school; other neighbors who are old friends from high school worked on her campaign, helping to raise funds and providing moral support. Many of Pam's acquaintances displayed campaign signs in their stores downtown or in their front yards. Her victory in the election reflects the strength of her ties to friends and neighbors, and her knowledge of their needs and opinions means she can effectively represent them on the school board.

Finally, Pam had the financial resources to go part-time and commit many hours to volunteer work. Although Pam's biotech company was facing an uncertain future during this period, her husband had a well-paying professional job and reasonable job security in a high-tech company. This "bottom-line" issue for Pam and Joseph provided the material basis for her increased community activism.

Many working parents who would like to get involved in their child's school or school system do not have all the factors Pam had working in their favor. Some are single parents, without partners with whom to share housework and childcare, or—even more important—the financial resources that would make part-time work feasible. Some are married low-wage workers who cannot afford even a slight reduction in the wages of either husband or wife. Some parents do not have employers willing to provide flexible hours, part-time positions, or job sharing. Some working parents live in urban or suburban communities where they do not know people and have few neighbors or friends to whom they could look for support. Finally, some working parents do not have extended family living nearby who can help with their children or support their volunteer work. However, by looking at how all these factors came together in Pam's life, we can begin to imagine—and perhaps even to plan for—socially supportive networks and work environments in which "community care work" can become more prevalent.

THE THIRD SHIFT: CARING FOR COMMUNITY IS NOT JUST "WOMEN'S WORK"

When I asked workers to draw maps of their work-family support networks, women had an easier time than men did. The idea of creating such a map seemed consonant with women's ideas about how they make the pieces of their lives fit, but this was not true for their male counterparts. Women also felt more comfortable introducing me to people in their family-community support networks, and more helpful in facilitating those contacts for further interviews. Whether they are working for pay or not, women see the process of forming connections with others as part of their "job." They are conscious and intentional about the size, membership, and reliability of the networks they are constructing.

The working fathers I met, by contrast, have limited involvement in caring for their families. When their children are young, some fathers drop them off and pick them up at childcare, feed and bathe them, and read bedtime stories. When their children are older, some fathers drop off and pick up at school, attend sports events, coach sports teams, or lead Scout troops. Most fathers go to parent-teacher conferences, some attend special school events, and two have participated in town-wide school committees. But the working mothers I met, and the wives of male biotech workers, do all that and much more. This is not to minimize the contributions that some fathers are making,[5] but to recognize that there are still significant gender differences in these working families, and that these are particularly visible when we look at differences in community involvement.

Mothers, whether they are stay-at-home moms or working, are the ones who are building and sustaining strong ties to community-based institutions. They not only do the pick-ups and drop-offs at childcare, but they are also the ones who research childcare providers. They are the ones to call a provider in the evening if there is a problem. They do the interpersonal work of fostering close ties between the center teachers or family daycare provider and their family. They organize parent pot-lucks and serve on parent committees. If there is a crisis at their childcare center or school, they attend special meetings. They seek out appropriate after-school activities and organize carpools or other transportation. They are mainly the ones who decide when it is time for the children to receive religious education, research different religious congregations near home, and choose one. They are the ones who volunteer to teach Sunday school. They keep family calendars in the kitchen and in their day planners. So while the composition of the workforce has changed, it is still women—within and outside the workplace—who are doing the hard work of building and maintaining the community-based support networks needed by their families.

The significant role of women in community care work has both a positive and a negative side. On the one hand, women in the past have made great contributions to their communities.[6] But is it fair to ask working women today, already doing two jobs, to do another unpaid job—a "third shift"? The effort launched by the contemporary women's movement to get men to share childcare and housework must now be expanded to the community sphere. The health and vitality of our community institutions are more important to the well-being of families than ever before. With traditional caregivers unavailable, we need both men and women to care for our communities and volunteer in community organizations.

RETHINKING GENDER ROLES AND WORKPLACE NORMS

There are several impediments to community involvement that are often go unnamed, though tacitly known. Volunteering is subject to gender stereotypes. The assumption persists that communicating with childcare providers, volunteering in schools, and being active in a religious institution is really "women's work." This persistent cultural message is internalized by working mothers and working fathers too. Every woman worker I talked with who has a school-age child expressed guilt, with a capital G, over not doing more in her child's school. The only exceptions are the few who have significantly changed their work lives—but hopefully *not* their career prospects by going from full-time to part-time work. I never heard this guilty feeling expressed by a father. In fact, fathers seemed to get "extra points" for coaching sports or volunteering otherwise in their communities. This "guilt differential" is a reflection of how well working mothers and fathers feel they are following or exceeding culturally sanctioned norms.

Family structure, and marital status in particular, also play a role in constraining community involvement. Some studies suggest that being married is associated with a higher rate of involvement, and being single with a lower rate.[7] It is striking that a number of two-parent families have consciously chosen to limit the wife's involvement in the paid labor force to permit community (particularly school) involvement, but this is not an option for single-parent families. This is not another indictment against single-parent families: most of the single parents I met do some form of volunteer work, mainly in religious institutions. Rather, it is a call for employers and community groups to be more sensitive to the special difficulties that single parents face in becoming actively involved in their communities. The presence of extended family members to help with childcare and other domestic chores can facilitate a single parent's involvement, but that is not enough. Community organizations themselves must consider special forms of outreach to single parents. For example, schools could institute home visiting programs (as nurses make home visits to mothers of newborns) in which teachers would come to a parent's home for an evening parent-teacher conference, if the parent chose.

The cultural norms that define community work as "women's work" are closely tied to traditional family structures, traditional gender roles, and the "separte spheres" model of male/female domains. Challenging these norms with new ideas about who is responsible for community work can bring more men into community volunteerism. Valuing the diversity of families and new family types can also expand the legion of community volunteers, especially fathers.[8] Making the responsibility for family care a community responsibility will diminish the public/private dichotomy in our lives *and* increase gender equality.

IMPEDIMENTS IN THE WORKPLACE

The current structure of paid employment, particularly full-time employment, is a problem for many working families. Survey research is somewhat contradictory on the issue of whether paid employment per se dampens women's involvement in volunteer activities.[9] However, my study of knowledge workers in the biotech industry shows that inflexible work schedules and limited leave and vacation policies negatively affect the level and scope of community involvement. Most of the parents who are active volunteers with childcare centers, schools, or faith-based institutions are women who have left the workforce, not entered the workforce to begin with, or significantly restructured their relationship to work through flexible hours, reduced hours, and/or job sharing. Those men who are involved in schools and after-school programs have not attempted, nor do they seem to feel compelled, to make any changes in their relationship to paid work. Thus, it is not surprising that they have lower involvement than women.

Additional impediments are tied to monetary rewards at work. Despite the passage of the Equal Pay Act more than 30 years ago, the gender gap in wages persists.[10] It is not surprising that the parent with the smaller paycheck—typically the mother—is the parent who "chooses" to go part-time so she can be more involved with family and community. When men's and women's wages reach parity, there will be no reason to assume that fathers should be the ones to work full-time and mothers should be the ones to work part-time and volunteer. A change in the wage structure can facilitate community involvement on the part of both men and women, and give working families real choices about who works how much for pay, and who volunteers how much.

Even current models of career advancement are incompatible with community involvement. The traditional model of professional career development is, not surprisingly, based on a male model. If one wants to advance in one's career, the expectation is that one will put in long hours and be physically present at the workplace as much as possible to demonstrate commitment. These expectations are particularly strong in the early stages of a career, frequently the time when people are also starting families and have a strong need and desire to spend time with young children. These requirements for professional success obviously do not include time for family care, and still less for community involvement. If, however, careers are restructured to follow the life course—as Phyllis Moen, former director of the Cornell Careers

Institute, has suggested[11]—then time invested in work can vary according to family needs, and time for community involvement can be an integral constituent of a fully realized career.

I have described these impediments in detail not to further discourage already weary and harried working parents, but rather to create a framework for thinking about solutions. For each impediment, there is a path toward change. In the closing chapter, I will explore these avenues for change and discuss how solutions must come not only from business and government, but also from community groups, religious organizations, and even working families themselves.

FROM COMMUNITY CONNECTIONS TO COMMUNITY INVOLVEMENT

This book and the stories that illustrate it lend weight to the idea that civil society is *not* in decline in 21st-century America. Communal and associational life is changing, to be sure, being reshaped by changes in the family, the nature of family care work, and the workplace. New forms of community involvement are taking shape in cities, suburban towns, and small rural communities; they look different from the PTA volunteerism of the 1950s, but they are no less important to the families involved. If we insist on narrow definitions of community involvement, we will miss seeing what community participation looks like today in the lives of "new economy" workers. It is true that only a small percent of the workers I met have engaged in "civic" affairs, defined as participating in a town, city, or state government body or in activities of the major electoral parties.[12] However, many biotech employees *are* involved in activities that link them to community-based services, programs, and institutions, and their experiences call for rethinking how "community involvement" is defined.

Pam Bodajian's story encompasses many forms of community participation, some recognized, some not. Like many working parents I met, she initially became involved with her community by meeting other parents who shared a common childcare provider. This expanded the number of people she knew in the city where she lived. These families began to socialize on the weekends, and some became active on the childcare center's Parents Committee. When Pam's son entered public school, this further expanded the number of parents she knew in her town. Like many parents with school-age children, early in her child's school years she attended back-to-school nights and parent-teacher conferences and occasionally helped out in the classroom. At that point, Pam wanted to do more. She joined the PTO but was dissatisfied with it. She eventually served on a committee initiated by her town's school board. This level of involvement is not the norm, and it required many kinds of community and workplace supports, as described.

Many working parents do not have the time or flexibility to run for a school board seat, but they are involved in the after-school activities of their children. These activities expand recreational opportunities for youth as well as strengthening ties between families. When parents become members of local YMCAs or send their children to gymnastics classes and music schools, they are supporting family-oriented programming in their communities. When they use senior centers, Meals on Wheels, and transportation services for the elderly, they are participating as clients in community–based programs. When they give a few hours of volunteer time to community programs and join their boards, they become involved in sustaining institutions necessary to build family-friendly communities. When working adults do things on their own—such as playing on town sports teams, joining health clubs, or taking adult education classes at community colleges—their participation supports community organizations.

In addition, more than half of the workers I interviewed are involved in faith-based institutions. They teach religious education classes and volunteer in activities aimed at helping the poor. They cook in homeless shelters, raise money for low-income youth to attend college, conduct clothing drives, and lead workshops for women transitioning from welfare into the workforce. There is also evidence of traditional forms of volunteer work and issue-based advocacy work. The families with adopted children from other countries serve as volunteers and/or board members of the adoption agencies that helped them become parents. A number of workers reported involvement with environmental issues—perhaps not surprising in a workforce with a large number of life scientists. These activities are evidence of an engaged citizenry, the building blocks of democracy.

This book makes visible the gamut of community-building activities that middle-class families engage in every day. These workers take as a given that the biotech industry is competitive and demanding, that their jobs and their company's future are uncertain, and that government is largely unresponsive to their needs. Because of these factors—or perhaps in spite of them—they have found a way to build networks of support and connection in their communities of residence and beyond that help their children grow and provide their families with some degree of security. It is this network of family and neighborhood connections that lays the foundation for institutional volunteerism and a healthy civil society.

CHAPTER TEN

FROM BACKYARDS TO CORPORATE BOARDROOMS AND BEYOND

ALL STAKEHOLDERS WELCOME

Our economic system pits people against each other in competition for educational opportunities, jobs, and promotions. The ethos of "work hard and play by the rules" is a deeply ingrained norm that promotes individual performance, merit, and rewards. Family life is extremely privatized. We are taught that the care of family members is the responsibility of each family on its own, and that it is shameful to ask for help with routine family care, no less serious family problems. Those in our society who do receive public support for family care are stigmatized. Community poses a fundamental challenge to the individualism and competition underlying our work lives, and it presents a radical alternative to the privatization of our family lives: it promotes a collective approach to problem solving and an expanded concept of social responsibility. Community is based on the idea that what we share exceeds what divides us, and that we gain more by working together than alone.

One way to alter the approach to work-family problems is to restructure the relationship between paid work and unpaid work in our society. If we want to raise healthy families, have a vibrant economy, and a strong civil society, then we have to stop privileging paid work over everything else. Of course, almost all of us have to earn a living; we cannot take time off to volunteer whenever we want to. This is especially true for people in low-wage occupations, who often have to work overtime or hold more than one job to support their families. But we must make it possible for more working people to engage in activities outside their paid jobs that will benefit their families and communities. We cannot expect work-family conflicts to disappear if we make changes only inside workplaces, and we certainly cannot ask families to do more themselves without changing the status quo. If we are going to give community greater priority in the overall design of our lives, we must redesign the other pieces.

The beginning of a movement for greater community engagement is already evident. We can see it in the involvement of Julie Taylor on the Parents Committee of her childcare center and in her church; in Mike Hallowell's leadership of after-school programs in his neighborhood; and in the work of Pamela Bodajian in her son's school and her city's school board. These workers are rethinking the place of paid work in their lives and making time for community. Working families know in their gut that they cannot "make it" on their own. They are agents for change in their own right, but they need institutional partners.

Working families need the resources and the commitment of players in the private, public, and nonprofit sectors to join in a concerted effort to strengthen families and facilitate community involvement. By learning more about the initiatives that have been started in these sectors, we can highlight the kinds of practices needed to resolve work-family problems and promote a stronger civil society. We can also imagine what our society might look like if these policies and practices were adopted by other institutions and widely available to working families.

WHAT CAN BUSINESS DO?

The role of employers in the resolution of work-family problems has been a subject of intense debate over the past 20 years, and three basic positions have emerged. Some groups, particularly labor unions, believe that employers should shoulder the major share of responsibility for addressing and paying for work-family programs for their employees. A number of unions have argued for an expansion of traditional wage and benefit packages to include work-family issues. Since the founding of the Coalition of Labor Union Women in 1973, an increasing number of unions have put forward an agenda in contract negotiations that includes support for childcare, elder care, family leave, and other family-friendly benefits.[1] Not all unions have incorporated work-family issues into their collective bargaining, but those with many women members and top leadership committed to family care needs have begun to make a difference.[2] Over the past decade, labor-management partnerships dedicated to work-family solutions have grown, and as a result,

unionized workplaces are more likely to have access to family-friendly benefits than nonunion workplaces.[3]

Another point of view has been espoused by a small but influential group
of large corporations who have voluntarily established family-friendly policies. These companies see themselves as "corporate champions" of innovative
programs for family care. They believe there are compelling reasons to offer
work-family benefits—an argument often called "the business case"—which
will aid employees and give employers a competitive advantage in their
industry. By providing family-friendly benefits they are better able to recruit
and retain qualified workers, as well as to enhance employees' commitment
and loyalty. There is an unstated quid pro quo in this scenario: employees get
support with their family care needs and employers have access to their
employees when and where they need them. These employers believe that the
"return on investment" in family-friendly policies is evident in the high
morale and low turnover of their workforce.

A third position is that the private sector is not responsible for these
"non-work" benefits. These employers are disinclined or opposed to offering
family-friendly benefits because they are often costly and may negatively
affect the bottom line. This position has been articulated most strongly by
small businesses and their trade associations and lobbyists. However, the
resistance of these employers is based on more than firm size and cost. Most
are philosophically opposed to government mandates and government regu-
lation of the private sector. This type of opposition was evident during the
eight years of Congressional debate that ultimately led to the passage of the
Family and Medical Leave Act (FMLA) in 1993. The proposed bill was
vociferously criticized by a number of employer trade associations, including
some businesses that already were voluntarily providing maternity leave and
other types of family leave.[4] They insisted the FMLA would negatively affect
their business performance—a point that was eventually disproved[5]—and,
more important, that they did not want the federal government telling them
how to run their businesses.

This three-way debate within the private sector has shaped the environment in which family-friendly policies have been tried and implemented.
The approach of family friendly employers has progressed from a human
resources/benefits package approach, based in a limited understanding of
family care, to a deeper examination of workplace culture and work organization. Issues of time and flexibility have received increased attention, and

some companies have renamed work-family policies to work-life policies to address a broader group of workers throughout the life course. However, these employers still represent a minority, and some workers have greater access to these benefits than others.[6]

I think we are ready for a new phase in the expansion of work-family policies that will require employers to look outside the walls of the workplace and into the community. Some work-family experts suggest that community is already an "emerging focus" among those companies that provide work-family benefits.[7] I would argue that if it is emerging, it is still in its infancy, and in many companies the idea has not even been born.[8] A community focus needs more attention from many more companies. Employers need to address community on several levels: to assess and respond to the needs of the community (or communities) in which their offices and plants are located; to make investments in the family support services on which their employees rely, usually located where employees live; and to encourage employee involvement in community volunteer work.

SOME BUSINESSES MAKE GOOD NEIGHBORS

There are several terms used to describe a positive and interactive relationship between companies and other institutions in our society. Sometimes these employers are called "neighbors of choice," meaning that "the corporation acknowledges the interdependence of its profitability and community well-being."[9] Some employers subscribe to the practice of "corporate social responsibility" or "corporate citizenship." These terms cover a broad array of policies, from the use of environmentally friendly materials in the production process, to fair and equitable treatment of employees, to annual contributions to the United Way. Businesses for Social Responsibility (BSR), the largest membership group of companies dedicated to this philosophy, states that corporate social responsibility entails "achieving commercial success in ways that honor ethical values and respects people, communities and the natural environment."[10] Some companies make only a superficial attempt to embrace this philosophy, offering an occasional business decision that promotes a positive public image. However, corporate citizenship is increasingly viewed as a comprehensive set of policies and decisions that are implemented not only because they will enhance the bottom line, but also because the company is genuinely committed to taking responsibility for the well-being of its employees, the communities in which they are located, and even the "global community." At this time, only a small percentage of U.S. companies put this more comprehensive definition of the term into practice, but it is a growing percentage.[11] These companies represent the vanguard of a nascent movement that could transform the relationship between corporate America and the cities, suburbs, and rural towns in which Americans live and work.

What kinds of things are socially responsible employers doing? Their focus has primarily been on environmental issues and labor standards.[12] Dumping contaminated or toxic waste into local water supplies, or depleting precious raw materials such as trees, is no longer acceptable policy. Recycling paper products and conserving energy in offices and production facilities is accepted practice. Many of these issues were ignored in the past and are now the focus of intentional policy making. These companies link their strategies for corporate growth to the goal of a sustainable development. Companies that are good corporate citizens also provide good jobs with decent wages and benefits, safe working conditions, and hiring policies based on nondiscrimination.

Unfortunately, being a good corporate citizen is not usually linked to a family-friendly agenda.[13] The list of "100 Best Companies" put out annually by *Working Mother* magazine provides a look at the "best practices" of companies who are committed to meeting the needs of working families. In a recent survey, the categories included are Child Care, Flexibility, Leave for New Parents, Work/Life (including elder care resource and referral, employee training, and job satisfaction), and Advancing Women.[14] There is no mention of community involvement or community investment. In a feature article shadowing four women who work at Merck, a company that has been on the "100 Best" list since 1986, these working moms complain about "overwork." They say work takes too much time from their families; they do not mention time for their communities.

Most companies do not see "community relations" projects—such as investing in community programs—as linked to work-family policies, but there are a few notable exceptions. Probably the oldest and most enduring is the American Business Collaboration for Quality Dependent Care (ABC). In 1992, a group of 22 large corporations partnered with service providers in the communities where they are located to provide quality childcare for their own employees and other community residents.[15] Their efforts have had a positive impact on the quality and the supply of childcare in 65 communities across the country. Over a ten-year period, ABC has funded more than 1,500 childcare and elder care projects and set up training programs for the community-based providers. In answering the question, "Why have competitive companies come together under the same umbrella?" ABC explains that its goal is to "ensure that programs meet the dual needs of employers and communities by building upon the existing dependent care infrastructure."[16] This is an important point for other employers to learn: there is an "existing infrastructure" in every community, for childcare, elder care, and other types of family support. Building the size, quality, and durability of that infrastructure enables employers to invest in something that will be there for current employees and generations to come.

LABOR/MANAGEMENT PARTNERSHIPS FOR WORKING FAMILIES

Businesses do not always have to go it alone to invest in community resources. They can join with other employers, and they can partner with labor unions. An initiative that addresses the family care needs of employees through a consortium of employers *and* a union is the 1199/Employer Child Care Fund. This consortium was formed in 1989 through the collective bargaining agreement between the 1199 Health and Human Services Employees Union and 17 healthcare employers in New York City. They established a childcare fund by putting in 0.5 percent of the gross payroll of each employer. By 1998, employers were contributing $8.5 million a year. By 2002, the number of employers involved had grown to 184 and the number of healthcare workers covered was about 45,000, about half of whom had children under age seventeen. By building a partnership linked to community organizations—from the YMCA to the Harlem School for the Arts—the consortium is able to provide a range of childcare options for all ages. They serve 7,000 children through many types of community-based services: early education centers for preschool children; school-age childcare programs; summer and holiday camps; a workforce skill development program for teenagers; and a Cultural Arts Center.[17]

One of the most far-reaching examples of a labor-management partnership focused on investing in community programs is an initiative by the United Automobile Workers (UAW) union and the Ford Motor Company. This partnership established a number of Family Service and Learning Centers in communities around the country where Ford has major production facilities. The first center was opened in the fall of 2001, and 31 centers were expected to be operational by mid-2003. The centers are multipurpose. The childcare component includes 24-hour center-based care designed to meet the needs of employees who work all three shifts, as well as licensed family childcare homes. The family service component includes the provision of after-school programs and summer camps, as well as classes and support groups for adults of all ages. Finally, the volunteer network—perhaps the most innovative aspect of the centers—is creating an intergenerational network of Ford employees who want to volunteer in community-based programs. Working closely with the United Way in each community, the network is designed to provide trained volunteers. Their activities include outreach to seniors and children who are home alone after school, as well as supporting established local and national programs. The assumption underlying the creation of these centers is simple yet bold: "Workers who feel good about their families and communities live happier more productive lives. It's our hope that every member of the Ford Motor Company family will have the opportunity to do just that."[18]

Both the 1199/multi-employer childcare fund and the UAW/Ford centers provide a window into what might be possible in the future if companies—both union and nonunion—expand their concept of the work-family needs to include the needs of the communities where they do business. The consortium model is a particularly important strategy for small and medium-sized firms that do not have the resources of large companies such as Ford. Pooling resources with other employers in their industry, city, or region makes new initiatives possible; as the ABC motto states, "To do together what none of us can afford to do alone."

It is important to recognize that labor unions are prime movers in the examples described, and that some of the most innovative programs are a result of labor-management partnerships, not just employer initiatives. Traditionally, unions focused on better wages and a small range of benefits like pensions, sick leave, and vacation. Since the mid–1980s, more and more unions have been negotiating for family-friendly benefits, especially childcare and paid leave. Now we are beginning to see unions look outside the walls of the workplace and seek partnerships with community programs that can support working families. This is an important new direction and, if developed further, will give energy to a labor movement struggling for members and a distinctive agenda.

PROMOTING COMMUNITY INVOLVEMENT

It is difficult to estimate how many companies actively promote volunteerism among their employees, and there are few scientifically valid surveys of firms available on this topic. For example, the Points of Light Foundation surveyed almost 2,800 companies and found that the proportion of employers that had incorporated an employee volunteer program went from 19 percent in 1992 to 48 percent in 1999.[19] The companies surveyed report several approaches to facilitate employee volunteerism: offering volunteer events on company premises (57 percent); providing community organizations with a list of employees who want to volunteer and describing their areas of skill and expertise (32 percent); providing release time for volunteering (21 percent); and encouraging retirees to volunteer (21 percent).[20]

The approach that holds the greatest promise for giving employees a meaningful volunteer experience and benefiting community-based programs is volunteer release time. Companies offer this option in one of three ways: as "work release," which allows employees to volunteer during regular business hours, in effect a short-term paid leave; as "matching time," which requires employees to match volunteer time during business hours with equal time during non-business hours; or as "social service leave," which gives employees paid time off to volunteer full-time for up to a year on a project of benefit to a community group approved by the company.

Companies provide these kinds of release time for different reasons. For some, it simply generates good will between the company and the community where they are located. On the business side, companies may want to develop new customers or clients, and community volunteer work may provide a way to expand their market base.[21] Offering meaningful volunteer experiences may also help companies retain valued employees and make it less likely that they will relocate. Employee volunteers may have work skills that are valuable to community groups and develop new skills transferable back to the workplace.

Those companies that offer employees paid time off for volunteer work sometimes do so on an informal, case-by-case basis, but increasingly it is part of a company's strategic approach to community investment.[22] The Center on Corporate Citizenship at Boston College, an international business membership group that helps companies strengthen their community relationships and investments, has published a report with examples of what it considers "best practices" on the part of employers who promote employee volunteerism.[23] Some of the companies they highlight include Lenscrafter, Inc., which extended its expertise in eye care to the needy, providing free optical services to the poor in the United States and developing countries; Time Warner, Inc., which established an adult literacy program linking employee tutors and adult learners; and Target Stores, which has participated in

"Family Matters," a Points of Light Foundation program that brings Target employees and their family members together in community service projects.

Although employers cannot be expected to solve all the social problems that beset communities today, they do have the resources to be a part of the solution. Corporate involvement in community life can make a difference both to the communities where they are located, and to the communities where their employees live and volunteer, by strengthening the capacity of local orgnizations to respond to the needs of working families. It may even have implications for how the United States treats other nations. In a speech on corporate social responsibility, Mary Robinson, the U.N. High Commissioner for Human Rights, said: "With globalization has come the growing sense that we are all responsible in some way for helping protect the rights of our neighbors, whether they live on the next street or on the next continent."[24] In essence, if an employer wants to be a "neighbor of choice," it should start in its own backyard.

WHAT CAN GOVERNMENT DO?

Long gone are the days of the New Deal and the Great Society, when federal government intervention was welcomed as a way to heal great social ills and lead us toward economic prosperity, equal opportunity, and civil rights. In the 1960s and 1970s, the Democratic Party stood for a strong activist central government, while the Republican Party argued for smaller federal government and more latitude ("rights") for the states. Since the election of Ronald Reagan in the early 1980s, there has been a growing convergence of views between the two major electoral parties in favor of a "smaller is better" model of federal government. When Bill Clinton was elected in 1992, after 12 years of Republican control of the executive branch, the calls for a leaner federal government came from the new Democratic president. The Clinton administration set out to "reinvent government," a way of downsizing the federal workforce without saying that the anti-big-government forces had won. During this period, the process of taking federal dollars and reallocating them in block grants to the states reached an unprecedented level. "Devolution," as this transfer is often called, was increased by welfare reform legislation passed in 1996. Known as the Personal Responsibility and Work Opportunity Act, this statute institutionalized a smaller federal role in providing support for the poor.

As America begins the 21st century with a president favoring an even smaller, less intrusive federal government, one can only wonder what role government will play in meeting the challenges faced by working families. So far, the distribution of block grants to states for childcare, transitional assistance to needy families, job training, and so on has not been entirely harmful. Many advocates for poor families and children have been wary of devolution—and with good reason[25]—however, block grants to the states have created opportunities for local voices and local concerns that would not have existed if the funds were controlled only from Washington, D.C. Community groups and the social service programs of faith-based organizations often have a better understanding of local problems and local conditions than "the feds." If given a seat at the table, these groups can often be a powerful force for change and for ensuring that community needs and perspectives are taken into account, and government data gathering can amplify their message.[26]

Although it is impossible to describe and assess in any comprehensive way the work of government agencies at the federal, state, and local levels, a brief look at a few initiatives directed at work, family, and community issues is useful for understanding the potential of the public sector as a partner in multi-sector problem solving.

GOVERNMENT AS MODEL EMPLOYER: BUILDING COMMUNITY CAPACITY

The U.S. Air Force has developed an innovative approach to work-family issues. Rather than a set of "family-friendly benefits" delivered at the workplace, the Air Force has instituted "Family Support Centers" for delivering human service programs to military families in their communities of residence. The Air Force method rests on four key components embodied in the acronym CARE, which stands for Creating Opportunities, Activating Interest, Removing Barriers, and Enabling Community Connections.[27] The Air Force develops each center by bringing together local stakeholders in community forums in which participants identify problems and design solutions. This process of discussion not only leads to formal partnerships linking community agencies and Air Force families, but also builds the informal social connections that make the service delivery system sustainable over time. The Air Force has moved away from a traditional human service model that views families as "clients" and "beneficiaries." Instead, they see Air Force families as "partners" and "assets."

The applicability of this model to the civilian population is difficult to calculate. Many people who work for the Air Force live on Air Force bases, and this spatial convergence of workplace and community of residence is not the case for most U.S. workers in other industries.[28] The Air Force is also different from most private-sector firms in that all enlisted personnel belong to a unit and have a "unit leader" who is responsible for their work and personal wellbeing. There is no question that the Air Force is a unique employer, requiring an unusual level of commitment from its workforce, yet its employees express many of the same feelings as civilian employees do.[29] They feel that "there are not enough hours in the day," given the time pressures they experience at work.

In the Air Force, the boundary between work and community is weak, but at the same time, reliance on community resources is strong. The importance of the Air Force's innovation lies less in the creation of specific centers in specific locations, and more in their community-oriented approach for addressing work-family issues—an approach worth consideration by civilian employers. Their strategy centers on building partnerships with community-based agencies, building the capacity of community groups, and recognizing that both informal relationships and formal networks are needed to build a sense of community for employees. If more employers adopted this approach, the strength and responsiveness of community organizations would increase, and working families outside the military could benefit.

PUBLIC POLICIES FOR WORKING FAMILIES

There are few public policies in America that support the new realities of work and family. In this, the United States currently lags far behind many other advanced industrial nations that have provided family policies. There is paid maternity leave in all but three industrialized countries around the world—the United States being one of them.[30] In France, there is a universal system of high-quality preschool programs which three- to five-year-olds can attend at minimal cost, and preschool teachers are well trained and well paid.[31] Many European countries provide child allowance programs that essentially pay parents to stay home and care for young children. Why the United States has not developed public policies of this kind has been the subject of considerable debate, and most agree that it's not about the money. Rather, there is a profound devaluing of family care work in general, and motherhood in particular, despite the rhetoric about "family values," that has contributed to a weak and impoverished set of family policies.[32] In addition, the needs of the elderly have been privileged over the needs of children, creating an unfortunate sense of competition between two groups that need care.[33]

Most of the existing government programs that support work and family are geared to low-income families or those transitioning from welfare to work. These are often referred to as "targeted" programs, and families must meet strict income eligibility requirements.[34] There is no question that these families need and deserve support, but there are several problems with developing family policies along these lines. First of all, children's needs are not a function of their parents' incomes, so developing public policies for children should begin with the needs of the child. Second, there are many middle-class families with moderate incomes who need public support but are not eligible because their households earn "too much." Finally, public support for targeted programs is limited. Like it or not, many middle-class families resent public policies for the poor at least in part because they themselves are struggling. On the other hand, they support "universal" programs like Social Security and Medicare that serve a broader cross-section of Americans suggesting that a universal approach to work-family issues would appeal to many Americans.[35]

One of the only public policies to address the needs of low-income *and* middle-class working families is the Family and Medical Leave Act (FMLA) of 1993, although it is far from universal. At present, the FMLA covers only 55 percent of the workforce because it includes only employers with 50 or more employees, and it has eligibility requirements for employees related to length of service and number of hours worked. The statute provides a job-protected leave of up to 12 weeks a year to care for a newborn or adopted child, to care for a parent, child, or spouse who is seriously ill, or for one's own serious illness. Approximately 3 million workers a year utilize this policy, and without it they would be forced to make excruciating choices between keeping their jobs and caring for their families.[36] The eligibility restrictions in the statute, however, limit its potential to support working families. Not only are 45 percent of all workers ineligible; in addition, the leave is unpaid. Only workers with some savings and/or a working spouse with a decent job can take advantage of this policy. A bipartisan commission that studied the impact of the FMLA on employers and employees found that 11 percent of workers who took unpaid leaves under the Act were forced to go on welfare as a result of lack of wage replacement.[37]

This commission, for which I served as executive director, recommended to Congress that an expansion of FMLA be considered, including some system of wage replacement.[38] There has been little action at the federal level, but there are now efforts underway in more than 20 states to introduce some vehicle for funding parental leave.[39] These efforts have been gaining ground, and in the summer of 2002 the state of California passed the first paid leave law.[40] It is likely that state statutes will precede and create momentum for more comprehensive federal legislation in the future.[41]

Although the FMLA creates leave for serious illness and other family crises, there are many other reasons why workers need job-protected leaves. For example, working parents need time off to get involved with their children's schools. To address this need, Patty Murray, senators from Washington state and a former PTA president, proposed the "Time Out for Schools Act." Unfortunately, it was not passed by Congress. A few states have tried to address these issues, too. For example, in 1998, the Massachusetts legislature passed the "Small Necessities Leave Act," which grants eligible employees a total of 24 hours per year of unpaid leave from work to participate in the school activities of a child, or to take a child or elderly relative for routine medical appointments.[42] Although the number of hours is small and the leave is unpaid, this is an example of state law expanding the parameters of federal legislation and setting promising new directions for public policy.

THE BULLY PULPIT: FROM RHETORIC TO ACTION

It is not often that we hear an in-depth analysis from our national leaders about the needs of working families, the health of our communities, or the importance of volunteerism. We may see a working mother or a community activist given a seat of honor at the president's State of the Union address, but that happens only once a year. Occasionally, a more considered and less publicity-conscious initiative is made based on a long-term strategy for action. For example, in 1997, President Clinton convened a "Summit for America's Future" in Philadelphia. It was both bipartisan and multi-sector, bringing together former presidents, 30 governors, 100 mayors, and business, religious, and community leaders. President Clinton and other speakers challenged America to take better care of its children and to teach children the importance of community service. To continue the spirit and intentions of the summit, a nonprofit organization was founded, called America's Promise, initially chaired by Colin Powell. This organization mobilized almost 500 national groups and more than 550 state and community partners to develop innovative programs for youth around "five promises." These include children's right to ongoing, caring relationships with adults, safe places to go during nonschool hours, quality healthcare, and quality education. The fifth promise, the "opportunity to give back through community service," emphasizes our collective responsibility for society. The summit is an example of elected leaders using the bully pulpit to advance the idea that care of children is a civic obligation of all sectors of society, not a private family matter, and to make plans to translate rhetoric into reality.

An important voice for working families at the state level is the bipartisan National Governor's Association (NGA). Much of its work is housed in the NGA Center for Best Practices, which gives technical assistance and policy guidance to governors and their staffs. The NGA is well known for its work on the importance of good early-childhood programs and on expanding the supply of childcare for working families. It was among the first to publicize brain research documenting the connections between the experiences children have during their first three years and their capacity for lifelong learning. More recently, the NGA Center has taken on issues of elder care, calling for new home- and community-based approaches to the complex financial and social issues involved in long-term care.[43] The NGA was also a leader in recognizing that devolution of funds and program responsibility from the federal to the state level required states to establish stronger relationships between state and county governments and local communities. They have been a strong voice in favor of the "outcomes movement," which promotes state-community collaboration to measure the impact of public programs on people's lives at the local level.[44]

An organization on the municipal level, paralleling the NGA, is the U.S. Conference of Mayors (USCM).[45] The USCM has played an important role in spurring local governments to better serve working families and community needs, focusing on the most at-risk and vulnerable residents of large urban areas. They have worked extensively on issues such as welfare reform, hunger, homelessness, affordable housing, and job training. In the past, they have given little attention to the needs of middle-class working families and workplace or community programs that could support their employment and family care needs. However, a new partnership between the USCM and the American Farm Land Trust holds promise for linking issues of poor and working poor families with those of middle-class families. These two groups are promoting "smart growth," a strategy for economic development that will benefit a broad cross-section of families living in cities, suburbs, and rural areas. As the partnership explains, "Assuring that people of all economic classes can afford attractive housing near good jobs is a cardinal principle of smart growth."[46]

In sum, there is a major contradiction shaping initiatives for working families by the public sector. On the one hand, there is little public support for the federal government to play a strong activist role or for increasing federal taxes to pay for social programs. On the other hand, there seems to be support for more activist government at the state and local level, and reforms to coordinate agencies with common missions.[47] There is a move toward weaving separately funded programs into better-coordinated systems, which not only is a more effective way to spend public dollars but also allows local communities to have input into how tax dollars are spent. It seems highly unlikely that the federal government alone can create universal programs for childcare and other community-based services that working families need.[48] Yet there are models developing at the state and local levels in which public dollars are merged with private and philanthropic dollars, and the results have helped working families.[49] The ability of government to assist working families will be different than it was during the 1930s and 1940s, with a smaller, weaker role for federal government and a larger, stronger role for state and local government. This may in the long run strengthen community voices, and it may be the best way to foster partnerships between government agencies and other sectors to improve the quality of family and community life.

WHAT CAN COMMUNITY-BASED ORGANIZATIONS DO?

Community-based nonprofit groups have always struggled for material and human resources. Full-time staff are often underpaid and volunteer labor inadequate. The capacity of community-based organizations is critically important to solving work-family issues, but our society is not doing enough to help these organizations grow and develop.

WORKING FAMILIES AND COMMUNITY SERVICES

Many community organizations provide social support services at the local level on which working families depend every day. They provide early care and education programs that serve young children from infancy until formal school begins. They run a variety of after-school programs through organizations like YMCA and YWCA, the Boys and Girls Clubs, Cub Scouts and Boy Scouts, or Brownies and Girl Scouts, to name just a few. They organize and sponsor sports teams and other extracurricular activities, including community service projects.[50] Faith–based institutions across many denominations also provide preschool and after-school programs, adult education classes, and social service programs. These organizations provide elder care services—community-based senior centers that provide meals, transportation, and adult daycare for those who are still living independently, home healthcare, visiting nurse services, and long-term care for the frail elderly. They include community health clinics and other preventive health programs (broadly defined) that deal with substance abuse, domestic violence, AIDS, hunger, and homelessness. There are also many nonprofit organizations in every community that work as advocates for children and families, education reform, high-quality, accessible healthcare, equitable workplaces, and a living wage.[51] These types of organizations provide educational materials and data to the public to increase awareness and set agendas for new public policies and grassroots action.[52]

Taken together, these organizations provide a set of family support services critical to working families. There are public dollars built into every city and town budget to build and maintain roads, bridges, and public transportation systems, but there is no comparable budget category for the family support infrastructure that is just as necessary in enabling employees to go to work. There are elements of this infrastructure, but most are unrecognized and underfunded. For example, most cities and some smaller towns have a childcare resource and referral (CCR&R) organization, which connects parents who need childcare with providers through individually tailored referrals. They offer consumer education to assist parents in picking quality childcare, and information on accessing government subsidies. They collect data on childcare supply and demand in particular communities to identify service gaps to be addressed. They provide training and resources to childcare providers to help them get licensed. These nonprofit agencies, serving 1.65 million working families a year, provide a critical set of services to working families, yet they constantly struggle for the funds to stay afloat.[53] These community-based organizations needed regular public and private investment if they are to provide some critically needed links between families and community support programs.

REDESIGNING COMMUNITIES

Some community-based organizations promote community planning and design processes that link the quality of our physical environment to our social environment. Using the skills of urban/community planners and architects, they work to strengthen community through attention to the physical layout of our cities, towns, and suburbs, and even our homes. These issues do not fall neatly into the baskets of private sector, public sector, and nonprofit (or NGO) sector. They require partnerships across multiple sectors, as well as citizen input to reassess our built environment and envision how it might be changed. For example, the tragic events of 9/11 catalyzed the formation of a group to develop plans for a new World Trade Center. The Civic Alliance to Rebuild Downtown New York, a coalition of community and urban planning groups gathered over 5,000 people to discuss plans that seek to balance citizen and commercial interests in an aesthetically pleasing design.[54] Another cross-sector group engaged in this process of reassessment and envisioning, sponsored by the Boston Society of Architects, is called "A Civic Initiative for a Livable New England." This project takes a regional approach both in defining problems and in seeking solutions. It has brought together a wide variety of citizens and community groups in public dialogues and "charrettes" to "redefine the process for growth and development in New England." Although primarily concerned with how economic development affects the environment, housing, zoning and transportation, it is developing a multi-issue agenda, and there may be opportunities to include work-family issues in its community context.[55]

Another response, based in innovative approaches to real estate development, is called "the new urbanism." The Congress on New Urbanism (CNU), founded in 1993, conducts public education on the problems associated with urban sprawl and the benefits of "smart growth" development strategies.[56] Its members are not against growth per se, but they believe that intentional planning can preserve open space, improve air and water quality, and bring our homes, workplaces, and services closer together. By redesigning urban environments, CNU hopes to entice suburbanites back into the cities. One such experiment is Celebration, Florida, one of a number of planned communities around the country that is struggling against the pressures of suburban growth and the erosion of urban neighborliness.[57] The planners have tried to re-create some of the older forms of residential neighborhoods by designing spaces that are "people-friendly" and less reliant on cars, and that have a range of services and institutions within walking distance of people's homes. New urbanism is against single-use facilities that provide only housing, retail, or office space. Buildings in their communities are designed for mixed use and a seamless integration of housing (including mixed-income and elder housing), workplaces, and stores. These communities have neighborhood centers with open civic spaces and pedestrian-friendly sidewalk grids. If a community can pass the "Popsicle test"—an eight-year-old should be able to walk from home to a store to buy a Popsicle without encountering fast-moving cars—then new urbanism has been realized.

"LIVEABLE" COMMUNITIES: AN ALTERNATIVE TO "NIMBYISM"

There are a number of community-based organizations whose work goes beyond a particular set of family support services, or a particular economic development and planning project, to provide a vision of what communities of residence should look like and feel like. These groups work to enhance the overall quality of life in communities by creating definitions of what it means to reside in a "livable" community. This term is somewhat vague, but it is becoming more concrete through initiatives in particular communities. A proliferation of research and action in the 1990s occurred to measure the quality of community life.[58] Some of these action-research projects are collectively referred to as the "Outcomes Movement" or the "Livability Movement." Whether or not these efforts constitute a movement is unclear, but the following examples—one at the state level, and one at the city level—give some idea of their purpose and goals.[59]

Oregon was the first state to get involved in monitoring and measuring the quality of community life. In 1989, it created an independent state planning and oversight agency called the Oregon Progress Board (OPB). This board, using citizen input, defined three strategic goals for the state to meet by 2010. They wanted to have the best-educated and best-prepared workforce, to preserve the state's natural environment, and to have an internationally oriented economy with good jobs paying high wages. The OPB released its first benchmarks in 1991 and set high but specific targets for the state. Benchmarking is intended not only to measure progress in terms of budget dollars expended or numbers of citizens served, but also to assess how programs are affecting the quality of people's lives. The state has a 20-year strategic plan called "Oregon Shines." The focus of the plan has expanded beyond economic development and the environment to a vision that includes health, caregiving, and citizen engagement.[60] With the current economic downturn, the OPB has encountered many difficulties meeting their benchmarking goals. Their mixed success to date is acknowledged in their recent report to the Oregon Legislative Assembly, as is their continued commitment to good jobs, excellent schools, and "engaged, caring and safe communities."[61]

In 1997, the mayor and city council of Tucson, Arizona, began a process of community participation to develop a vision of what the citizens of Tucson wanted in their community. They developed a set of indicators to help both city officials and citizens measure whether their community was becoming more "livable." Their efforts rely on a model of sustainable development that is gaining ground in both the United States and many less developed nations. Most of the resources of the Livable Tucson Program go into surveying citizens, holding workshops and other educational forums on the concept of sustainability, and creating a library of resources on sustainability and information about what other communities are doing. Their emphasis on taking time to bring many voices into the planning process shows their commitment to grassroots democracy.

These are just two examples of what is being done by community-based nonprofits to challenge and change serious deficits in community life at the local level. They provide models that can be replicated in other communities according to local needs and conditions. They are significant in several respects. First, they provide an alternative position to the NIMBYists (an acronym for "not in my backyard") who use the claim of community rights to exclude people they don't want in their communities, and to thwart public facilities they don't wanted sited in their "backyards."[62] NIMBYism reproduces class and racial segregation, and it often results in the poorest communities bearing social burdens that should be distributed across all communities. Second, the livability movement promotes communities built on inclusion and equity, linking issues that are often dealt with separately, and players who often work separately. It creates public conversations about what kinds of places people want to live in and actively solicits citizens' input. These local policy-action organizations can empower working families to achieve their long-term economic and community goals.

WHAT CAN WORKING FAMILIES THEMSELVES DO?

As the stories of the biotech workers I met demonstrate, many working families—with their first-hand experience of daily conflict between holding a job and caring for their loved ones—are already trying to resolve work-family problems. They are building community–based support networks and volunteering in community institutions, trying to shift private burdens into the public realm.

ON THE HOME FRONT

Some families are experimenting with ways to restructure paid work, family care, and housework on a more egalitarian basis. A shift in gender relations is needed to allow both men and women the time for involvement in family care. One pioneering group that is working to create this shift is the Third Path Institute, based in Philadelphia. Jessica DeGroot, its founding director, is promoting the practice of "shared care," defined as a family arrangement in which "parents maximize the use of parental care while staying actively engaged with work. They accomplish this by reconfiguring work around the needs of family and sharing in their involvement with work, home and children."[63] Third Path tries to catalyze change by holding workshops and training sessions, and by publicizing the experiences of couples that practice the "shared care" philosophy. DeGroot advocates a model of marriage in which men and women participate as equally as possible in the number of hours of paid work each does and the numbers of hours of unpaid caregiving work. While the vision of Third Path is large in scale, their approach is currently based on work with small groups of families, limiting their impact to individual households and leaving discussions with employers to individual negotiations. Although there is little mention of shared community volunteerism, the Third Path model is clearly applicable to an equitable approach to community care work. Third Path hopes eventually to have an impact on organizations outside the family, as well as on public policy; their perspective is urgently needed in these less privatized arenas.

The issue of who does what work in the family has a spatial component as well, and the physical configuration of the home is also a site ripe for change.[64] Historians have shown how profoundly our domestic spaces affect the sexual division of labor in the family, and some scholars in architectural history, like Delores Hayden, have made suggestions for home redesign, promoting collective approaches to childcare, housework, and cooking.[65] Others have formed community-based food cooperatives and co-housing units that share dining and kitchen facilities among several families. These are pioneering, bold experiments to make family life less privatized and family care a collective responsibility.

THE POTENTIAL OF PARENT POWER

Despite the prevailing belief that family problems are a private matter, some parents have begun to join together and organize around work-family issues. Labor union members have done this by encouraging their bargaining committees to add family-friendly benefits to contract negotiations. Other parents have worked around specific issues such as childcare. Parents United for Child Care (PUCC) is a grassroots organization that advocates affordable, high-quality childcare in communities of the Boston area and in the Massachusetts state legislature. One of the most important aspects of their work is training parents to become active leaders on early care and education and school-age childcare issues. They teach parents how to speak publicly, write opinion pieces for their local newspapers, and build networks. Their founding director, Elaine Fersh, strongly argues that the empowerment of parents is a key to the creation of a better-funded and coordinated childcare system.

Another single-issue group that has grown dramatically since its founding is Mothers Against Drunk Driving (MADD). These parents have used their grief and frustration to mount one of the most effective public education campaigns in the country. Their activism has improved the chance that the public can travel without being endangered and that young adults are taught responsible alcohol use.

An organization of parents that operates with a multi-issue agenda is the National Parenting Association (NPA). Founded in 1993, the NPA "is working to make parenting a higher priority in our private lives and on the public agenda." The organization works on stopping gun violence, building high-quality schools and after-school programs, and promoting television programs that send positive messages to kids. The rationale for this organization is presented in *The War against Parents*, by Sylvia Hewlett, the NPA executive director, and Cornell West. The authors state: "Contemporary moms and dads are trapped between the escalating requirements of their children, who need more resources (in terms of time and money) for longer periods of time than ever before, and the signals of a culture that is increasingly scornful of efforts expended on others."[66] NPA believes that way out of this trap begins by building partnerships with parent groups across the country at the community level. For example, the Council for Civic Parent Leadership, a group based in Minnesota, connects parents with the programs that serve their families and children. They hold local town meetings for parents, survey parents about what their children need, and bring the responses to state and local officials.

POWER IN NUMBERS, ROOTS IN COMMUNITY

What these organizations have in common is their belief that working families themselves, and parents in particular, can make a difference in solving some of the toughest issues facing our businesses and communities today. Historically, unions have been a vehicle for working parents to make their voices known, and this tradition has been expanded in recent years by bringing issues of family care into the bargaining process. What is new is the effort of working parents to create family-based civic organizations to reform schools, improve childcare, and make communities safer. The need for these organizations to flourish has been argued by the sociologist and political scientist Theda Skocpol in *The Missing Middle*, where she calls for "a process of connecting centers of family activity across communities and states into a nationwide civic association of, by, for and the vast majority of America's families."[67] Although the emergence of a national association of families may still be years away, it will grow only if and when working families themselves begin to build strong connections at the local level—in their communities—around issues of common concern. As the stories in this book show, that process has begun to take shape in cities, suburbs, and rural towns around issues of pre-school care, after-school programs, education, and engagement in faith-based institutions. If employers and others actively support this kind of involvement, then a national association of families based in communities across America may soon become a reality.

CHAPTER ELEVEN

THE CALL OF COMMUNITY

VOCATION AND AVOCATION

The changes that have accompanied the burgeoning of the "new economy" have challenged the old employer-employee contract and have deprived working families of job security. In these uncertain times, the ability of communities to support family needs is more urgent than ever. The ability of workers to form a sense of community, in many parts of their lives, is critical. The workers interviewed for this book understand this at an intuitive level. When I asked them "Is it important to you to be part of a community?" almost to a person they answered "Yes!" Listening to their stories, I began to understand community as the connective tissue that makes their work and family lives possible. It is the invisible framework that connects families to the people and institutions that provide care, services, and support. And like human tissue, it is living and changing. In fact, it is the ability of a community—however one defines the term—to adapt to change that makes it durable.

COMMUNITY IN THEIR OWN TERMS

When asked to share a recent experience that gave them the feeling of belonging to a community, workers gave an interesting range of examples.

Colleen McCarthy, an associate scientist from BioPrima, said, "At a recent town election, I realized that I personally knew several of the candidates running for the various offices. I grew up in [a city] and never even knew my neighbors, so seeing so many names of people I knew on the ballot sheet really gave me the sense that within our town we all knew each other and we're all connected."

Hank Bartholet, a production worker from BioSegunda, said, "I did a ride sponsored by a local hog [Harley Davidson] chapter to raise money for the Muscular Dystrophy Association."

Beth Finley, a senior scientist and manager from BioSegunda, said, "My father-in-law's wake and funeral last year [gave me a feeling of belonging to a community]. Many of my friends from church came for support, even though they didn't know my father-in-law."

Julie Taylor, a postdoctoral research scientist at BioPrima, said, "One of the September 11th victims was a resident of our town, and the father of two children, one a kindergartener, in the school . . . my children attend. In his memory, the kids and the teachers organized a walk to raise money for a group called Seeds of Peace (which brings together teenagers of nations in conflict)—remarkably *all* of the kids joined the walk—over 500!—and the school community came together with a memorial ceremony after."

It is striking that all these experiences involve feelings of being connected to others—around a cause or charity, at a time of loss, or in an act of citizenship—in an emotionally intense way. It is also significant that three out of four of these experiences took place in the communities where people live.

When I asked why these experiences were important to them, their responses eloquently explained the meaning of community in their lives.

Colleen said, "Because my children are just forming friendships now and their world is centered around our town. I think it's important for them to be part of a community. . . . And I need to know the children, parents, coaches, teachers, and priest that my children will be associating with."

Hank said, "The camaraderie and the feeling that I am making a difference make [community] important."

Beth said, "To have close relationships, be able to serve one another and be served."

Julie said, "[There are] many reasons . . . a support group for me, knowing that I have a group of people that I can rely on to help out when I need help—especially given that my extended family is far away—and who I can help out in return. For my children—a 'known' group of kids to play with and hang out—whose families I know and who share similar values. Having groups of people in different contexts—church, scouts, school—that I can work with cooperatively to make our town a good place to live."

These reasons speak to both the personal and social value of community involvement. Community connections have a practical value. They are a method for coping with the daily challenges of working and family care, linking individual children and their parents to relatives, to other families, and to non-family members who care for them. These relationships taken together are seen as the basis for advancing a larger social good, such as creating "good places to live." Community involvement also has a transcendent, nonmaterial value, giving an expanded meaning, even purpose, to our lives. It can make a difference to an organization or cause outside the family where there are unmet needs. A number of workers, like Julie and Colleen, spoke of community as important for their children, not just themselves or other adults. The idea of "reciprocity"—to serve and be served—is also a strong theme. Working parents need to be there for one another. Communities need to provide programs to support working families, *and* working families need to volunteer time to keep these institutions strong and responsive.

As this book has documented, some workers I met are engaged with their communities, while others only aspire to be. Their lack of involvement is *not* an individual or private problem. I have argued that it has multiple sources. Part of the problem is in the workplace, where employer policies are inflexible and inadequate to meet the needs of a workforce that is no longer composed only of male breadwinners without family responsibilities. Another problem is a stalled gender revolution in the family; the paid work roles of men and women have changed dramatically, but their roles inside the family have shifted only slightly. A third part is the design of our communities, the spatial separation between workplace and home, and the fact that many cities and suburbs do not have the services and infrastructure to accommodate the needs of working families. There is still little recognition that most adults are out of their community most of the day, and most children and elders in their community all day. A series of institutional obstacles impede broader engagement in the communities where we live and in the community organizations we value. Conversely, a series of institutional changes could facilitate community involvement that would, in turn, strengthen the civil society.

RESPONDING TO THE CALL OF COMMUNITY

A movement to build livable, family-friendly communities is within our grasp. It will take the work of many individuals and organizations developing a common vision and mobilizing the resources to turn that vision into reality. Given the changing realities of work and family, it will require new thinking for this movement to take root. In particular, we need to rethink the relationship of paid to unpaid work. The current model of economic and social provision revolves around paid work. It is the most valued kind of work, taking up most of the hours in a day, for most adults. But this cannot continue if we are also serious about family well-being and community health. We need to create a new set of priorities that challenges the dominance of paid work in our lives, and values unpaid family and community care work. Receiving support through established residence in the community where one rents or owns a home could provide a new paradigm for the provision of health insurance and other benefits to support families. The terms of eligibility would need to be defined, just as they are for employer-provided benefits. But it is well worth considering a new method for distributing work-family benefits given the fragility of jobs in the "new economy," and the ups and downs of our global economic system. What will it take to move in this direction?

A NEW TOWN COMMONS

In colonial New England, settlers built new villages around a shared public space, the town commons. The buildings around the commons were central to community life—a town hall, an inn for travelers, a church, a school, and the houses of town leaders and ordinary citizens. This space was a crossroads for local residents. They exchanged information, sold and traded goods, and conversed about the issues of the day. In contemporary America, we lack comparable public spaces and comparable conversations among our neighbors, friends, teachers, and clergy. Neither a church spire nor a band shell is required; however, we do need public meeting places that are accessible and comfortable for all kinds of families, regardless of race, ethnicity, or income. We need to leave our individual cars and kitchens and create spaces where families can go for information, resources, and support. Some might say we could do this over the Internet, but there is no substitute for meeting face to face; the goal is to create family-to-family ties and strong community institutions.

Within these spaces, we could conduct local conversations about the needs of working families, share unsolved problems, and seek innovative solutions. We need these conversations to challenge deeply entrenched cultural messages that family problems are private problems. We need them because there are so many meanings of community, and because many kinds of community care work are invisible and undervalued. We need conversations to open up ideas about what role community can play in people's lives. We need forums and groups to help us be more intentional in creating the practical and material aspects of community—what I have called the "social infrastructure" of work-family support. We also need to discuss the existential or spiritual aspect of community. By acknowledging our longing for human connections that can sustain us not just day to day, but year to year, we can build social relationships that give our lives purpose and meaning.

This kind of space would make it easier for families who are newcomers in a community to meet other families in similar work situations with children of similar age. Such a meeting place would have made it easier for Colleen McCarthy to find a play group for her preschool sons when she moved into a new suburban community, and to meet people from the two churches where she was considering membership. Helen Rafferty might have found other working mothers in her suburb more easily, and been spared the indignity of feeling like an oddity in a town with many stay-at-home moms. Malika Shaheed might have found a comfortable place to meet other Afro-Caribbean parents and discuss ways to bring an appreciation of the cultural traditions of their homeland into the public schools. Jessica Bromfield's in-laws might have met other retirees concerned about the new development plans for their town and encouraged them to get involved in the battle to preserve open space.

EMPLOYERS WHO INVEST IN COMMUNITY

We need employers to break out of conventional corporate thinking. Currently, family-friendly benefits are delivered through the human resource department, and contributions to the community are made through the United Way and the community relations department—but never the twain shall meet. A "family-friendly" workplace is a necessary but not sufficient part of creating a healthy social environment for children and families. We need employers who are both family-friendly and community-friendly, willing to link these two objectives across the labor-management divide. Only one employer I have heard about—an HMO linked to a hospital—created a job called "director of work, family and community." Unfortunately, when the economy took a downturn and layoffs were required to offset losses, the position was eliminated.[1] Companies need people whose job it is to link work-family policies, community investment, and community involvement at an operations and strategic level.

We also need employers to provide release time or other leave policies for community work in schools, childcare centers, senior centers, and faith-based institutions, just a few of the organizations crying out for volunteers. Workers should not be penalized for doing unpaid work that benefits their community;

they should be rewarded, because this work benefits everyone. There are release-time programs in a small number of companies, but most of them are for volunteering once a year in a charity chosen by the employer. What is needed is quite different. Employees need regular time, over multiple years, to build long-term relationships with the community-based groups that help them care for their family. Giving employees time to volunteer, in the organizations they choose, would do more to strengthen families and communities than many of the existing forms of volunteer work. An approach to employee volunteerism that maximizes employee choice should be a hallmark of family-friendly employers.

Imagine how different Lily Huang's life would be if her employer recognized and valued her desire to volunteer in her son's preschool during the work day. She could have become a regular presence at the center and not had to worry about how her performance as a research scientist was being evaluated, or bring work home. Many of the workers I met agonized about whether even to mention to their supervisor their desire to leave work early, or to have a five-hour day once a month. These kinds of options should be presented to employees when they are hired. Employees with many hours of community volunteerism should be given bonuses or other forms of employee recognition, not penalized and stigmatized.

We also need more employers willing to form partnerships with community groups and invest in their programs, through both financial and human capital. Adapting a Family Support Center model, such as the Air Force has, is one option. Establishing an employer consortium to expand childcare programs, such as 1199 and healthcare employers in New York have done, is another. Nurturing cross-institutional partnerships and building the capacity of community organizations are at the heart of what employers can do to address work-family issues.

Some employers might prefer a looser partnership with community programs—one that could vary in location, focus, and services depending on the needs of the workforce, or that might simply involve a regular financial commitment. For example, BioSegunda could support Mike Hallowell's work coaching sports teams and leading Cub Scout troops with a monetary contribution. In this case, when Biosegunda moved it's facilities out of the city where Mike lives it could have made a contribution to community groups providing after-school programs. BioSegunda could have become a "community-friendly employer" rather than an employer whose relocation made it difficult for Mike to sustain his community volunteer work.

LABOR UNIONS WILLING TO EXPERIMENT

Although labor unions only represent 9 percent of the private sector workforce today—and there are no unionized workplaces in biotech that I know of—the influence of collective bargaining agreements often goes beyond the particular workplace in which it is negotiated. Nonunion employers in biotech can learn from unionized employers in other sectors. The efforts of some labor-management partnerships, such as that of the UAW and Ford, described in the previous chapter, are truly innovative because they are based on building partnerships with community programs and encouraging employee volunteerism.

Some union members may say that their local should stick to negotiating wages, health insurance, and other traditional benefits, especially during an economic recession, but that will be to the detriment of the future of the labor movement. I think we need more union leaders to insist on the importance of work-family benefits, and to look beyond the workplace and into the community to resolve work-family issues. We need more union leaders willing to rethink concepts like seniority in light of work-family pressures, and recognize that it is often the families of young workers with young children who are the most vulnerable to layoffs, rather than workers with many years of seniority.[2] We need new strategies for organizing the unorganized that understand the importance of building a sense of community and friendship among workers, both inside and outside the workplace.[3] Those unions willing to work with employers in seeking community partners can set in motion a new approach to collective bargaining—an approach that benefits working families and strengthens the capacity of community programs—that can be replicated by union and nonunion employers alike.

GOVERNMENT TAKING A UNIVERSAL APPROACH

We need public policies that support working families, regardless of whether these families have been deemed "at risk" by some government agency. Too many of our public policies are limited to those seeking or holding low-wage jobs. There is no question that these families have the greatest financial need, but many middle-class families are also "at risk" and in need of supportive public policies. Even families making at or above the median income may find it difficult to pay for childcare and mortgages, to save for college and for retirement. We need to meld the "targeted" approach and the "universal" approach so that the greater economic needs of low-income families are addressed while not ignoring the needs of moderate-income families. Work-family problems are cross-class issues affecting the majority of American families today. Our public policies must be realigned to address that reality.

Despite the flaws in Social Security and Medicare and their need for reform, we do have universal programs for elders and retirees. Now we need comparable programs to support children from birth to adulthood, such as universal preschool and all-day kindergarten. We need programs to support adults during the years they are gaining skills, forming families, and raising children. Some may say it's too expensive to create universal work-family public policies, but I think that the costs of not providing them may be higher.[4]

For example, we need to expand the Family and Medical Leave Act to all workers regardless of firm size. Those who work for small employers give birth and have seriously ill parents just as often as those who work for large employers. The family care needs of workers cannot be measured by the size of their company. It should be possible to accommodate the difficulties of small employers through tax incentives or other supplements. We also need public policies for paying workers while they are on leave. Again, the difficulties of small firms need to be taken into account and a system set in place that is not administratively cumbersome. The Temporary Disability Insurance system, which covers workers affected by nonjob-related disabilities including pregnancy-related disability, has been operating "in the black" in five states, is one model for funding paid leave. The Unemployment Insurance system, historically used to cover workers during employer-initiated layoffs, is another. These two existing systems, developed at different periods in history, would need to be adapted if used for this purpose, but the fundamental approach to paid leave—which has been missing in many debates on this issue—is a cost-sharing model.[6] Everyone who benefits from paid family and medical leave—workers, employers, and government—should pay into a common fund. This is both workable and fair, and could be piloted in a small number of states to test its impact on the business environment and on working families.

This kind of approach could work in the biotech industry and would address many business concerns. On the one hand, many biotech firms are not in a position to fund paid leaves by themselves, especially those in a start-up mode or still without commercially viable products, like BioPrima. This means they need institutional partners to share the cost and enable them to remain competitive. On the other hand, given the youth of the biotech workforce and the number of workers with children, biotech companies regardless of size ought to have a paid leave benefit. If BioPrima, for example, were to join a consortium with other small biotech firms to provide paid leave, not only would they be helping the workers they employ with young families, they would also be giving talented workers a reason to stay with their firm.

A host of new public policy initiatives are needed, but I want to address one in particular. I think Congress should pass a "Community Service Leave Act" that parallels the FMLA. Any employee who needs leave time to volunteer in a childcare center, senior center, school, faith-based institution, or adoption agency (just to name a few) could get a job-protected leave to do so, up to a reasonable number of days a year. This type of leave is not for the one-shot "Community Cares Day." It would facilitate a regular monthly donation of volunteer time to a group that is important to each employee and his or her family. This kind of policy initiative would not tinker at the margins of work-family conflict, but would dramatically restructure the options that working families have for family time and community volunteerism. Again, one can imagine the difference such a public policy could make to the life of a worker like Julie Taylor, who struggles to get time off to volunteer in her daughter's elementary school.

Finally, when the government promotes volunteerism, programs such as AmeriCorps should be developed and expanded. These programs are *not* a substitute for government involvement in strengthening communities—as proposed by former president George H.W. Bush and his "Thousand Points of Light" initiative—but rather a significant supplement to the programs of an activist government. We cannot allow the social safety net that poor families rely on to unravel, and then send in some volunteers to feed the hungry. Rather, we must think about what families and communities need to build a sustainable future, and then make it possible for citizens to take time off work, or pause in their careers, to help make that a reality.

TOOLS FOR BUILDING LIVABLE COMMUNITIES

We need to put tools in the hands of community-based groups and families to help them envision the kind of communities they want to live in, develop strategies to create them, and give them methods to set goals and measure their progress. Developing a tool like the Family-Friendly Community Index would enable families and community groups to recognize existing community assets and set benchmarks for developing livable communities. The work of compiling information can engage the institutional partners needed to make changes and assess outcomes. It can also facilitate a community-based dialogue in which affordable housing, better public transportation, and more open space become part of the same agenda as flexible work schedules, high-quality childcare, and more after-school programs—not competing agendas.

When I first interviewed Malika Shaheed, a single mother of three and an Afro-Caribbean immigrant, she went on at some length about how difficult her life had been until she had been able to buy a used car. She explained that there was no public transportation that connected the school where she dropped off her older two sons and the childcare center where she dropped off her youngest son. She either had to do a good deal of walking—difficult with a four-year-old—or take a cab to another bus line, which she could ill afford. In her experience, the "hard" issue of a better transportation system and the "soft" issue of delivering children to school and childcare were inextricably bound. By listening to the experiences of parents like Malika, we can begin to make connections between issues that are often unconnected, and redesign communities according to the needs of working families.

CROSS-SECTOR SOLUTIONS

The extent of work-family problems is so great that it is unfair to expect any one sector in our society to solve them.[7] The experiences of the biotech workers in this book—and the fact that so many of the services and supports they use to manage work and family cluster around their communities of residence—suggest that workplace and community supports need to be coordinated. These spheres are now quite bifurcated, but they could be effectively woven into a single system. We need to rethink whether work-family resources should be delivered only through the workplace via a benefits model tied to individual employees, or, alternatively, whether they could be delivered through a partnership among businesses, government, and community institutions. In this model, work-family supports would be based on the household and family needs of employees, not just one individual paid by his or her company. Employers would give support to the community programs their employees use, and local government—with federal and/or state dollars—would be charged with building an integrated service delivery system. Community groups, both secular and religious, could contribute their knowledge about how to meet family needs in culturally appropriate ways, with sensitivity to differences in child-rearing approaches, food preferences, and language differences. This is an approach to resolving work-family conflict that has rarely been tried, but I believe it is the kind of collaboration between public, private and non-profit organizations worthy of experimentation.

Partnerships are needed not only to develop better ways of delivering family-friendly benefits, but also to address the social problems that underlie work-family conflict. For example, the mismatch between work hours and school hours, a problem raised by almost every biotech worker I spoke with who has school-age children, is not a problem employers alone can solve. Some employers may be willing to give some employees a reduced work day schedule so they can be home with their kids after school, but this is not a systemic solution, and it would not be economically viable for low-income families. What is needed is a partnership that brings together employers, school principals and superintendents, and community organizations that provide after-school programs to devise a better system, a system that could vary according to the needs of particular businesses, schools, and communities.

A variety of solutions might emerge from such a cross-sector conversation. For example, what if Barbara Feldman's employer, BioTertia, were willing to shorten her work day one day a week, and one day a week her daughter's elementary school and her son's preschool would stay open until 5:45. In this scenario, the need to be flexible would not fall solely on Barbara's employer. Each institution would make a change to accommodate the needs of families with young children: Barbara, a single mother who worries about the safety of her children in the afternoon, could be assured of being home with her kids one afternoon a week, and on another day her children would have structured activities at school until she could pick them up.

In another scenario, BioTertia might work with the school system in the large city where they are located and expand after-school programs based in the elementary schools. Perhaps some neighborhood sports teams could use school facilities for their activities and get extra help from staff when parents are not available. If there were not enough money for many staff positions, maybe the Council on Aging in that city could organize some regular senior volunteers for the after-school programs.

These are just two examples of solutions that might be possible if more than one institution were grappling with a problem. Cross-sector solutions are effective because they keep costs affordable for each participating institution, while at the same time they develop systemic approaches that go beyond what any single stakeholder institution could accomplish.

"THE HEARTLESS WORLD"

It is time to bring issues of community building and civil society into the daily struggle of working and caring for our families. The framework used to develop work-family policies in the past was very dualistic. Employees were either "at work" or "at home," as if there were no significant larger context of social relationships and institutions to which we all belong. But it is the very embeddedness—or lack of embeddedness—of families and individuals in a community of some type that may determine whether anyone can success-fully negotiate the current work-family system. Similarly, it may be the very connections—or lack of them—of businesses to the communities where they are located that determine their success in recruiting and retaining workers, in selling their products, and in having the confidence of their shareholders. And it may be the connections—or lack of them—that public sector agencies and elected officials have to real people living in real communities that deter-mines whether ordinary citizens feel that government is representing the interests of working families rather than special interests.

It is time to ask ourselves some hard questions. If we value our families so much, why do we spend so little time with them? For some families, long work hours are the only way to pay for basic necessities. But why do other famlies seek bigger homes and multiple cars, if these require more hours at work? Many share the feeling that what is most fulfilling in life comes from our family and community relationships, yet these receive little priority in terms of our time. In this post-September 11th world, we hear that people's priorities are changing. A recent study found that 41 percent of working adults reported changing their work and life priorities since the 9/11 attacks.[8] They say they want to put less emphasis on work and more on family. But where is community in this scenario? Are the events of September 11, 2001 simply going to lead us back into the private world of our own families, and reify the home as "the haven from the heartless world"?

For me, and I think for many other working Americans, "the heartless world" is the world without community—the world where people are isolated and separated and share no common purpose. It is possible to dismantle the roadblocks to community involvement, whether they are at work or at home. Employers can redesign benefits so that family care becomes a shared respon-sibility that utilizes and builds community resources. We can redesign the spaces where we live and the way our work is organized. We can rethink the place of paid work in our lives, a challenging task that may be unsettling at first, but ultimately rewarding. It is still a question of both hearts and minds. If we change our minds—the frameworks we use for thinking about work and family—then we can follow where our hearts are leading, toward others, at work, at home, and in our communities.

APPENDIX ONE

RESEARCH DESIGN AND METHODOLOGY

Field work for this book began in the spring of 1997 and concluded in the spring of 2001. The book is based primarily on participant observation and interviews with 40 workers and their families. More than 100 interviews were conducted for the project, using the following process:

SITE SELECTION AND FIRM ORIENTATION

Three biotechnology firms were selected based on diversity of size, their interest in work-family issues, and their willingness to provide access to their workforce. In the first several months of the project, interviews were conducted with CEOs, human resource directors, and other senior managers about company history and formal work-family policies. During this time, direct observation of workers and the work process at each site was also completed, including scientific research work and the manufacture of biotechnology products.

MAPPING INTERVIEWS

Thirty-three mapping interviews were conducted with workers in three biotechnology firms. Those interviewed included research scientists, senior and middle managers, and production workers. These interviews covered daily work-family routines, allocation of family care and housework tasks, dependent care arrangements, criteria for choosing a community of residence, experiences in communities of residence with services and neighbors, and involvement—formal and informal—in community groups. Interviewees were asked to draw "maps" of their work-family support systems and "communities" as they defined them. The maps were used to elicit further information about the kind of support being provided, the extent of reciprocity in key relationships, and other issues. At the end of the interview, each biotech worker was asked to identify the two or three most important people on his or her map, and whether he or she would feel comfortable facilitating contact between the interviewer and those persons for a follow-up interview. Additional interviews with workers were conducted without the mapping component.

FAMILY-COMMUNITY NETWORK INTERVIEWS

Using a "snowball sampling" method facilitated by introductions from workers who completed mapping interviews, follow-up interviews were conducted with 35 individuals, including spouses, extended family members, non-relative childcare providers, including preschool and after-school care, community service professionals, and clergy of several denominations. The focus of these interviews was to learn about the relationship between workers and their key support people from another person's perspective, and to gain further insights into how each biotech worker constructs a work-family support system and sense of community. (No worker offered to facilitate an interview with a school-based professional.)

PARTICIPANT OBSERVATION

This included spending time in the homes of biotech employees, and/or their extended family members, at different times of day and evening, as well as attending a variety of sports and community events and religious services at the invitation of biotech employees. It included site visits to the childcare programs used by some families. It also included observation of the workday of some workers who completed mapping interviews and/or tours of their work areas.

COMMUNITY PROFILES AND SECONDARY DATA ANALYSIS

Data were gathered from state agencies, town websites, and the Massachusetts Municipal Association on the 36 home communities (34 in Massachusetts, 2 in other states) of 40 families. Utilizing secondary data analysis, community profiles were compiled, including population figures by gender, age, and race, figures on employment and wages, percentage of home ownership, value of homes, cost of rent, availability of recreational and sports facilities, houses of worship, library facilities, councils on aging, and public and private family care services and programs.

APPENDIX TWO

CONSTRUCTING A FAMILY-FRIENDLY COMMUNITY INDEX

The Family-Friendly Community Index is constructed by collecting town-level data on the ten social indicators listed below, and each indicator is composed of several sub-indicators to enhance the assessment. A weight is assigned to each sub-indicator, with the entire set totaling 100 points. For each indicator, the maximum number of points is assigned to the "best in class" city/town, and zero points to the "worst in class," and communities in between are allocated points proportionally. Additionally, using data on statewide averages, the state of Massachusetts was allocated points for each sub-indicator using the same system. This provides a way to assess the communities of the families studied in comparison with other communities in the state (the two communities outside Massachusetts are not included). Communities are then ranked, including the state as a whole, to evaluate the accessibility, quality, and affordability of community-based programs available to families, and the extent of public investment in both services and infrastructure.

The following weights are assigned to each indicator and sub-indicator:

1. Economic self-sufficiency and housing affordability = 20 points
    (a) Percent of families earning above $50,000/yr. = 5
    (b) Housing affordability gap = 7
    (c) Percent of families with children under 18 living at 100% of poverty = 4
    (d) Percent of families with college education = 4

2. Preschool childcare = 10 points
   (a) Availability = 3
   (b) Quality = 4
   (c) Affordability = 3

3. School-age childcare = 10 points
   (a) Availability = 3
   (b) Affordability = 4
   (c) Transportation = 3

4. Quality of education = 12 points
   (a) Per-pupil expenditures = 4
   (b) Advanced or proficient 4th grade MCAS English scores = 2
   (c) Advanced or proficient 4th grade MCAS Math scores = 2
   (d) Advanced or proficient 10th grade MCAS English scores = 2
   (e) Advanced or proficient 10th grade MCAS Math scores = 2

5. Elder care = 8 points
   (a) Per capita expenditures on senior centers = 4
   (b) Percent of population 60 and over served = 2
   (c) Number of volunteer hours per capita = 2

6. Public libraries = 5 points
   (a) Per capita expenditures = 2
   (b) Availability of family programs = 3

7. Parks, recreation, and open space = 6 points
   (a) Per capita expenditures on parks and recreation = 3
   (b) Percent of open space =

8. Transportation services = 6 points
   (a) Access to public transportation system = 2
   (b) Access to commuter rail = 2
   (c) Availability of para-transit (town-based services) = 2

9. Public safety and neighborhood stability = 10 points
   (a) Violent crime = 3
   (b) Property crime = 3
   (c) Percent of population living in community 6 years or more = 4

10. Integrated health and family support = 13 points
   (a) Participation in/access to health & family support services and
       programs

The results of these calculations are summarized in Table 1.

TABLE 1. FAMILY-FRIENDLY COMMUNITY INDEX

City/Town Ranking	Type of Community	Median Income	Total
1	SUBURB, residential	$130,339	70.28
2	SUBURB, economically developed	$108,189	63.32
3	SUBURB, residential	$108,926	60.65
4	SUBURB, economically developed	$89,076	59.79
5	SUBURB, economically developed	$77,674	59.74
6	SUBURB, economically developed	$92,993	58.07
7	SUBURB, residential	$84,878	56.12
8	RURAL community	$64,202	55.95
9	SUBURB, residential	$86,341	55.51
10	SUBURB, economically developed	$82,904	54.89
11	SUBURB, economically developed	$70,565	54.49
12	URBAN center	$61,029	53.52
13	SUBURB, economically developed	$66,396	53.18
14	SUBURB, economically developed	$91,105	53.13
15	SUBURB, economically developed	$81,826	52.89
16	SUBURB, economically developed	$71,334	52.80
17	SUBURB, residential	$102,550	52.48
18	SUBURB, economically developed	$66,486	52.00
19	SUBURB, economically developed	$65,633	51.48
20	SUBURB, economically developed	$72,330	50.83
21	SUBURB, residential	$77,604	49.42
22	SUBURB, economically developed	$61,942	49.01
23	URBAN center	$59,423	48.56
24	URBAN center	$59,735	48.28
25	URBAN center	$67,441	47.91
26	RURAL community	$67,173	47.68
27	State of Massachusetts	$61,664	44.27
28	URBAN center	$55,557	41.48
29	RURAL community	$58,973	41.02
30	URBAN center	$42,998	40.55
31	RURAL community	$61,663	39.34
32	URBAN center	$51,243	38.39
33	RURAL community	$59,309	35.94
34	URBAN center	$48,898	32.27
35	URBAN center	$41,863	26.44

Methods for point allocation and data sources for each sub-indicator are summarized below.

1. ECONOMIC SELF-SUFFICIENCY AND HOUSING AFFORDABILITY

(a) Percentage of families earning $50,000/year or more: the higher the percentage, the higher the ranking. Data are from Census 2000, U.S. Census Bureau.

(b) The "affordability gap" is calculated by using the U.S. Department of Housing and Urban Development's (HUD) standard that consumers should spend no more than 2.5 times their annual income on housing costs. To arrive at the "income needed" to buy a home in each community, the median home price is divided by 2.5. The affordability gap in dollars is calculated by subtracting the median family income from the income needed. The affordability gap is then converted into a percentage: the lower the percentage, the higher the ranking. Median family income and the median home price data come from Census 2000, U.S. Census Bureau.

(c) Percent of families with children under eighteen living at 100 percent of poverty: the lower the percentage, the higher the ranking. Data are from Census 2000, U.S. Census Bureau.

(d) Percent of families with college education: the higher the percentage, the higher the ranking. Data are from Census 2000, U.S. Census Bureau.

2. PRESCHOOL CHILDCARE

(a) Availability: The preschool availability rate is calculated by dividing the number of licensed preschool slots available in each community by the preschool population. The higher the availability rate, the higher the ranking. State and local population figures for children under age five and median family income come from Census 2000, U.S. Census Bureau.

(b) Quality: The quality of preschool care (three months to five years) is based on the percent of NAEYC-accredited centers in the community; to calculate this percentage, the number of NAEYC centers is divided by the total number of state-licensed centers per city/town. The higher the percentage of accredited centers, the higher the ranking. (Figures for NAEYC-accredited centers do not include any licensed and/or accredited public school preschool programs or family-run childcare programs.)

(c) Affordability: Affordability is calculated by determining the percentage of median family income spent on childcare for one child; the average weekly cost of five-day, full-time care is divided by the weekly median family income. The lower the percent of family income needed to pay for care, the higher the ranking. Income data are from Census 2000, U.S. Census Bureau.

Data on number of slots, accredited centers, and average weekly cost for the three items above come from surveys conducted by the Early Learning Services division of the Massachusetts Department of Education.

Note: Measuring the quality of infant, toddler, and preschool childcare requires data on child/staff ratios, staff turnover, staff training, and other factors. Unfortunately, data on these aspects of quality are not available on the community level, thus the use of NAEYC accreditations as the sole measure of quality.

3. SCHOOL-AGE CHILDCARE

(a) Availability: The school-age program availability rate is calculated by dividing the school-age capacity (number of slots) by the school-age population. The school-age childcare capacity includes only slots from private, state-licensed centers and does not include capacity from public school programs. State and local population figures for children ages 5–14 come from Census 2000 U.S. Census Bureau. The higher the availability rating, the higher the ranking.

(b) Cost: School-age childcare cost for each town represents the average weekly costs across kindergarten, elementary, and middle school grades, and includes both private and public school-age programs. To arrive at the school-age cost as percentage of income, the median weekly family income is divided by the average weekly school-age cost. The lower the percentage, the higher the ranking.

(c) Access to transportation: The percentage of programs with transportation services covers both public and private programs. The higher the percentage of such programs in a town, the higher the ranking.

Data on number of slots, cost, and transportation come from surveys conducted by the Early Learning Services division of the Massachusetts Department of Education.

Note: Even though four towns have no school-age childcare capacity, they do have cost and transportation figures, owing to the fact that the capacity/availability data cover only private, center-based, school-age programs, while the cost and transportation data cover both private and public school-age programs. As a result, the school-age childcare availability rates calculated for these towns are a bit lower than in reality.

4. QUALITY OF EDUCATION

(a) To arrive at per-pupil expenditures, total student expenditures per town are divided by total student enrollment: the higher the expenditures, the higher the ranking. State and local data for student enrollment and total student expenditures come from the Massachusetts Department of Education.

(b–e) The MCAS (Massachusetts Comprehensive Assessment System) statewide exam scores for fourth graders and tenth graders come from the Massachusetts Department of Education. The percentage of students with "advanced" or "proficient" English/math scores is calculated by aggregating the top two categories as designated in the state MCAS data. The higher the percentage of students with advanced or proficient scores in each town, the higher the ranking.

Note: Measuring school quality is controversial and complicated. MCAS scores are an imperfect and/or partial measure of high quality of education but are included in the index because the data is available at the community level and the scores are used by the state in its evaluation of public schools.

5. ELDER CARE

(a) To calculate per capita expenditures, population figures for people sixty and over are divided by yearly Council on Aging expenditures: the higher the percentage, the higher the ranking. Expenditure figures come from the Municipal Data Bank of the Division of Local Services of the Massachusetts Department of Revenue.

(b) Percentage served is calculated by dividing the number of seniors served in senior centers in each city/town by the number of residents sixty and over: the higher the percentage, the higher the ranking. A senior center is defined as a facility that has at least one full-time employee and offers elder-related programming such as fitness, health screening, information and referral, and outdoor and other recreational activities. Centers that are exclusively meal sites are not included. These data come from the Massachusetts Executive Office of Elder Affairs.

(c) To arrive at the number of volunteer hours per capita (sixty and over), the number of hours worked by volunteers at the senior centers in each community is divided by the elder population per town: the higher the per capita hours, the higher the ranking. Data come from the Massachusetts Executive Office of Elder Affairs.

6. PUBLIC LIBRARIES

(a) Per capita expenditures are calculated by dividing the yearly library allocation in the state budget by the city/town population figures: the higher the percentage, the higher the ranking. The public library expenditures for the state and the cities/towns come from the Municipal Data Bank of the Division of Local Services of the Massachusetts Department of Revenue.

(b) City/town library websites are used to gather data on whether a library has preschool programs, after-school programs, and family/adult programs on its event calendar. A "yes" in each category gives the city/town 1 point, for a possible maximum of 3 points.

7. PARKS, PECREATION, AND OPEN SPACE

(a) To calculate expenditures per capita, the total parks and recreation expenditures are divided by the total population. Data for the state's and town's parks and recreation expenditures come from the Municipal Data Bank of the Division of Local Services of the Massachusetts Department of Revenue. Population figures come from Census 2000, U.S. Census Bureau. The higher the expenditures per capita, the higher the ranking.

Note: Some towns have low expenditures per capita because they are located next to bigger towns and use those facilities. Some towns have low expenditures on recreation because the figures are buried in the public works budget and cannot be disaggregated. Some towns do not have large expenditures on parks for the same reason.

(b) The percentage of open space is calculated by taking the amount of recreational and open space in a city/town and dividing it by the total amount of land in that city/town. Data on the amount of recreational and open space in each of the towns are from the Geographic Information System of the Massachusetts Executive Office of Environmental Affairs. Data on the total land area in each city/town is obtained from profiles of "Commonwealth Communities" compiled by the Office of the Secretary of Massachusetts. The higher the percentage of open space, the higher the ranking.

8. TRANSPORTATION SERVICES

The data on each community's available public transportation come from profiles compiled by the Massachusetts Department of Housing and Community Development.

Each town is given 2 points for availability of commuter rail, 2 points for availability of public transportation services, and 2 points for the availability of para-transit services, such as transportation for the disabled and elderly within a town, for a total of 6 possible points. The higher the total number of points, the higher the ranking.

9. PUBLIC SAFETY AND NEIGHBORHOOD STABILITY

(a) To arrive at the crime rate, the total number of crimes in each community is divided by the total population, and converted to a percentage: the lower the crime rate in each category, the higher the ranking. "Violent crimes" include murder, rape, robbery, and aggravated assault. "Property crimes" include burglary, larceny, and motor vehicle theft. The state's crime data are from the Federal Bureau of Investigation's 2000 edition of "Crime in the United States." The city/town crime data are from the Crime Reporting Unit (CRU) of the Massachusetts State Police. State and local population figures are from Census 2000, U.S. Census Bureau.

Note: The crime data for these cities/towns are from 1998 or 1999 because crime data for 2000 were either incomplete or unavailable at the time of this study. Data on Neighborhood Watch Groups were unavailable.

(b) Data on percentage of population living in a community for six years or more are from Census 2000, U.S. Census Bureau, for each city/town: the higher the percentage, the higher the ranking.

10. INTEGRATED HEALTH AND FAMILY SUPPORT SERVICES

This indicator is compiled by allocating 1 point to communities with the following programs, each of which involves a lead agency coordinating the services of more than one other state agency and/or nonprofit: Massachusetts Family Literacy Program of the Massachusetts Department of Education (DOE); Parent Education Program of Children's Trust Fund (CTF); Community Partnerships for Children (DOE); School-Linked Services (DOE); Community Connections, Department of Social Services (DSS); Mass Family Centers (CTF); Healthy Families (CTF); Mass Family Network (DOE).

Communities received 1 to 3 points depending on the level of coordination and strength of collaboration in the Community Health Networks run by the Department of Public Health.

For the provision of Early Intervention services, communities received 1 point if they were serving 50–75 percent of families in need of services, and 2 points if they were serving 76–100 percent of families in need of services. Detailed information on the goals of each program and services provided are found on the websites of each state agency listed above.

Note: The scores for the State of Massachusetts are largely based on publicly available state averages. In a few cases, indicators 5(c), 6(b), 8 and 13, the state was allocated points by taking the median of the scores of the other communities in the Index. Although the 34 communities in the Index are not statistically representative of all Massachusetts cities and town, they are diverse, and the median provided the best available way to approximate a state average.

ACKNOWLEDGMENTS

There are many people who generously helped make data available for this index. I would like to express my appreciation to the following individuals: at the Massachusetts Department of Education, Alice Barton, Arlene Dale, Nancy Doyle, Dean Elson, Kyla McSweeney, Kathy Rodriguez, and Jason Sachs; at the Massachusetts Department of Public Health, Cathy O'Connor, Jean Shimer, and Kristen Noonan; at the Massachusetts Department of Social Services, Brian Cummings; at the Massachusetts Executive Office of Environmental Affairs, Scott Costello and Jane Pfister; at the Massachusetts

Executive Office of Elder Affairs, Emmett Schmarsow; at the Massachusetts Department of Health Care Finance and Policy, Susan Kennedy; and at the Children's Trust Fund, Sarita Rogers and Karole Rose.

The job of compiling and organizing all of this data, and doing the calculations for the Index, was accomplished with remarkable dedication and professionalism by Kevin Choi, MIT Class of 2002.

NOTES AND REFERENCES CITED

INTRODUCTION

1. All proper names of biotech workers used in this book are pseudonyms. In some cases, to protect people's privacy, small details about their lives have been slightly altered. However, the events and dialogue are taken either from interview transcripts, field notes, or direct observation.

2. In order for biotechnology companies to sell products, they need approval from the Food and Drug Administration. This requires three stages of clinical trails (see www.clinicaltrials.gov). From the inception of the research and development phase to producing a marketable product takes from 12 to 15 years. See F. Carré, P. Rayman, et al. *Professional Pathways: Examining Work, Family, and Community in the Biotechnology Industry*, Report to the Alfred P. Sloan Foundation (Cambridge, MA: Radcliffe College, 1999), p. 181.

3. According to a monthly survey of households conducted by the Census Bureau, in 2001, the overall labor force participation rate for mothers with children under 18 years of age was 72.1 percent (78.7 percent for unmarried mothers and 69.6 percent for married mothers). See *Labor Force Statistics from the Current Population Survey*, "Employment Characteristics of Families, Table 5." (Washington, D.C.: Bureau of Labor Statistics, U.S. Department of Labor, 2002).

4. See Arlie Hochschild, *The Time Bind: When Work Becomes Home and Home Becomes Work* (New York: Metropolitan Books, 1997).

5. See Robert Putnam, *Bowling Alone: The Collapse and Revival of American Community* (New York: Simon and Schuster, 2000).

6. For an excellent presentation of the evidence of a growing movement for community and civic engagement, see Carmen Sirianni and Lewis Friedland, *Civic Innovation in America: Community Empowerment, Public Policy, and the Movement for Civic Renewal* (Berkeley: University of California Press, 2001).

7. See Jody Heymann, *The Widening Gap: Why America's Working Families Are in Jeopardy—and What Can Be Done about It* (New York: Basic Books, 2000), pp. 113-118.

8. See Joan Williams, *Unbending Gender: Why Family and Work Conflict and What Can Be Done about It* (New York: Oxford University Press, 2000); and Eileen Applebaum et al., *Shared Work, Valued Care: New Norms for Organizing Market Work and Unpaid Care Work* (Washington, D.C.: Economic Policy Institute, 2002).

9. There is a fairly large literature on men's involvement with housework and childcare. The findings are quite contradictory. Some focus on the increase in men's participation in family care; see B. J. Kramer and Edward Thompson, eds., *Men as Caregivers: Theory, Research, and Service Implications* (New York: Springer, 2002). Others focus on the persistence of the traditional gendered division of labor; see Francine Blau, Marrianne Ferber, and Anne Winkler, *The Economy of Women, Men, and Work* (Saddle River, NJ: Prentice Hall, 2002). In a sense, both are true. The question is whether men's participation is continuing to increase, and if not, why not? The sociologist Kathleen Gerson suggests that attention to social context, institutions, and social arrangements is needed to assess changes in men's domestic roles (see her book *Generative Fathering: Creating Social Supports for Parenting Equality* [Newbury Park, CA: Sage, 1996].) When this kind of approach is used, the results lend weight to the concept of a stalled gender revolution inside the family. For example, Susan Bianci found that although men's share of housework increased to about one-third during the early 1990s, it has now leveled off; see "Is Anyone Doing the Housework?: Trends in the Gender Division of Household Labor," *Social Forces* 79.1 (2000), 191-228. In a study of men's involvement in childcare, fluctuations in the economy and differences in men's and women's wages appear to affect the durability and sustainability of men's involvement; see Lynne Casper and Martin O'Connell, "Work, Income, the Economy, and Married Fathers as Childcare Providers," *Demography* 35.2 (1998), 243-250.

10. See Richard Moe and Carter Wilkie, *Changing Places: Rebuilding Community in the Age of Sprawl* (New York: Henry Holt, 1997). As in most books on sprawl, neither community involvement nor the work-family issues of community residents are mentioned.

CHAPTER 1

1. See Hortense Powdermaker, *Stranger and Friend: The Way of an Anthropologist* (New York: W.W. Norton, 1966) on the tension between observation and participation in the practice of ethnographic field work. Ethnography is a method for the study of a small group of subjects in their own environment: in this book, a small group of knowledge workers in their workplaces, homes, and communities of residence. Ethnographic accounts are both descriptive and interpretive: descriptive, because closely observed detail is a major source of data; and interpretive, because the ethnographer must determine the significance of what she observes. The anthropologist Clifford Geertz uses the term "thick description" to capture the essential methodology of the ethnographer; see "Thick Description: Toward an Interpretive Theory of Culture," in *The Interpretation of Cultures: Selected Essays* (New York: Basic Books, 1973), pp. 9-10.

2. This group includes families with one biotech worker who has been interviewed at least once and who has provided basic demographic and socio-economic data about self and family. For more information on methodology, see Appendix 1.

3. This project was funded by the Alfred P. Sloan Foundation's program on "Dual-Earner Middle Class Families," directed by Dr. Kathleen Christensen.

4. See Susan Moeller Okin, *Justice, Gender, and the Family* (New York: Basic Books, 1989).

5. See Sirianni and Friedland (2001), p. 24.

6. *Ibid.* In the case studies of community organizing and community health in a variety of inner-city areas, children's health is mentioned once, but issues of childcare and elder care are not included.

7. This is a theme I explored in an edited collection based on ethnogrpahic case studies of workplace and community organizing. See Ann Bookman and Sandra Morgen, eds., *Women and the Politics of Empowerment* (Philadelphia: Temple University Press, 1988).

8. See Sidney Verba, Kay Schlozman, and Henry Brady, *Voice and Equality: Civic Voluntarism in American Politics* (Cambridge, MA: Harvard University Press, 1995), pp. 251-263.

9. The community work of women I met is less leadership-oriented and more informal. Working women today are less involved with broad civic education, such as the League of Women Voters, and more involved with organizations they rely on for the education and care of their own children and elders.

10. There is a rich line of research among social historians that has made visible the unrecognized volunteerism of women. See, e.g., Anne Firor Scott, *Making the Invisible Woman Visible* (Urbana: University of Illinois Press, 1984); Lori D. Ginzberg, *Women and the Work of Benevolence, Politics, and Class in the Nineteenth Century United States* (New Haven: Yale University Press, 1990); Anne M Boylan, *The Origins of Women's Activism, New York and Boston, 1790-1840* (Chapel Hill: University of North Caroline Press, 2002); Karen J. Blair, *Joining Together: Exploring the History of Voluntary Organizations* (Melbourne, FL: Krieger, 2003); and Susan Porter, *Engendering Benevolence: Orphan Asylums in Antebellum America* (Baltimore: Johns Hopkins University Press, forthcoming).

11. "Social capital" has been defined as "features of social organization such as networks, norms and social trust that facilitate coordination and cooperation for mutual benefit." See Robert Putnam, "Bowling Alone: America's Declining Social Capital," *Journal of Democracy* 6 (January 1995), 67.

12. For more on the impact of alternative work schedules—particularly part-time work—see chapter 9.

13. For a discussion of the impact of maternal employment children and families, see Francis Ivan Nye and Lois W. Hoffman, *The Employed Mother in America* (Chicago: Rand McNally and Company, 1965), and Lois Hoffman and Lise M. Youngblade, *Mothers at Work: Effects on Children's Development* (Cambridge: Cambridge University Press, 1999).

14. For data on progress and barriers encountered by certain groups of professional women, see *Good for Business: Making Full Use of the Nation's Human Capital,* Report of the Glass Ceiling Commission, U.S. Department of Labor, Washington, D.C., 1996.

15. See Denise Venable, "The Wage Gap Myth," National Center for Policy Analysis, Brief Analysis No. 392, April 2002. The author concludes, "Those who still cite women's 76 cents for every male dollar as evidence of sexism fail to take into account the underlying role of personal choice. The 'wage gap' is not so much about employers discriminating against women as about women making discriminating choices in the labor market."

16. According to the Current Population Survey, the wage gap persists. In 2001, average annual earnings for men with a high school diploma were $33,037, whereas for women they were $24,253. Average annual earnings for men with a B.A. were $53,108; for women, $39,865. See U.S. Census Bureau, Current Population Reports (Washington, D.C.: Department of Commerce, March 2002).

17. Tamar Lewin, "A Child Study Is a Peek: It's Not the Whole Picture," *New York Times,* July 21, 2002.

18. See Jeanne Brooks-Gunn, Wen-Jui Han, and Jane Waldfogel, "Maternal Employment and Child Cognitive Outcomes in the First Three Years of Life: The NICHD Study of Early Child Care," *Child Development* 73 (2002), 1052-1072. The authors conclude that there were negative effects on the reading readiness of three-year-olds when the mother worked 30 hours or more per week in the first nine months of the child's life, even when controlling for the quality of the home environment, the quality of the childcare arrangement, and the mother's sensitivity. Although the authors are careful to say that the data do not prove that the lower reading readiness scores were *caused by* maternal employment in the first nine months, this point was not made by the media. The authors' call for improving the quality of childcare,

having longer maternity leaves with pay, and expanding family friendly benefits were also not reported.

19. See Wendy Kaminer, *A Fearful Freedom: Women's Flight from Equality* (Boston: Addison Wesley, 1991).

20. See Felice N. Schwartz, "Management Women and the New Facts of Life," *Harvard Business Review* (January-February 1989), 65-76.

21. The term "mommy track" first appeared in an article in the *New York Times* critiquing Schwartz's article in the *Harvard Business Review* (see Tamar Lewin, "'Mommy Career Track' Sets Off Furor," *New York Times*, March 8, 1989). Schwartz always felt her ideas had been misunderstood, and that she was really proposing a "parent track," as explained by her son Tony Schwartz in an article in *Fast Company* (1999) published after her death.

22. There are other scholars who have made substantial contributions to our thinking about family care and women's place; see particularly Emily K. Abel and Margaret Nelson, eds., *Circle of Care: Work and Identity in Women's Lives* (Albany, NY: SUNY Press, 1990), and Joan Toronto, *Moral Boundaries: A Political Argument for an Ethic of Care* (New York: Routledge, 1993). For an excellent collection of recent scholarship on carework, see Francesa Cancian et al, eds., *Child Care and Inequality: Rethinking Carework for Children and Youth* (New York: Routledge, 2002).

23. See Mona Harrington, *Care and Equality: Inventing a New Family Politics* (New York: Knopf, 1999), p. 24.

24. *Ibid.*, p. 48.

25. For discussion about how the work-family field has evolved, see Marcie Pitt-Catsouphes, "A Coming of Age: Work/Life Flexibility," in Eileen Applebaum, ed., *Balancing Acts: Easing the Burdens and Improving the Options for Working Families* (Washington, D.C.: Economic Policy Institute, 2000). See also R. Barnett, "A New Work-Life Model for the Twenty-First Century," *Annals of the American Academy of Political and Social Sciences* 562 (1999), 143-158, and D. Friedman and A. Johnson, *Moving from Programs to Culture Change: The Next Stage for the Corporate Work-Family Agenda* (New York: Families and Work Institute, 1996).

26. See *Workforce 2000: Work and Workers for the 21st Century US* (Washington, D.C.: U.S. Department of Labor, 1987). This report made the following projections about the 21st century: the American economy will grow at a relatively healthy pace; U.S. manufacturing will be a much smaller share of the economy; most new jobs will be created in the service industries and will demand higher skill levels; the workforce will grow slowly, becoming more female, and will include more minorities and older persons.

27. It is difficult to get an accurate estimate of the number of employers that provide on-site childcare. A study by the Families and Work Institute found that 12 percent of employees with children under six years of age "have access to a child care center operated or sponsored by their employer at or near the worksite." See *Ahead of the Curve: Why America's Leading Employers Are Addressing the Needs of New and Expectant Parents* (New York: Families and Work Institute, 1998), p. xviii.

28. See Hochschild (1997), pp. 27-34.

29. For a report on their projects at Xerox, Corning, and Tandem Computer, see Rhona Rapoport and Lotte Bailyn, *Relinking Life and Work: Toward a Better Future* (New York: Ford Foundation, November 1996), p. 27.

30. See discussion in Lotte Bailyn, *Breaking the Mold: Women, Men, and Time in the New Corporate World* (New York: Free Press, 1993).

31. See Rhona Rapoport, Lotte Bailyn, Joyce Fletcher, and Bette Pruitt, *Beyond Work-Family Balance: Advancing Workplace Performance and Gender Equity* (San Francisco: Josey Bass, 2002).

32. Some scholars in the work-family field have recently begun to bring the issue of community into their research. This kind of research is more advanced in the United Kingdom than in the United States, as evidenced by publication of the journal *Community, Work, and Family*. In the United States, several important articles have appeared, notably Patricia Voydanoff, "Conceptualizing Community in the Context of Work and Family," *Community, Work, and Family* 4.2 (2002), 133-156. See also Patricia Voydanoff, "Community as a Context for the Work-Family Interface," in *Resources for Teaching: Work and Family Encyclopedia*, Sloan Work and Family research network, available at www.bc.edu/be_org/avp/wfnetwork. Research-in-progress on community issues by Shelley MacDeramid, Marcie Pitt-Catsouphes, and Rosalind Barnett promises to further advance the integration of work, family, and community. Their work was presented at the NICHD/Sloan Conference on "Workforce/Workplace Mismatch?: Work, Family, Health and Well Being," Washington, D.C., June 16–18, 2003.

33. This observation is based in part on a review of the Sloan Work and Family Research Literature Database. Out of a total of more than 4,500 citations, only 103 are related to community. Of those that focus on the community-family interface, the majority are studies of schools and parental involvement in education. A similar point on how community has (or has not) entered the work-family field has been made by Patricia Voydanoff in "Incorporating Community into Work and Family Research: A Review of the Basic Relationships," in *Human Relations* 54.12 (2001), 1609-1637.

34. See two important articles by Rosalind Barnett that look at both aspects of spillover; "Home to Work Spillover Revisited: A Study of Full-Time Employed Women in Dual-Earner Couples," in *Journal of Marriage and Family* 56 (1994), 647-656; and "Positive Spillover Effects from Job to Home: A Closer Look," *Women and Health* 19.2/3 (1992), 13-41.

35. See James T. Bond, Ellen Galinsky, and Jennifer E. Swanberg, *The 1997 National Study of the Changing Workforce* (New York: Families and Work Institute, 1998), pp. 131-139.

36. Wellman has shown how these three views of community are linked with different historical periods: "lost" communities are linked to the transition from preindustrial to industrial society; "saved" communities are linked to the period of industrialization; and "liberated" communities are part of the postindustrial period. See Barry Wellman, Peter J. Carrington, and Alan Hall, "Networks as Personal Communities," in Barry Wellman and S. D. Berkowitz, eds., *Social Structures: A Network Approach* (Cambridge: Cambridge University Press, 1988), p. 134.

37. *Ibid.*, p. 135.

38. NIMBY stands for "not in my backyard" and NIMBYism is used to describe a community response based on narrow self-interest rather than broader notions of social responsibility.

39. For an excellent ethnographic account of the complex and often unexpected reactions of residents in a diverse, upscale urban neighborhood faced with locating an AIDS clinic in their midst, see Jane Balin, *A Neighborhood Divided: Community Resistance to an AIDS Care Facility* (Ithaca: Cornell University Press, 1999).

40. Alexis de Tocqueville, *Democracy in America*. Translated by George Lawrence and edited by J.P. Mayer. (New York: Harper Perennial, 1988).

41. Robert Bellah, Richard Masden, Willliam Sullivan, Ann Swidler, and Steven Tipton, *Habits of the Heart: Individualism and Commitment in American Life* (Berkeley: University of California Press, 1985).

42. Robert Putnam, "Bowling Alone: America's Declining Social Capital," *Journal of Democracy* (January 1995); and *Bowling Alone: The Collapse and Revival of American Community* (New York: Simon and Schuster, 2000).

43. See Alan Wolfe, *One Nation, after All: What Americans Really Think about God, Country, Family, Racism, Welfare, Immigration, Homosexuality, Work, the Right, the Left, and Each Other* (New York: Penguin, 1998), pp. 250-263.

44. See Theda Skocpol, *Protecting Soldiers and Mothers: The Origins of Social Policy in the United States* (Cambridge, MA: Harvard University Press, 1992). For a discussion linking historical data with contemporary activism, see Theda Skocpol and Morris P. Fiorina, eds., *Civic Engagement in American Democracy* (Brookings Institution and Russell Sage Foundation, 1999).

45. Robert Wuthnow, *Loose Connections: Joining Together in America's Fragmented Communities* (Cambridge, MA: Harvard University Press, 1998).

46. See Robert Wuthnow, "The United States: Bridging the Privileged and the Marginalized?" in Robert Putnam, ed., *Democracies in Flux: The Evolution of Social Capital* (New York: Oxford University Press, 2002), pp. 59-102.

47. Amatai Etzioni, *The Spirit of Community: The Reinvention of American Society* (New York: Simon and Schuster, 1993).

48. The debate on the merits of communitarianism, and particularly the way it subverts or revitalizes liberalism, depending on your point of view, is beyond the scope of this book. See Stephen Mulhall and Adam Swift, *Liberals and Communitarians* (Oxford: Blackwell, 1992); Jean L. Cohen and Andrew Arato, *Civil Society and Political Theory* (Cambridge, Mass.: MIT Press, 1994); and Gershon Shafir, ed., *The Citizenship Debates: A Reader* (Minneapolis: University of Minnesota Press, 1998).

49. *A Nation of Spectators: How Civic Disengagement Weakens America and What We Can Do about It*, Final Report of the National Commission on Civic Renewal, 1998.

50. See the Commission's "Index of National Civic Health."

51. E. J. Dionne, ed., *Community Works: The Revival of Civil Society in America* (Washington, D.C.: Brookings Institution Press, 1998).

52. See Robert Putnam, "Bowling Together: The United State of America," *American Prospect* (February 11, 2002), 20-22.

53. *Ibid.*, p. 22.

54. Sirianni and Friedland (2001).

55. *Ibid.*, p. 8.

56. On the evolution of the term "social capital," see Robert Putnam, ed., *Democracies in Flux: The Evolution of Social Capital in Contemporary Society* (New York: Oxford University Press, 2002), pp. 4-12.

57. Sirianni and Friedland (2001), p. 33.

58. "New economy" refers to both the structural changes that occurred in our economy owing to the globalization of business, and to the dramatic impact that innovations in information technology have had on many industries. When the term was first used, it generally referred to the computer industry per se, but it now refers to the many industries that use and are affected by innovative networked technologies, such as telecommunications, finance, and biotech. For a discussion of the "old economy" and the "new economy" and its impact on working families, see Paul Osterman, Thomas Kochan, Richard Locke, and Michael Piore, *Working in America: A Blueprint for the New Labor Market* (Cambridge, MA: MIT Press, 2001), pp. 6-10.

59. For excellent studies on working families in another segment of the new economy workforce, the high-tech industry in Silicon Valley, see Judith Stacey, *Brave New Families: Stories of Domestic Upheaval in Late Twentieth Century America* (New York: Basic Books, 1991); and J. A. English-Lueck, *Cultures@Silicon Valley* (Stanford: Stanford University Press, 2002).

60. See the final report of the project, Carré et al. (1999).

61. All workers at each site were informed about the project and given the opportunity—on a completely voluntary and confidential basis—to be interviewed. When the initial project finished in February 1999, I continued interviewing and doing field work until the spring of 2001.

62. Carré (1999), p. 38.

63. See Appendix 1.
64. The percentage of workers who hold a college degree in Massachusetts is 27.2 percent according to the 2000 Census, while in this sample a little over 75 percent hold a college degree.
65. These estimates are drawn from biotechnology industry salary surveys. I did not collect data on per capita income for this sample, but rather household income.
66. It is very difficult to get accurate data on the demographic characteristics of the biotech workforce, partly because it is such a new industry and biotech jobs are not captured in the Standard Industrial Classification (SIC) Index. For a discussion of estimates of the number of women working in biotech, see Carré (1999), p. 18.
67. There are no reliable data available on the percentage of minorities in the Massachusetts biotechnology industry. This industry estimate is drawn from conversations with individual members of the Massachusetts Biotechnology Council (MBC) Human Resource Committee.
68. In 2001, 11.7 percent of American families were living in poverty. The Census Bureau defined the poverty threshold for a family of four with two children under eighteen years of age as $17,960 (see Bernadette Proctor and Joseph Palaker, "Poverty in the U. S.: 2001," in *Current Population Reports, Consumer Income* [Washington, D.C.: U.S. Department of Commerce, September 2002]). In 2001, the median family income for a family of four was $42,228 (see Carmen DeNavs-Walt and Robert Cleveland, "Money Income in the U.S.:2001," in *Current Population Reports, Consumer Income* [Washington, D.C.: U.S. Department of Commerce, September 2002).
69. The following figures are based on self-reported annual household income (N=33). Interviewees were given five categories with ranges. Twenty percent report annual household incomes between $20,000 and $50,000 (only one worker reported an annual income between $20,000 and $30,000); 9 percent between $50,000 and $75,000; 48 percent between $75,000 and $100,000; 15 percent above $100,000.
70. Arlie Hochschild uses this term to describe the "Taylorization" of home life in which "numerous activities formerly done at home now go on outside the home." See Hochschild (1997), pp. 49–50.

CHAPTER 2

1. For a more detailed description of the U.S. biotechnology industry, see W. Hernandez, F. Carré, and S. Resnick, "The Industry," in Carré (1999), pp. 11-26.
2. An accepted industry definition for biotechnology is "the understanding of living systems and the application of advanced technologies to solve problems and develop products—in essence the commercialization of modern biology." See *Massachusetts Biotechnology Directory, 2000 Edition* (Cambridge, MA: Massachusetts Biotechnology Council, 2000), p. 19.
3. *Biotech 99: Bridging the Gap*, Ernst and Young's Annual Industry Report, 1999.
4. A spokesman for the Massachusetts Biotechnology Council said in the summer of 2002 that the state's biotech workforce is now up to 28,000 "as new startups continue to form and biotechnology firms add manufacturing and marketing skills." See Sherwood Ross, "Talent Hunt Is Still On in Biotech," *Boston Globe*, August 11, 2002.
5. These groups have worked together to create long-term strategies for workforce development at every occupational level of the industry, from production workers with vocational education training certificates to postdoctoral research scientists.
6. *Massachusetts Biotechnology Directory*, 2000 Edition, p. 30.
7. *Ibid.*, p. 31. The total workforce was reported as 23,596, but nine companies in the state with large numbers of employees did not respond to the survey on which these statistics are based.
8. While the number of small companies still remains numerically the largest sector of the

industry, medium-sized companies have declined and large biotech companies (more than 150 employees) have increased by 42 percent (*ibid.*, p. 34). For the argument on future job growth, see *Massbiotech 2010: Achieving Global Leadership in the Life Sciences Economy* (Cambridge: Massachusetts Biotechnology Council, 2003).

9. In 1999 and 2000, seven large pharmaceutical companies established sites in Massachusetts, including UCB Pharma, Pfizer, Merck, LION/Bayer Bioscience Research, Amgen, Hoescht, and American Home Products (*ibid.*, p. 5).

10. Some large pharmaceutical companies have acquired smaller biotech firms with promising products, while many biotech firms have struggled for survival and autonomy. Some biotech firms have been forced into acquisition or merger arrangements as a result of the economic risks and cost of sustaining the long-term product development research period.

11. The percentage of men is 54 percent, and of women 46 percent; see Carré (1999), p. 21.

12. See "Survey of Human Resource Departments in the Massachusetts Biotechnology Industry" (Cambridge, MA: Radcliffe College, May 1998). Surveys were sent to 113 companies and the response rate was 29.2 percent.

13. 1997 Human Resource Survey, Figure 19.

14. The layoff rate among the firms surveyed is approximately 25 percent; 1997 Human Resource Survey, p. 2.

15. 1997 Human Resource Survey, p. 2.

16. Of survey respondents, 91 percent report having parental leave, 88 percent report having personal sick days. There is no documentation available on the extent of parental leave and sick days among the companies that did not respond to the survey, and it may be quite a bit lower.

17. The FMLA mandates that companies with 50 or more employees provide unpaid leave for one's own serious illness, birth, adoption, or the serious illness of a parent, child, or spouse.

18. Only 3 percent have on-site childcare, and only 7 percent have community service leaves. 1997 Human Resource Survey, p. 3.

19. This survey was conducted in 1999 by the Survey Group of Wakefield, Massachusetts, for the Massachusetts Biotechnology Council (MBC). Sixty-five companies responded to the survey, and it is likely that those who responded one offering more work-family benefits that those who did not respond.

20. For example, 32 percent of employers provided a telecommuting option to their employees, but only 18 percent allowed employees to job-share. The number of companies that allowed leaves beyond the FMLA mandate was small—a third or less of companies surveyed. 1999 Human Resource Survey.

21. See *Working Mother*, "The 15th Annual Survey of the 100 Best Companies for Working Mothers," October 2003.

22. In a 1996 publication on "Prevalence of Work Family Programs in Companies," only 5.3 percent are reported to be engaged in "corporate foundation giving," which could include donations to community groups, and 1.6 percent as "consortium centers for child care," which could include community groups in a partnership with companies. Community involvement per se is not listed among 30 policy options. See Friedman and Johnson (1996), p. 25.

23. Most of the survey respondents (54 percent) are small businesses with 50 or fewer employees, mirroring the size of many biotech firms in the state. Of the remaining respondents, 29 percent had 51-500 employees, and 17 percent had more than 500 employees. See "Biotechnology's Involvement with Its Communities: Community Relations Benchmarking Survey" (Cambridge, MA: Massachusetts Biotechnology Council, 2001). Out of 206 full or associate MBC members, the committee received 48 surveys back (a 23 percent response rate).

24. See Joyce Tait, "Beyond NIMBYism: The Evolution of Social Attitudes to Biotech," in T.C. Smout, ed., *Nature, Landscape, and People* (East Linton, UK: Tuckwell Press, 2001).

25. It is not clear whether those leave times were paid or unpaid, but they appear to be unpaid.

26. This company is headquartered out of state and has a major production facility some distance from the new industrial park.

27. An "adjuvant" is a drug or agent added to another drug or agent to enhance its effectiveness. It can also be a substance injected along with an antigen to enhance the immune response.

28. For an excellent discussion of the parameters of flexibility in biotech and its impact on work-family, see Susan C. Eaton, "If You Can Use Them: Flexibility Policies, Organizational Commitment, and Perceived Productivity," in *Industrial Relations*, 42(2), April 2003, pps. 145–167.

29. Information on BioTertia's Community Relations Office is taken from an interview in February 2001 with a member of the Community Outreach Committee of the Massachusetts Biotechnology Council.

30. According to the American Medical Association, in 1969-1970, 9 percent of those enrolled in medical school were women, whereas in 2001-2002, 44.1 percent were women. In 1970, 7.6 percent of all physicians were women, whereas in 2001, 24.6 percent of physicians were women. See "Women in Medicine Data Source, " 2003 Edition, Tables 1 and 2. In law, in 2001, 29.7 percent of all lawyers were women, and 48 percent of all law school students were women; see "A Current Glance at Women in the Law," Commission on Women in the Profession, American Bar Association (2002).

31. See Carré (1999), p. 207.

32. See Susan Eaton and Lotte Bailyn, "Reconceptualizing Careers and the Employment Contract in Changing Organizations," in Carré (1999), pp. 51-59.

33. This finding accords with national survey data on the use of parental leave. See *A Workable Balance: Report to Congress on Family and Medical Leave Policies*, Commission on Leave (Washington, D.C.: U.S. Department of Labor, May 1996).

34. For an overview of work-family policies vs. practice at the three firms, see Susan Eaton and Lotte Bailyn, "The Work-Family Boundary: A More Fluid Conception," in Carré (1999), pp. 92-95.

35. Human resource policies in the biotech industry in Massachusetts cover the gamut of possible adoption leave policies, but the majority are less generous than the one Rachel got, according to a member of the MBC Human Resource Committe.

36. Data from interview by a member of the Radcliffe biotechnology project.

37. The uneven accessibility of flexible scheduling options is a pervasive problem. Lonnie Golden's research, using national samples, has shown that if you are a woman, a person of color, or a person with little or no higher education, you are less likely to have access to flexible schedules than other workers. See Lonnie Golden, "Flexible Work Schedules: Which Workers Get Them?" *American Behavioral Scientist* 44.7 (2001), pp. 1157-1178.

CHAPTER 3

1. See Juliet B. Schor, *The Overworked American: The Unexpected Decline of Leisure* (New York: Basic Books, 1992).

2. For an excellent discussion of the myriad ways in which time affects work and family life, see Phyllis Moen, ed., *It's About Time: Couples and Careers* (Ithaca: ILR Press, of Cornell University Press, 2003). For a discussion of the bifurcation of the workforce between those who work too many hours and those who work too few, see Jerry A. Jacobs and Kathleen Gerson, "Overworked Individuals or Overworked Families: Explaining Trends in Work, Leisure, and Family Time," *Work and Occupations* 28.1 (1998), 40-63. For documentation about who works too many hours, see Ellen Galinsky, Stacey Kim, and James T. Bond, *Feeling Overworked: When Work Becomes Too Much* (New York: Families and Work Institute, 2001),

and S. Jody Heymann, "Low Income Parents and the Time Famine," in Sylvia Hewlett et al., eds., *Taking Parenting Public* (Lanham, MD: Rowman and Littlefield, 2002).

3. Data from a nationally representative sample show that married mothers spend more time caring for and doing things for children than fathers on both work days and non-work days. See James T. Bond et al., *The 1997 National Study of the Changing Workforce* (New York: Families and Work Institute, 1998), p. 39.

4. See Susan Faludi, *Backlash: The Undeclared War against Women* (New York: Crown, 1991).

5. See Linda Waite et al., "Trends in Men's and Women's Well-being in Marriage," in *The Ties That Bind: Perspectives on Marriage and Children* (New York: Aldine De Gruyter, 2000).

6. See Lotte Bailyn, Thomas Kochan, and Robert Drago, *Integrating Work and Family: A Holistic Approach*. Sloan Work-Family Policy Network Report (Cambridge, MA, September 2001).

7. See Phyllis Moen and Yan Yu, "Effective Work/Life Strategies: Working Couples, Work Conditions, Gender and Life Quality," *Social Problems* 47.3 (2000), pp. 291-326.

8. This group represents about 21 percent of those families with whom I conducted in-depth interviews (N=33) and 18 percent of the whole sample (N=40).

9. There are no families among these workers in which the husband is staying home to care for the children while the wife works full-time.

10. The lack of part-time opportunities was corroborated by interviews of other researchers on the Radcliffe Biotechnology Industry Project. See S. Eaton and L. Bailyn, "The Work-Family Boundary: A More Fluid Conception," in Carré (1999), p. 93. Efforts to get data on the prevalence of part-time work from the Massachusetts Biotechnology Council (MBC) and Biotechnology Industry Organization (BIO) were unsuccessful. Neither industry trade organizations nor the Bureau of Labor Statistics collect this data for biotech workers.

11. For a discussion of the cultural resistance to part-time work, see Cynthia Fuchs Epstein, Carroll Seron, Bonnie Oglensky, and Robert Saute, *The Part-Time Paradox: Time Norms, Professional Life, Family, and Gender* (New York: Routledge, 1999), especially chapter 4.

12. Several workers with families living out of state did use far-flung family members for dependent care, usually at times of childbirth or emergencies. See chapter 6.

13. Janet Gornick, a political scientist, and others argue that shifts in relations between men and women will come about only with changes in employment policy and public policy. See Janet Gornick, Marcia Meyers, and Katrin Ross, "Public Policies and the Employment of Mothers: A Cross-National Study," *Social Science Quarterly* 79.1 (1998), pp. 53-54.

CHAPTER 4

1. Despite the fact that most people's commute was going to increase substantially, and that some people live near one another, a carpool proposal from one worker was not of interest.

2. See Stephanie Coontz. *The Way We Never Were: American Families and the Nostalgia Trap* (New York: Basic Books, 1992).

3. For discussion of the territorial versus social meanings of community, see Patricia Voydanoff, "Conceptualizing Community in the Context of Work and Family," *Community, Work, and Family* 4.2 (2001).

4. Some scholars "define community from the standpoint of the focal individual and equate it with the personal network of social ties." See Michael E. Walker, Stanley Wasserman, and Barry Wellman, "Statistical Models for Social Support Networks," in Stanley Wasserman and Joseph Galashiewicz, eds., *Advances in Social Network Analysis* (Thousand Oaks: Sage Publications, 1994), p. 72.

5. See Gerson Shafer, ed., *The Citizen Debates* (Minneapolis: University of Minnesota Press, 1998).

6. See Anita Blanchard and Tom Horan, "Virtual Communities and Social Capital," *Social Science Computer Review* 17 (1998), 293-307.

7. Robert S. Lynd and Helen Merrell Lynd, *Middletown: A Study in Modern American Culture* (New York: Harcourt Brace, 1929), and a sequel, *Middletown in Transition: A Study in Cultural Conflicts* (New York: Harcourt Brace Jovanovich, 1937).

8. See Herbert J. Gans, *Urban Villagers: Group and Class in the Life of Italian Americans* (New York: Free Press, 1962).

9. See William Julius Wilson, *When Work Disappears* (New York: Vintage, 1997); also Katherine S. Newman, *No Shame in My Game: The Working Poor in the Inner City* (New York: Vintage, 2000).

10. See Carol Stack, *All Our Kin: Strategies for Survival in a Black Community* (New York: Harper and Row, 1974).

11. See Leith Mullings and Alika Wali Klumer, *Stress and Resilience: The Social Context of Reproduction in Central Harlem* (New York: Academic/Plenum, 2001); Steven Gegory, *Black Corona: Race and Politics of Place in an Urban Community* (Princeton: Princeton University Press, 1999); Roger Sanjek, *The Future of Us All: Race and Neighborhood Politics in New York City* (Ithaca: Cornell University Press, 1998); and Ida Susser, *Norman Street: Poverty and Politics in an Urban Neighborhood* (New York: Oxford University Press, 1982).

12. See William Whyte, *The Organization Man* (New York: Doubleday, 1956).

13. See Herbert Gans, *The Levittowners: The Ways of Life and Politics in a New Suburban Community* (New York: Vintage, 1967); John R. Seeley, R. Alexander Sim, and Elizabeth Loosley, *Crestwood Heights: A Study of the Culture of Suburban Life* (New York: John Wiley, 1963); and S. D. Clark, *The Suburban Society* (Toronto: University of Toronto Press, 1966).

14. See Kenneth T. Jackson, *Crabgrass Frontier: The Suburbanization of the United States* (New York: Oxford University Press, 1985); M. P. Baumgartner, *The Moral Order of the Suburb* (New York: Oxford University Press, 1988); John Palen, *The Suburbs* (New York: McGraw Hill, 1995); and Roger Silverstone, ed., *Vision of Suburbia* (New York: Routledge, 1997).

15. See Sam Bass Warner, *Street Car Suburbs: The Process of Growth in Boston, 1870-1900* (Cambridge, MA: Harvard University Press, 1978); David Contosta, *Suburb in the City: Chestnut Hill Philadelphia, 1850-1990* (Columbus, OH: Ohio State University Press, 1992); Barbara Marsh, *Expanding the American Dream: Building and Rebuilding Levittown* (Albany: SUNY Press, 1993); and Margaret Marsh, *Suburban Lives* (New Bruswick, NJ: Rutgers University Press, 1990).

16. Rosalynd Baxandall and Elizabeth Ewen, *Picture Windows: How the Suburbs Happened* (New York: Basic Books, 2000), p. xxi.

17. See John Paul Jones et al., eds., *Thresholds in Feminist Geography: Difference, Methodology, Representation*, (Lanham, MD Rowman and Little, 1997), and Catherine Stimpson et. al, eds., *Women and the American City* (Chicago: University of Chicago Press, 1981), which includes Delores Hayden's classic, "What Would a Non-Sexist City Be Like?"

18. Melissa Gilbert's research critiques essentialism and brings a spatial perspective to debates about poverty and the underclass. See M. Gilbert, "Feminism and Difference in Urban Geography," *Urban Geography* 18.2 (1997), pp. 166-197.

19. See Susan Hanson and Geraldine Pratt, *Gender, Work and Space* (New York: Routledge, 1995). The authors show how women work closer to home than men, and how job opportunities and labor markets are spatially clustered by gender.

20. See Delores Hayden, *Redesigning the American Dream* (New York: Norton, 1984).

21. Matthew E. Kahn, "The Environmental Impacts of Suburbanization," *The Journal of Policy Analysis and Management* 19.4 (2000), 569-586.

22. See Charles C. Euchner, ed., *Governing Greater Boston: The Politics and Policy of Place, 2002 Edition* (Cambridge, MA: Rappaport Institute of Greater Boston, 2002), p. 3.

23. See Anthony Flint, "Planning the Fragmented Metropolis: Acting Regionally and Locally," in *Governing Greater Boston* (2002), p. 196.

24. *Ibid.*, p. 8.

25. A classification system, developed by a working group of Massachusetts states agencies, describes five types of communities. Suburbs are either "economically developed suburbs" with high levels of economic activity, social complexity and relatively high incomes, or "residential suburbs," affluent communities with low levels of economic activity; "urban centers" have high population density, cultural diversity, and a concentration of commercial and manufacturing activity; rural communities are either "historic manufacturing sites" or "small towns that are sparsely populated and economically undeveloped."

26. The development of "edge cities" began in the 1980s when jobs moved out of cities and into the suburbs where many middle-class families live. See Joel Garreau, *Edge City: Life on the New Frontier* (New York: Doubleday, 1988).

27. Of the 40 families profiled, only 10 percent work within five miles of their home, whereas almost two thirds work over 20 miles from home. Within the sample as a whole, 20 percent work over 30 miles from home.

28. Hanson and Pratt (1995), p. 155.

29. For a discussion of suburban racial segregation, see J. Eric Oliver, *Democracy in Suburbia* (Princeton: Princeton University Press, 2001), pp. 99-105.

30. Of the 40 families profiled in this book, 20 percent do not own their own homes. This group includes largely young married workers with low-income jobs, and single-parent families.

31. See chapter on "The Economic Fall Out of Divorce," in Sylvia Ann Hewlett, *A Lesser Life: The Myth of Women's Liberation in America* (New York: Morrow, 1986).

32. For a moving ethnography of a 1970s California community composed of elderly Jewish immigrants, see Barbara Myerhoff, *Number Our Days* (New York: E. P. Dutton, 1978).

33. This pattern has been documented for many knowledge workers. "The knowledge society is the first human society where upward mobility is potentially unlimited. Knowledge differs from all other means of production in that it cannot be inherited or bequested. It has to be acquired anew by every individual, and everyone starts out with the same total ignorance." *The Economist*, November 3, 2001.

34. See *Working Mother* and *Business Week*.

35. There are few studies that assess "family-friendliness" using objective measures. For interesting findings on how dual-earner couples themselves rate their communities, see Raymond Swisher, Stephen Sweet, and Phyllis Moen, "The Family-Friendly Community and Its 'Life Course Fit' for Dual-Earner Couples," BLCC Working Paper #01-09, June 2001.

36. See Marc Miringoff and Marque-Luisa Miringoff, *The Social Health of Nations: How America Is Really Doing* (New York: Oxford University Press, 1999), on developing "social indicators" to assess the health of American families and society. Government efforts to compile this kind of information include the U.S. Health and Human Services report, *American Children: National Indicators of Well-Being* (Washington, D.C., 1996). Philanthropic organizations such as the Annie E. Casey Foundation produce an annual *Kids Count Data Book: State Profiles of Child Well-Being*.

37. For a full explanation of each indicator, see Appendix 2.

38. 27 percent of communities lie inside Route 128 (including Boston and Cambridge), 35 percent of communities lie between Route 128 and Route 495, and 38 percent of communities are located west of Route 495 (including Worcester).

39. One attempt to remedy this problem in Massachusetts is the "Boston Children and Families Database" (see FN 52, page 295).

CHAPTER 5

1. See Appendix 1 on methodology for more detail on interviewing methods.
2. Many social network researchers take individual players as a starting point and generate models that include other resources and actors. One study estimated that many people have social networks of 1,500 informal ties and 20 active ties to significant individuals; see H. R. Bernard and P. Kilworth, *Report to the Anthropology and MMDI Programs* (Washington, D.C.: National Science Foundation, 1990). See also C.S. Fisher, *To Dwell among Friends: Personal Networks in Town and City* (Chicago: University of Chicago Press, 1982); and Barry Wellman and S. Wortley, "Different Strokes for Different Folks: Community Ties and Social Support," *American Journal of Sociology* 96 (1990), 558-588. However, the emphasis remains on the "personal," as the title to a very influential article by Barry Wellman, Peter J. Carrington, and Alan Hall reveals, "Networks as Personal Communities" in Barry Wellman and S. D. Berkowitz, eds., *Social Structures: A Network Approach* (Cambridge: Cambridge University Press, 1990), pp. 130-184.
3. For an analysis of how institutions in the larger society affect the size and shape of personal and family-based networks, see Moncrieff Cochran et al., *Extending Families* (Cambridge: Cambridge University Press, 1990).
4. The social network analysts focus on "ties" and "social support" that are necessary for day-to-day reproduction, as well as for emergencies. The assets-mapping scholars and practitioners talk about capacity and social capital, and creating the conditions for social change.
5. Social support is defined as "the way in which people and households get resources that do not come from exchanges in the market economy, distributions from the state, or distributions from charity." Social support has also been defined as "a generalized resource available from one's network of friends and acquaintances (the social network) that helped one to deal with everyday problems or more serious crises." See Michael E. Walker, Stanley Wasserman, and Barry Wellman, "Statistical Models for Social Support," in *Advances in Social Network Analysis*, (1994), p. 53.
6. The content and transfer of social support comprises much of what is also called "social capital" in our society. There is an extensive literature on social capital. For a useful discussion of this term, drawing on comparative case studies, see Robert Putnam, ed., *Democracies in Flux: The Evolution of Social Capital in Contemporary Society* (New York: Oxford University Press, 2002).
7. See John P. Kretzman and John L. McKnight, *Building Communities from the Inside Out: A Path toward Finding and Mobilizing a Community's Assets* (Chicago: ACTA, 1993). The objective of assets mapping is the "quest for transformation" in which communities can build their capacities and develop and strengthen partnerships among individuals, associations, and institutions, thereby creating whatever change is needed. Assets mapping has been further developed by the Madii Institute in Minnesota which emphasizes the inclusion of the "cultural knowledge" of community residents as an asset.
8. The concept of "weak ties" was introduced by Mark Granovetter, "The Strength of Weak Ties," *American Journal of Sociology* 78 (1973), 1360-1380. He shows that certain ties that appear weak, such as professional acquaintances, are critical in helping people get jobs.
9. For supporting documentation that social netowrks are not static, see Cochran (1990), p. 31.
10. See Alan Dawley, *Class and Community: The Industrial Revolution in Lynn* (Cambridge, MA: Harvard University Press, 1976), on how living in a company town affects workers' sense of community.
11. In this group of 40 families, both biotech production workers and managers live in multi-generation households.

12. See the stories of Mike Hallowell (pp. 173–175), and Steve Lombardi (pp. 80–81) for further evidence of this pattern.
13. This finding differs significantly from a study that found "a long commute is associated with a reduction in women's neighborhood networks." See Penny Edgell Becker and Heather Hofmeister, "Work Hours and Community Involvement in Dual-Earner Couples: Building Social Capital or Competing for Time?", Bronfenbrenner Life Course Center Working Paper #00-04, February 2000.
14. The only exceptions were two families with children in federally subsidized slots in childcare centers outside their community of residence.
15. Phyllis Moen, ed., *It's About Time: Couples and Careers* (Ithaca: ILR Press of Cornell University Press, 2003), pp. 9–13.
16. The maps of single-parents appear similar to those of married parents, but more cases are needed to understand differences at each stage for single-parent families.
17. See Hochschild (2000), pp. 36-40, 171-172, 186.

CHAPTER 6

1. Annual turnover rates for teaching staff average 36 percent, and among assistant teachers and aides they average 52 percent. See Suzanne Heilbrun and Barbara Bergmann, *America's Childcare Problem: The Way Out* (New York: Palgrave, 2002), p. 190. This is linked to low wages: in 2000, the median wage for a childcare worker was $7.43, and the median wage for a preschool teacher was $8.56 (Bureau of Labor Statistics, U.S. Department of Labor, Occupational and Employment Statistics Survey, 2000).
2. See Introduction.
3. For information on accreditation by the National Association for the Education of Young Children (NAEYC), see Heilbrun and Bergmann (2002), pp. 146-154.
4. See Heymann (2000).
5. Joan Lombardi, the founding director of the Child Bureau, argues that during the 20th century, preschool childcare programs (birth to age five) and school-age childcare programs (six to seventeen) have been "strained and underfunded," providing limited assistance with minimum coverage. See Joan Lombardi, *Time to Care: Redesigning Child Care to Promote Education, Support Families, and Build Communities* (Philadelphia: Temple University Press, 2003), pp. 39-42, 57-58, 170-171.
6. Lombardi (2003), pp. 16–17.
7. Holly Jo Hair Hunts and Rosemary Avery, "Relatives as Child Care Givers: After Hours Support for Nontraditional Workers," *Journal of Family and Economic Issues* 19.4 (1998).
8. 27–35 percent of children are cared for by relatives. See M. Brown-Lyons, A. Robertson, and J. Layzer, *Kith and Kin—Informal Child Care: Highlights from Recent Research* (New York: Center for Children in Poverty, 2001).
9. S.W. Helburn, ed., *Cost, Quality, and Child Outcomes in Child Care Centers*, Technical Report (Denver: University of Colorado at Denver, Department of Economics, Center for Research in Economic and Social Policy, 1995).
10. See S. Kontos, C. Howes, E. Galinsky, and M. Shinn, *Quality in Family Child Care and Relative Care* (New York: Teacher's College Press, 1995).
11. See Sharon L. Kagan and Nancy E. Cohen, *Not by Chance: Creating an Early Care and Education System for America's Children*, Full Report of the Quality 2000 Initiative (New Haven: Bush Center in Child Development and Social Policy, Yale University, 1997), p. 66.
12. Margaret Blood, *Our Youngest Children: Massachusetts Voters and Opinion Leaders Speak Out on Their Care and Education* (Boston: Strategies for Children, 2000), p. 16.

13. See J. P. Shonkoff and D.A. Phillips, *From Neurons to Neighborhoods: The Science of Early Child Development*, by the Board on Children and Families of the National Research Council, Institute of Medicine (Washington, D.C.: National Academy Press, 2001).

14. Estimates on NAEYC accreditation vary from 20 to 35 percent. See N. Marshall et al., *The Cost and Quality of Full Day, Year Round Early Care, and Education: Pre-School Classrooms* (Wellesley Centers for Research on Women, 2001), p. 34.

15. See *Securing Our Future: Planning What We Want for Our Youngest Children*, Future Trends, vol. 6, Early Services Learning Department, Massachusetts Department of Education, March 2001, p. 22.

16. For information on community-based childcare resource and referral agencies, see www.naccrra.org.

17. Center-based care costs $5,000–$10,000 a year for one child, and non-center care costs about 10 percent less. See Heilbrun and Bergmann (2002), p. 4.

18. The involvement of relatives reinforces traditional notions of famial obligation and reciprocity. See Nancy Folbre, *The Invisible Heart: Economics and Family Values* (New York: New Press, 2001), pp. 36-38.

19. Relatives, particularly grandmothers, provide approximately 53 percent of care for employed parents. See Harriett Presser, "Some Economic Complexities of Child Care Provided by Grandmothers," *Journal of Marriage and Family* 51 (1989), pp. 581-591.

20. See pages 152–153 on the role of grandparents in community affairs. Other studies have shown that unpaid community service brings great rewards to men and women during retirement. See Phyllis Moen, "The Gendered Life Course, " in *Handbook of Aging and the Social Sciences* (New York: Academic Press, 2001), p. 187.

21. The families that go outside of their communities for childcare are using federally subsidized slots made available by income eligibility.

22. For children 6-17, 69 percent of married parents work outside the home, 79 percent of single-mother families, and 84 percent of single-father families (U.S. Department of Labor, Bureau of Labor Statistics, 2001).

23. U.S. Bureau of the Census, 1998.

24. U.S. General Accounting Office, "Fact Sheet on School-Age Children's Out of School Time" (Washington, D.C., 1998). Of those children who are in kindergarten to third grade, a recent study extimates that 17 percent are cared for by relatvies, 14 percent are in a center-based program, and 10 percent are cared for by non-relatives.

25. *Bringing Education into the After School Hours*, U.S. Department of Education (Washington, D.C., 1999). For an insightful study on being home alone, see Deborah Belle, *The After-School Lives of Children: Alone and with Others While Parents Work* (Mahwah, NJ: Lawrence Erlbaum Associates, 1999).

26. See B. M. Miller, "Out of School Time: Effects on Learning in the Primary Grades" (Wellesley, Mass.: Wellesley College, Center for Research on Women, National Institute for Out of School Time, 1995). Also see S. L. Hofferth et al., "Self Care Among School-age Children," paper presented at meeting of the Society for Research on Adolescence, 2000, Minneapolis.

27. D. L. Vandell, and K. M. Pierce, "Can After-school Programs Benefit Children Who Live in High Crime Neighborhoods?" Symposium at meeting of the Society of Research in Child Development, 1999.

28. Judith Bender et al., *Half a Childhood: Quality Programs for Out of School Hours* (Nashville, TN: SchoolAge Notes, 2000), p. xv.

29. A study conducted by Mathematica Policy Research for the U.S. Department of Education found that the 21st Century Community Centers "had limited influence on academic per-

formance, no influence on the safety or the number of 'latchkey' children, and some negative influences on behavior." See *When School Are Open Late: The National Evaluation of the 21st Century Community Learning Centers*, U.S. Department of Education, Office of the Under Secretary (Washington, D.C., 2003). These findings have been challenged by many organizations that have worked on expanding the availability and quality of after-school programs.

30. Report of Mass 2020 and the Keeping Kids on Track Campaign, *No Time to Lose: Children and Their After School Hours* (Boston, 2002).

31. School-based after-school programs include those operated by public school systems, available in 53 communities (data courtesy of Nancy Doyle, MA Department of Education), and those that use public school facilities but are independently run, available in 30 communities (data courtesy of Carol Resnick, MA Department of Education).

32. This is not unique to the two agencies described, especially for families who have adopted children from China. See Adam Pertman, *Adoption Nation: How the Adoption Revolution Is Transforming America* (New York: Basic Books, 2000), pp. 53, 57.

33. See John Paul Marosey, *A Manager's Guide to Elder Care and Work* (Greenwood, 1999).

34. Among the families I met, men are more involved with elder care than with childcare.

35. For a summary of community-based initiatives to support childcare provided by kith and kin, see Deborah Stahl, et al., *Sparking Connections: Community-Based Strategies for Helping Family, Friend, and Neighborhood Caregivers Meet the Needs of Their Children and Employees*. (New York: Families and Work Institute, 2000) pp. 24–27.

36. This position is elaborated in a community-based study of childcare in a Chicago neighborhoods. See Maya Carlson and Felton Earls, "Childcare as the Cradle of Democracy," paper presented at Conference on Work Family and Democracy," November 29-December 1, 2000.

CHAPTER 7

1. According to the Mott Foundation, 92 percent of Americans support organized programs for children and teens in the after-school hours. See Charles Stewart Mott Foundation, *Special Report: 21st Century Schools* (1999).

2. Some research shows that juvenile crime rates triple between the hours of 3:00 p.m. and 6:00 p.m. See J. A. Fox and S. A. Newman, *After-School Crime or After-School Programs?*, Report to the U.S. Attorney General (Washington, D.C.: Fight Crime, Invest in Kids, 1997).

3. In 1999, the U.S. Department of Education established a commission to assess math and science education. The commission found that "whether we look at comparisons of our young people to those of other nations or look simply to the progress our students are making at home, the nation keeps getting the dismal message about mathematics and science achievement: our students are losing ground"; *Before It's Too Late: A Report to the Nation from the National Commission on Mathematics and Science Teaching for the 21st Century* (Washington, D.C.: U.S. Department of Education, September 2000), p. 11.

4. There is a great deal of evidence linking after-school programs with improved academic performance. See J. Spielberger and R. Halpern, *The Role of After-School Programs in Children's Literacy Development* (Chicago: University of Chicago, Chapin Hall Center for Children, 2002); and D. Huang, B. Gribbons, K. Kim, C. Lee, and E. L. Baker, *A Decade of Results: The Impacts of LA's BEST After-School Initiative on Subsequent Student Achievement and Performance* (Los Angeles: University of California at Los Angeles, Graduate School of Education and Information Studies, Center for the Study of Evaluation, 2000).

5. Two-thirds of the families profiled in this book have school-age children.

6. Putnam (2000), p. 63.

7. Susan Crawford and Peggy Levitt, "Social Change and Civic Engagement: The Case of the PTA," in Theda Skocpol and Morris Fiorina, eds., *Civic Engagement in America* (Washington, D.C.: Brookings Institution Press, 1999), pp. 249-296.

8. *Ibid.*, p. 250.

9. Sonya Michel, "The Limits of Maternalism: Policies toward American Wage Earning Mothers during the Progressive Era," in Seth Koven and Sonya Michel, eds., *Mothers in a New World* (New York: Routledege, 1990).

10. Crawford and Levitt (1999), p. 262.

11. Bender et al. (2000), p. xiii.

12. See Barbara Schneider and James Coleman, eds., *Parents, Their Children and Schools* (Boulder, CO: Westview, 1993).

13. This type of parental involvement is argued to be less effective than the actions of a federated structure like the PTA. But for working parents, volunteer activities that give them extra time with their child are understandably preferred.

14. Crawford and Levitt (1999), p. 269.

15. I am using the term "modest income" for households at or below the national median income. Median family income for a family of four was $42,200 in 2001. See "Selected Measures of Household Income Inequality; 1967-2001," Bureau of the Census, U.S. Department of Commerce, 2001.

16. These gender differences mirror those found in other studies of home-based parental involvement, even though many mothers work in scientifically related positions. See J. S. Eccles and R. D. Harold, "Family Involvement in Children's and Adolescent Schooling, " in Alan Booth and Judy Dunn, eds. *Family-School Links: How Do They Affect Educational Outcomes* (Mahwah, NJ: Lawrence Erlbaum, 1996).

17. The fathers I interviewed do not voice regret when reporting about school events they missed, and are often self–congratulatory about making it to a school play or science fair.

18. George is referring to instability at BioPrima in the late 1990s when a potential partnership with another company fell through.

19. The LaLeche League is a national organization with local chapters that supports breastfeeding.

20. For statistics on the number of children who need after-school care versus the number of programs available, see chapter 6.

21. Nationwide, 28 percent of after-school programs are at public schools, 35 percent at childcare centers, and 14 percent at faith-based institutions. Bender et al. (2000), p. xvii.

CHAPTER 8

1. The *bima* is the raised platform in the front of a synagogue from which the rabbis speak and from which the Torah is read. A *yod* is a pointer stick used to point out each word in the Torah as it is read aloud. *Yod* means "hand" in Hebrew, and often is used to refer to the hand of God.

2. For discussion of the debate on the "charitable choice" provision, see Martha Minow, "Choice or Commonality: Welfare and Schooling after the Welfare State," in Mary Jo Bane, Brent Coffin, and Ronald Thiemann, eds., *Who Will Provide: The Changing Role of Religion in American Social Welfare* (Boulder, CO: Westview, 2000), pp. 182-187.

3. The Jeremiah Project studies, promotes, and replicates the work inner-city ministers are doing to restore civil society in poor communities. See Byron R. Johnson, "The Role of the African American Churches in Reducing Crime among Black Youth," CRRUCS Report 2001-2;

Jeremy Whyte and Mary de Marcellus, "Faith-based Outreach to At Risk Youth in Washington, DC," TJP Report 98-1 (1998); and David Larson and Byron Johnson, "Religion: The Forgotten Factor in Cutting Youth Crime and Saving At-Risk Urban Youth," TJP Report 98-2 (1998).

4. A recent ruling by the Supreme Court that government funds can be used to fund parochial schools adds credence to this concern. On June 28, 2002, the Supreme Court decision in the Louisiana case *Mitchell v. Helms* overturned two prior Supreme Court decisions, and permits the use of taxpayer money for computers and other instructional materials for use in parochial schools.

5. See Bane, Coffin, and Thiemann, (2000), p. 5.

6. The recent crisis in the Catholic Church in the United States, related to the sexual abuse of children and women by clergy, has spurred a new level of lay Catholic involvement, such as the formation of the Boston-based group, Voice of the Faithful.

7. In surveys done by Gallup in 1990, about two thirds of Americans reported membership in a church or synagogue, 40 percent attended services regularly, and 85 percent received religious training in their childhood; see *Emerging Trends* 12 (September 1990).

8. The word "Havurah" comes from the Hebrew word *haver*, which means "friend."

9. This has been corroborated in a national study of civic and religious voluntary activity. The authors found that "Not only are women more likely than men to go to services regularly, they are more likely to give time to educational, charitable, or social activities associated with their church or synagogue and to contribute money to their religion." See Sidney Verba, Kay Lehman Schlozman, and Henry Brady, *Voice and Equality: Civic Volunteerisn in America Politics* (Cambridge: Harvard University Press, 1995).

10. CCD classes constitute the standard religious education curriculum for Catholic children.

11. Data taken from a nationally representative survey of congregations conducted in 1998. See Mark Chaves, "Congregation's Social Service Activities," Policy Brief No. 6, Urban Institute (December 1999).

12. Programs which address basic human needs, related to an issue like employment, represent only 1-3 percent of congregational social service work. See Chaves (1999), p. 4, Table 2.

13. Chaves (1999), p. 3.

14. For a discussion of belief in the orderliness of the world and how it helps people cope with the materialistic world of work, see Robert Wuthnow, *Poor Richard's Principle: Recovering the American Dream through the Moral Dimension of Work, Business, and Money* (Princeton: Princeton University Press, 1996), pp. 311-312.

CHAPTER 9

1. For more on Pam's perspective on the PTO, see page 217.

2. For a description of their job share arrangement, see chapter 2, pp. 34–36.

3. For a discussion of the benefits and disadvantages of part-time work for employers and employees, see H. Hartmann, Y. Yoon, and D. Zuckerman, *Part-time Opportunities for Professionals and Managers: Where They Are, Who Uses Them, and Why* (Washington, D.C.: Institute for Women's Policy Research, 2000), pp. 3-4.

4. For a discussion of how the variables of time and money shape civic voluntarism, see Verba, Schlozman, and Brady (1995). The authors find that men and women have equivalent amounts of "free time" (p. 294) to invest in these activities, although men have more money to contribute. However, they acknowledge a contradiction in their data. When controlling for certain gender-based differences in education and income, "men have significantly more free

time than women." They explain, "The data on time constraints make clear that life circumstances have a different impact on free time for women than for men. . . . This is not the
result of greater time spent on the job, but of the fact that women who work full-time continue to assume disproportionate responsibility for caring for home and children" (pp. 302-
303). People employed part-time have more "free time" than people employed full-time,
although there is no gender breakdown for these figures that would accentuate the gap given
that many more women than men work part-time (p. 295).

5. Although there is a sizable literature on fathers' increasing contributions to their families in
   childcare and housework, there is almost no mention of fathers' participation in community
   work.

6. See Daphne Spain, *How Women Saved the City* (Minneapolis: University of Minnesota Press,
   2001), p. 44.

7. Crawford and Levitt report that married women are more likely to participate in school serv-
   ice groups than single women, and that as income increases the impact of marriage increases.
   In contrast, income has no impact on the likelihood of single mothers' participation. See
   S. Crawford and P. Levitt (1999), pp. 287-288, 292.

8. See W. Bradford Wilcox, "Good Dads: Religion, Civic Engagement, and Paternal
   Involvement in Low Income Communities, " CRRCUS, Report 2001-4 (December 2001).
   Wilcox concludes that fathers who are involved in religious institutions are more likely to be
   involved in community-based youth programs.

9. Working full-time seems to decrease volunteerism. See David M. Almeid and Daniel A.
   McDonald, "The Time Americans Spend Working for Pay, Caring for Families, and
   Contributing to Community," Paper presented at the Conference on Work Family and
   Democracy, November 29–December 1, 2000. However, the findings are contradictory on the
   impact of working part-time, and some studies say it enhances participation. (See Nicholas
   Zill, "Family Change and Student Achievement: What We Have Learned, What It Means for
   Schools," in Booth & Dunn (1996). Others say it has no effect (see Crawford and Levitt, p. 271).

10. According to the U.S. Census Bureau, the median earnings of year-round, full-time workers
    in the year 2000 were $37,057 for men and $27,194 for women. See "Profile of Selected
    Economic Characteristics: 2000," U.S. Census Bureau, Census 2000, Summary File 3.
    Journalist David Leonhardt wrote, "Women's pay still lags behind men's in virtually every sec-
    tor of the economy. Full-time female workers made 77.5 percent of what their male counter-
    parts did last year" (*New York Times*, February 17, 2003).

11. See Phyllis Moen and S. K. Han, "Gendered Careers: A Life Course Perspective," in Rosanna
    Hertz and Nancy Marshall, eds., *Work and Family: Today's Realities and Tomorrow's Visions*
    (Berkeley: University of California Press, 2001).

12. One is a production worker who served as a member of his town's board of health. The other
    two are a manager and a research scientist who served on their town's school committee.

CHAPTER 10

1. See N. Firestein, "Labor Unions Speak for Working Families," in Eileen Applebaum, ed.,
   Balancing Acts: Easing the Burdens and Improving the Options for Working Families
   (Washington, D.C.: Economic Policy Institute, 2000); and N. Dones and N. Firestein,
   "Labor's Participation in Work-Family Issues: Successes and Failures, " report to the Johnson
   Foundation, Labor Project for Working Families (Berkeley, 2001).

2. See Naomi Gerstel and Dan Clawson, "Unions' Response to Family Concerns," *Social
   Problems* 48.2 (2001), pp. 277-298.

3. With only 9 percent of private sector workers, and 14 percent of all workers, unionized, these achievements affect only a small sector of the workforce. See Osterman et al. (2001), pp. 196-197.

4. Between 1986 and 1992, several major business groups opposed the FMLA, including the U.S. Chamber of Commerce, the National Federation of Independent Businesses (NFIB), and the National Association of Manufacturers (NAM). See Steve Wisensale, *Family Leave Policy: The Political Economy of Work and Family in America* (New York: M.E. Sharpe, 2001), pp. 143-145.

5. See *A Workable Balance* (1996). Two nationally representative random sample surveys, one of employees and one of employers, found that the FMLA was not the burden to business many had predicted. The new law had no noticeable effect on costs (p. 126), or on various measures of business and employee performance (p. 131).

6. In 1998, the Families and Work Institute surveyed a representative sample of for-profit and nonprofit businesses: 68 percent provided flextime; 33 percent allowed employees to work off-site; 36 percent provided resource and referral services to locate childcare; 5 percent provided referrals for elder care; 9 percent provided on-site or near-site childcare; and 5 percent provided support for after-school programs. See E. Galinsky and J. T. Bond, *The 1998 Work-Life Study: A Sourcebook* (New York: Families and Work Institute, 1998).

7. See Ellen Galinsky and Arlene A. Johnson, *Reframing the Business Case for Work-Life Initiatives* (New York: Families and Work Institute, 1998).

8. In the 1998 Business Work-Life Survey, only 1 percent of employers provided support for community programs and only 11 percent reported involvement in public-private partnership to support childcare, parent education, and public education (Galinsky and Bond, 1998, p. 79).

9. See Marcie Pitt-Catsouphes, Irene Fassler, and Bradley Googins, *Enhancing Strategic Value: Becoming a Company of Choice* (Boston College Center for Work and Family with Boston College Center for Corporate Community Relations, 1998).

10. See "Overview of Corporate Social Responsibility," Issue Brief, Businesses for Social Responsibility, 2003, p. 1. For an excellent discussion on the need for businesses to be socially responsible, see Chapter 2, in Robert B. Reich, *I'll Be Short: Essentials for a Decent Working Society* (Boston: Beacon Press, 2002).

11. It is very difficult to get a scientific estimate of the number of U.S. companies that have embraced the corporate citizenship approach to business practices. Most surveys are not based on nationally representative random samples, but rather on the policies of companies that are already a part of the Corporate Citizenship movement. See publications of the Center on Corporate Citizenship, Boston College, Carroll School of Management, for information on their 300 corporate members.

12. Groups that monitor and collect data on these activities include the Global Reporting Initiative, Social Accountability 8000, Principles for Global Social Responsibility, and the Sunshine Standards of the Stakeholders Alliance.

13. See Pitt-Catsouphes et al. (1998) on the case for companies being both "family-friendly" and "community-friendly."

14. See *Working Mother*, October 2002.

15. Utilizing the expertise of Work/Family Directions (now WFD Consulting), they began with an investment of $25 million and expanded their commitment to $125 million in 1995.

16. See the website of the American Business Collaboration for Quality Dependent Care, www.abcdependentcare.com.

17. Information from the Child Care Partnerships Project of the National Child Care

Information Center, a program of the Child Care Bureau in the U.S. Department of Health and Human Services.

18. See the Family Service and Learning Center's website, www.familycenteronline.org.

19. This upward trend is encouraging, but the overall response rate to their survey was only 9 percent, and the sample was not representative.

20. See "The Corporate Volunteer Program as a Strategic Response" (Points of Light Foundation, 1999).

21. In 1996, AT&T gave all of its 127,000 employees one paid day off a year for volunteer work, or 1 million hours of volunteer time worth approximately $20 million. The Xerox Corporation offers "sabbaticals," paying up to 20 employees to take up to 12 months of volunteer leave. The GAP, Inc., gives their full-time employees five hours a month to volunteer, and includes part-time employees in their program.

22. See Susan Thomas and Brenda Christoffer, *Corporate Volunteerism: Essential Tool for Excellence in Corporate Community Involvement* (Boston College Center for Community Corporate Relations, 1999), p. 5.

23. *Ibid.*, information on Lenscrafter programs, p. 15; on Time Warner programs, p. 19; on Target programs, p. 22.

24. Speech by Mary Robinson, U.N. Commissioner for Human Rights, "Beyond Good Intentions: Corporate Social Responsibility and for a New Century," presented to the Royal Society for the Encouragement of Arts, Manufactures and Commerce, London, England, May 7, 2002.

25. See Sandra Morgen, "The Agency of Welfare Workers: Negotiating Devolution, Privatization and the Meaning of Self Sufficiency," *American Anthropologist* 103.3 (2001), 747-761; and Timothy Conlan, *From New Federalism to Devolution: Twenty-Five Years of Intergovernmental Reform* (Washington, D.C.: Brookings Institute Press, 1998).

26. The new "American Community Survey" (ACS) of the Census Bureau assists communities by gathering data to support the "planning and evaluation of programs for everyone from the newborn to the elderly."

27. See Gary L. Bowen, Dennis K. Orthner, James Martin, and Jay Mancini, *Building Community Capacity: A Manual for U.S. Air Force Family Support Centers* (Chapel Hill: Better Image, 2001), p. 81.

28. This model raises many questions for private sector employers. Do Family Support Centers make sense when employees are scattered over a large area? Where should centers be located to be fair to all employees in a company? Seeking answers should be pursued before dismissing the concept behind these centers.

29. See Gary L. Bowen, James A. Martin, and Jay A. Mancini, *Communities in Blue for the 21st Century* (Fairfax: Caliber Associates, 1999), p. 24.

30. Although the United States was not always a "laggard" in the provision of public support for families, see Skocpol (1992), the United States was the last industrial country to adopt an unpaid leave policy. See Wisensale (2001), p. 239.

31. See Gail Richardson and Elizabeth Marx, *A Welcome for Every Child: How France Achieves Quality Child Care, Practical Ideas for the United States* (New York: French-American Foundation, 1989).

32. See Ann Crittenden, *The Price of Motherhood: Why the Most Important Job in the World Is Still Devalued* (New York: Henry Holt, 2001), especially chapter 5.

33. See Theda Skocpol, *The Missing Middle: Working Families and the Future of American Social Policy* (New York: W.W. Norton, 2000), p. 8.

34. Targeted programs include the Child Care and Development Block Grant, which provides

poor and low-income families subsidies for childcare; Head start, which provides family support services and prepares low-income children for kindergarten; and the Child Health Insurance Program, which provides health insurance to poor uninsured children.

35. Skocpol (2000), pp. 109.

36. An "Employer Survey" found that 3.6 percent of workers, or 1.75–2.5 million workers, utilized family and medical leaves a year. See *A Workable Balance* (1996) pp. 83-84.

37. Nine percent of all leave takers, and 20.9 percent of low-wage leave takers, were forced to go on public assistance to cover lost wages. See *A Workable Balance* (1996), p. 111.

38. The Commission on Leave urged employers, unions, and states to give "serious consideration" to voluntarily adopting "a uniform system of wage replacement." See *A Workable Balance* (1996), pp. 198-199.

39. At least 28 states have introduced legislation to establish paid leave. See "State Family Leave Benefits Initiatives in 2001-2002 State Legislatures: Making Leave More Affordable," National Partnership for Women and Families (Washington, D.C., 2002). This information is current in June 2003.

40. The California law (SB 1661) allows workers to collect partial wage replacement (55-60 percent of salary) for up to six weeks to care for seriously ill family members or for parental leave by expanding the state's existing Temporary Disability Insurance (TDI) system. Workers covered by the program will pay $27 a year in disability insurance to cover the costs.

41. State-level action also occurred at the time that the FMLA was stalled in Congress from the mid-1980s to early 1990s. When the FMLA was signed into law in 1993, there were already 32 state statutes covering some aspect of family and medical leave. See Weisensale (2001), p. 127.

42. See Massachusetts General Law (M.G.L.) Chapter 149, section 52D, for specific definitions and provisions of the Small Necessities Leave Act.

43. Testimony by Governor Howard Dean of Vermont, representing the National Governors' Association, before the Senate Special Committee on Aging, June 20, 2002.

44. See Cornelius Hogan, "The Power of Outcomes: Strategic Thinking to Improve Results for Our Children, Families, and Communities," prepared for the NGA Center on Best Practices, June 2001.

45. Founded in 1932, the U.S. Conference of Mayors' role has evolved to meet the changing needs of the 1,139 cities with populations over 30,000. See http://usmayors.org/uscm.

46. "Smart growth" is defined as "the kind of growth that uses land efficiently, does not entirely rely on the auto, revitalizes cities, protects farmland to strengthen agriculture, and makes communities safe, diverse, pleasant places to live and work." See *Town Meets Country: Farm City Forums on Land and Community*, Joint Project of the U.S. Conference of Mayors and the American Farmland Trust, March 2002.

47. See Mary M. O'Brien, *Financing Strategies to Support Comprehensive Community-based Services for Families and Children* (National Child Welfare Center for Organizational Improvement, October 1996).

48. Free childcare for all families is estimated to cost $123 billion a year. See Heilbrun and Bergmann (2002), p. 216.

49. See Anne Mitchell and Louise Stoney, *Financing Child Care in the United States: An Illustrative Catalogue of Current Strategies* (Ewing Marion Kaufman Foundation and the Pew Charitable Trusts, 1997) especially the section on public/private partnerships.

50. A group that combines service, advocacy, and community volunteerism is Citizen Schools. It provides after-school programs to middle-school students in Boston, using an apprenticeship model.

51. "Living Wage Campaigns" are grassroots efforts of low-wage workers, labor unions, and com-

munity groups to help families obtain a decent standard of living. See Osterman et al. (2001), pp. 135-138.

52. The "Boston Children and Families Data Base" was created with support from three NGOs—the Boston Foundation, Northeastern University, and the Metropolitan Area Planning Council—to enable municipal agencies to serve families and children.

53. See statement of Yasmina Vinci, executive director of NACCRRA, Testimony before the Subcommittee on Human Resources of the House Ways and Means Committee, April 11, 2002, on the need to increase funding for childcare resource and referral agencies.

54. See Edward Wyatt, "5,000 Meet to Discuss the Next Phase for Ground Zero," *New York Times*, July 21, 2002.

55. For more information on "A Civic Initiative for New England," see www.architects.org/civic/evaluation.html.

56. See report of a Congress on New Urbanism conference, *An American Challenge*, 2000; Peter Katz, *The New Urbanism: Toward an Architecture of Community* (New York: MacGraw-Hill, 1994); and Kenneth B. Hall and Gerald A. Porterfield, *Community by Design: New Urbanism for Suburbs and Small Communities* (New York: McGraw-Hill, 2001).

57. For an in-depth study of Celebration, Florida, see Andrew Ross, *The Celebration Chronicles: Life, Liberty, and the Pursuit of Property in Disney's New Town* (New York: Ballantine Books, 1999).

58. See Miringoff and Miringoff (1999).

59. Other "liveability" projects include *Minnesota Milestones,* created in 1991 to involve the public in setting goals for Minnesota's future; and 1000 Friends of Washington, which issues a "Sprawl Watch Report Card" on the quality of community life around central Puget Sound.

60. See Pamela Varley, "The Oregon Benchmarks Program: The Problem of Restoring Political Support," Kennedy School of Government, Case 16-99-1554, 1999.

61. See "Is Oregon Making Progress? The 2003 Benchmark Performance Report," Report to Oregon Legislative Assembly, Oregon Progress Board, March 2003.

62. NIMBY stands for "Not In My Backyard" and describes communities who protect their privileges while accepting little responsibility for the greater social good.

63. See the website of the Third Path Institute, at www.thirdpath.org

64. See Polly Wynn Allen, *Building Domestic Liberty: Charlotte Perkins Gilman's Architectural Feminism* (Amherst: University of Massachusetts Press, 1988).

65. See Delores Hayden, *Redesigning the American Dream* (New York: W.W. Norton & Co., 1984).

66. Sylvia Ann Hewlett and Cornell West. *The War against Parents* (New York: Houghton Mifflin, 1998), p. 36.

67. Skocpol (2000), p. 166.

CHAPTER 11

1. Private conversation with Karen Liebold, January 2002.

2. This example is based on a union that took an innovative approach to negotiating layoffs at a hospital. See Kris Rondeau, "Connecting Work and Family in the Higher Education Workplace: Past Successes, Future Directions," in *Labor-Management Partnerships for Working Families*, Susan Cass, ed., (Cambridge: MIT Workplace Center, Sloan School of Management, October 2003), p. 27.

3. Kris Rondeau, "Relational Practice: Illustrations from Union Alliance-Building," presentation at the Center for Gender in Organizations, Simmons College, May 4, 2000.

4. This kind of argument was made when the FMLA was being debated in Congress and many parties were saying that the United States could not afford to institute that kind of public policy. Economist Heidi Hartmann and sociologist Roberta Spalter-Roth showed that there are real costs to society—increased welfare payments, lost income, diminished pensions—when public policies are *not* created. See H. Hartmann and R. Spalter-Roth, *Unnecessary Losses: Costs to Americans of the Lack of Family and Medical Leave* (Washington, D.C.: Institute for Women's Policy Research, 1990).

5. Four states have passed legislation to establish universal pre-kindergarten programs in Florida, Georgia, New York and Oklahoma. In Massachusetts, comparable legislation has been filed, *An Act Establishing Early Education for All* (H.1838/S.239), and has received considerable bipartisan support.

6. See Ann Bookman, "Parenting without Poverty: The Case for Paid Leave," in Janet Hyde and Marilyn Essex, eds., *Parental Leave and Child Care: Setting a Research and Policy Agenda* (Philadelphia: Temple University Press, 1991).

7. See L. Bailyn, T. Kochan, and R. Drago, *Integrating Work and Family: A Holistic Approach* (2001), for more discussion on the importance of cross-sector approaches.

8. This finding comes from a survey by Maritz Research. They also found that 52 percent of those surveyed said they had decided to use flextime or work from home in order to spend more time with family. See Vivian Marino, "Reordering Priorities," *New York Times*, June 30, 2002.

INDEX